MRS. MORHARD
and THE BOYS

MRS. MORHARD
and THE BOYS

One mother's vision.
The first boys' baseball league.
A nation inspired.

RUTH HANFORD MORHARD

CITADEL PRESS
Kensington Publishing Corp.
www.kensingtonbooks.com

CITADEL PRESS BOOKS are published by

Kensington Publishing Corp.
119 West 40th Street
New York, NY 10018

All the photographs that appear in this book were collected by Al Morhard.

All Kensington titles, imprints, and distributed lines are available at special quantity discounts for bulk purchases for sales promotions, premiums, fund-raising, educational, or institutional use. Special book excerpts or customized printings can also be created to fit specific needs. For details, write or phone the office of the Kensington sales manager: Kensington Publishing Corp., 119 West 40th Street, New York, NY 10018, attn: Sales Department; phone 1-800-221-2647.

ISBN-13: 978-0-8065-3887-7
ISBN-10: 0-8065-3887-2

First hardcover printing: March 2019

10 9 8 7 6 5 4 3 2 1

Printed in the United States of America

Library of Congress CIP data is available.

Electronic edition:

ISBN-13: 978-0-8065-3889-1 (e-book)
ISBN-10: 0-8065-3889-9 (e-book)

For Al,
My Inspiration
*

And in memory of
MRS. JOSEPHINE MORHARD
1891–1978

CONTENTS

The one constant through all the years
has been baseball.
America has rolled by like an army of steamrollers.
It's been erased like a blackboard, rebuilt, and erased again.
But baseball has marked the time.
This field, this game, is a part of our past.
It reminds us of all that once was good,
and what could be again.

—*Field of Dreams*, 1989

The Big Day

League Park, Cleveland, Ohio

On September 28, 1941, Boston Red Sox slugger Ted Williams became the last Major Leaguer to hit over .400. It happened in Philadelphia's Shibe Field, home of the Philadelphia Athletics. Williams crushed a ball into the right-field speaker to lift his average to .406. It was a monumental achievement, but the newspapers at the time gave it scant notice.

It was another game in another Major League ballpark that had people buzzing that day. One team had a shortstop with a .600 batting average who could field like Lou Boudreau, pitch right- or left-handed, and was nearly impossible to hit either way. The opposing team's hurler had fanned seventeen and walked none in winning his last game.

It was the first-ever Little World Series in League Park, the storied weekday home of the Cleveland Indians and pro football Cleveland Rams. But this day, it was the Little Indians, champs of the Junior American League, playing the undefeated Little Cardinals, the Junior National League winners. Associated Press stories in newspapers from Florida to Maine to New Mexico extolled the heroics of the young boys they said, "play a brand of baseball far beyond your expectations."

There was nothing like it anywhere. Boys from nine to fourteen looking and playing like mini-versions of their big league heroes captivated the Depression-weary public. Today, Ted Williams's historic achievement is legendary, but only a few former players remember that Little World Series game in League Park—or the leagues—or the woman behind it all.

Her name was Mrs. Josephine Morhard, and she was the founder and undisputed "commissioner" of the boys' leagues, where good deeds mattered as much as the number of wins. Her achievement was grounded in her own turbulent life and driven by a fierce determination to free her son from the clutches of his father's alcoholism and violence that had scarred his early life.

On that day in 1941, she stood in the middle of the Cleveland Indians home team dugout, a commanding figure despite her short stature, surrounded by young boys in Little Indians uniforms just like those of their big league namesakes—white uniforms and navy caps sporting the big red Cleveland Indians "C" on the front of their shirts. The Little Cardinals were across the field in the visitors' dugout, proudly wearing replica uniforms that had two red birds on a branch above the name "Cardinals."

The two-decker stands of the big league park shook with cheering kids, their moms, dads, brothers, sisters, aunts, uncles, grandparents, friends, and fans, many of them from other teams in the boys' leagues. In Mrs. Morhard's brand of baseball, everyone participated in one way or another. They were all family.

At fifty, Mrs. Morhard was the same age as the ballpark. She'd added weight over the years, and her waist now was indistinguishable from her bosom. She wore her long reddish-brown hair piled high in a bun, topped with a plain baseball cap so she didn't show favoritism. Only her dress and high heels looked out of place in the concrete domain of Indians manager Roger Peckinpaugh. Otherwise, she was at home. Her bright eyes fastened on the game. Her left hand rested on a fungo bat almost as tall as she was. Her right hand clutched a scorecard. A silver whistle hung around her neck, ready to signal any infringement of her rules or sign of bad behavior among the boys.

The Little Indians had defeated the Little Cards by a score of 2–1 in a preliminary game the week before. It was a pitcher's duel, and Little Indians pitcher Jackie Heinen was the winner. Today Heinen was playing third base and the Indians other ace pitcher,

Dick Kusa, was on the mound. Mrs. Morhard's son Junior was at second base, his best buddy Joey Phipps in right field.

It wasn't looking good for the Little Indians. The Little Cards' Jim Fronek was pitching a no-hitter. His team was ahead 4–2, with two outs. The only Indians runs were unearned. He'd kept the hard-hitting Little Indians in check. But the Cards' best player, arguably the best in either league, shortstop Marlo Termini, didn't have a hit yet either.

The game was in the bottom of the sixth inning. Junior was at the plate for the Little Indians. It was the biggest game of his young life. He was eleven years old and playing for the "Little World Series" championship in League Park, the same place where Babe Ruth belted his five hundredth home run, Joe DiMaggio hit safely in his record fifty-sixth straight game, and Junior's hero Bob Feller was pitching his way to Cooperstown.

Junior was younger and smaller than most of his teammates, but he was a good second baseman. He had a strong throwing arm, and he was fast. So far in the game, he'd made an out and a couple of assists, but he didn't have a hit in two at-bats and he wanted one. Badly.

The count was 1 and 2. With just one inning to go, this would likely be his last chance to get on base. He looked at Little Cardinals pitcher Fronek winding up. The pitch looked high, the type of pitch that always gave him trouble. It whizzed by. The umpire called, "Strike three." Junior looked up at him quizzically, certain the ball came in outside the strike zone, but, for once, he didn't challenge the call. He said nothing. The inning was over.

Disappointed, he walked slowly toward the dugout, his forehead crinkled into a frown, his head down.

Mrs. Morhard didn't flinch as he passed by on the way to the field with his teammates. She was proud of the way he handled himself. A few years earlier, his temper would have taken over and he would have acted very differently in a situation like this.

She checked her scorecard. A couple of the boys on the Little Indians hadn't played yet, and she had a league rule that every boy needed a chance to play, so she juggled the Little Indians lineup to make sure all the players on the team would get in. Then, she bolted from the dugout, blew her whistle, and marched across the field to the Little Cardinals dugout. She told the Little Cardinals' manager he needed to get all his players in the game too. The Cards manager objected, his hands flying in the air, his head bobbing up and down as he talked. His best players were on the field. They needed to stay in if they were to win the game! Mrs. Morhard insisted. That was the rule. Every boy on both teams needed a chance to play.

Her unconventional approach to boys' baseball had its roots in her own unconventional life. She was one of seventeen children of an immigrant farmer who kept having children so he'd have enough help on the farm. She left home when she was still a child, fighting her way through the black holes of poverty, misogyny, sexual assault, and thievery that often devoured young girls on their own. She married outwardly successful men and hobnobbed with celebrities only to watch her husbands throw away their good fortune on liquor and women. She was a twice-divorced mother of two in a time when that was a rarity and women like her were often stigmatized. She struggled to run a meat market and raise her two children on her own through the Great Depression. Her life was a microcosm of the extraordinary times in which she lived.

In her leagues, women as well as men managed baseball teams (and sometimes scoured the local bars for their wayward husbands). There were rules every player had to abide by, and sportsmanship, respect, and fairness were mandated on the field and off. To her, baseball was more than a game. It was a way to help her son recover from a childhood marred by his father's drunken, violent eruptions. It was a way to help all her young boys avoid the perils she'd encountered, and teach them fundamental values to help them grow up to become good men. Winning wasn't all that mattered. Baseball was a way to help the boys grow up right.

Mrs. Morhard headed back across the field to the home team dugout for the seventh and last inning. She knew the Little Cardinals' manager was angry with her, but both teams had the same rules, and she was making sure the Little Indians complied too.

As she looked around the vast ballpark, she was proud—and happy. She was making a difference in these boys' lives, especially Junior's. He was eleven, going on twelve, almost the same age she was when she walked away from her home and family. She was giving him the childhood she never had.

It was an unseasonably warm 84 degrees at the ballpark. The score remained 4–2 in favor of the Little Cardinals. There was one inning to play.

I: Early Life

Tomboy, they called me, because I loved to do the things boys did. We were a large family, seventeen to be exact. And therefore we all learned to make ourselves useful one way or another, very early in life.
—JOSEPHINE MATHEY MORHARD

CHAPTER ONE

A Cruel Winter

February 1899, League Park, Cleveland, Ohio

Mounds of snow piled onto the empty League Park seats, forming a silent crowd of snowmen. The wooden rafters shuddered as the north wind plowed through the open end of the ballpark. Long fingers of ice drooped down from the stands. People said it was the coldest winter they'd ever seen in Ohio. It had also been the worst baseball season ever for the ballpark's resident team, the Cleveland Spiders. During the season, few fans had occupied these seats to cheer on the home team. They had good reason. Their team had been decimated. The future of the ballpark was uncertain.

Just a couple of weeks before opening day in 1898, the team's owner, a streetcar mogul named Frank Robison, had shipped the Spiders' best players—including future Hall of Famers Cy Young, Jesse Burkett, Bobby Wallace, and the team's entire starting rotation—to a second team he'd purchased at a sheriff's sale, the St. Louis Browns. The Spiders went on to become the worst baseball team in Major League history, ending with an embarrassing 20-134 record, a .130 winning percentage. There would be no more opening days, no more Cleveland Spiders. It was to be the team's last season.

Ninety miles to the south, near the Ohio-Pennsylvania border, a sad eight-year-old girl stared out the kitchen window of the farmhouse at the mounds of snow piling up near the shed where the pigs were kept. She knew nothing of League Park or the Spiders, or that she would one day stand in the dugout of the same ball field cheering on her own teams, with crowds of kids and their families filling these seats, the sky a glorious blue.

Poland, Ohio

Josephine bolted from the farmhouse. She felt her tears freeze as they rolled down her cheeks. The biting cold raced along her spine and stung her nose as she hurried toward the pig shed. She pushed her way through the knee-high snow, holding her own as the wind thundered across the fields, nearly lifting her into its icy arms.

She was bundled in her warmest woolen clothing. A knit hat covered her head, but the shrill cold made her ears ache. With every breath, the frigid air dried her mouth and seared its way into her lungs. She pulled her hat down over her nose and mouth and stuffed her mitten-covered hands back in her pockets. She could barely feel her feet through her two pairs of heavy wool socks and thick rubber four-buckle arctics.

Winter had painted its monochromatic hues over her family's farm. The grass and trees and fields, the farmhouse, barn and sheds wore a fresh coat of snow. The bright sun that had warmed Josephine's face as she planted rows of now-harvested wheat hid its face behind shapeless, colorless clouds. It looked like a typical winter day, but it was far from normal, certainly for the Mathey family. Inside the small two-story farmhouse, influenza threatened the lives and sapped the spirit of the family. The frigid cold was making it worse.

Josephine's mother, Elizabeth Mathey, now forty-two and a grandmother, had delivered her seventeenth child, Eugene, on January 13, nearly a month earlier. With her body already weak from bearing so many children, she caught the flu. Now, aided by the extreme cold, her influenza had turned to pneumonia. Several other children also had the flu. Most were recovering, but Josephine's two youngest siblings, the baby and the one-year-old, were still braving high fevers and seemed to be getting worse.

Josephine couldn't bear to stay in the house with her mother and the babies so sick. She hurt inside. Her older sister Ellen admonished her not to go out, but Josephine, as usual, didn't pay attention. She needed to get away. Being with the piggies always made her feel better. She wanted to watch them, pat their heads, cradle the tiny ones, and tickle their snouts.

But this was not the day to play with the animals. By the time she reached the shed, she couldn't stop shaking. Her face and hands and toes were burning with the cold. She couldn't linger, no matter how much she wanted to stay.

The temperature was brutal—it had plummeted down to 20–30 degrees below zero in the night. Just southwest of Poland in Milligan, Ohio, the thermometer hit –39 degrees—an Ohio record that still stands.

A newspaper in nearby Hamilton, Ohio, reported, "the ears of many hogs dropped off—they being so badly frozen that the least lurch caused them to fall to the ground . . . sportsmen claim the bad weather killed more quail than did all the hunters. Thousands have frozen."

Other newspapers in the state reported businesses "paralyzed," schools dismissed, laborers refusing to work, people frozen to death in their sleighs, coal shortages, boats sinking in icy rivers, a boy nearly frozen to death on his way to school, and hundreds of people with frozen noses, ears, and fingers.

One report said it was as bitter "as any man ever knew." Meteorologists and weather historians called the February chill "the mother of all cold waves" and "the greatest Arctic outburst in history."

For two full weeks, the eastern half of the United States was in the grip of some of the lowest temperatures ever recorded. NASA/Goddard's Laboratory for Atmospheres attributed it to a series of cyclones and a final massive anti-cyclone that moved steadily southward from the Arctic. Even southern cities felt its fury. It was –15 degrees Fahrenheit in Washington, D.C., and –20 degrees in Lexington, Kentucky. The temperature in Tallahassee, Florida, hit –2 degrees.

Blizzards of snow descended along with the cold. More than a foot of snow piled on the coastal regions from the Carolinas to Maine. In Florida, traces of snow fell as far south as Fort Myers. On the southern tip of New Jersey, Cape May received 34 inches of snow. Washington, D.C., had even more, at 34.2 inches.

Josephine only knew she'd never been so cold. She could only spend a few minutes with her beloved piggies before she shivered her way back to the farmhouse as fast as she could.

The old farmhouse was unusually still. The daily sounds of children laughing, arguing, playing, slamming doors, and noisily stomping up and down the stairs were muted. It was cold, even in the kitchen where the black coal-fired iron stove gave off the home's only heat.

Josephine drew as close to the stove as she could, leaving her outerwear on and crowding several siblings who were momentarily forgetting their chores. Her month-old baby brother Eugene lay pale, coughing, swaddled in a basket on a shelf in the oven to keep him warm.

In the big bedroom, Elizabeth lay nearly motionless in the plain metal bed she usually shared with her husband Joseph. Streams of sweat rolled down her flushed cheeks despite the cold. When she coughed, her whole body shook. She normally kept the windows wide open to let in the brisk air, even in winter. Now the windows were tightly shut—the white curtains no longer billowing, hanging limp.

The older girls checked on her regularly, gently placing cool cloths on their mother's forehead, giving her water to bring the fever down, and handing her the tablets of quinine they hoped would restore her health. The family feared Elizabeth was near death.

Josephine's usually rambunctious nature was subdued. With all her heart, she wanted to go back to the shed, to pretend everything was okay, to be comfortable and play with the piggies.

She was used to normal winter cold. From the time she was five years old, she'd driven the horse and wagon five miles to and from Rogers' Coal Bank whenever the family needed a load of coal for the kitchen stove. A bucket full of coal and a small shovel stood next to the stove, to keep the stove replenished. When the bucket was empty, one of the children would go to the basement to get more coal from the coal bin where it was stored. There was no coal delivery, and usually it didn't matter to Josephine whether it was the dead of winter or a blizzard was raging. She would get the coal. But this was different.

For one of the few times in her life, she didn't do what she wanted. This day, February 10, 1899, was simply too frigid.

Her mother Elizabeth lingered near death for weeks, but, as the extreme cold subsided, she gradually regained her strength. Josephine's little sister and baby brother weren't as fortunate. They slowly lost ground, their tiny bodies too weak to fight off the illness. First one, then the other, died, taking a piece of Josephine's heart with them. They were laid to rest in tiny caskets near the children the family had lost earlier—Joseph Felix, Mary, and Henry Mathey. Only twelve of the seventeen children now remained.

Josephine was learning just how cold the world could be.

Josephine was the eleventh of Joseph and Elizabeth Mathey's seventeen children. She'd often say, only partly smiling, that her father wanted lots of kids so he could have enough help around the farm.

Joseph was a tenant farmer with a modest plot of land where he raised horses, cows, pigs, sheep, and chickens, and grew wheat, corn, potatoes, and other crops. A large barn housed the horses and cows; sheds sheltered the pigs and chickens; an oversized doghouse catered to the family's shaggy black Newfoundland, Rover.

Joseph had come to America as a teenage orphan. He'd grown up on a farm in Champagney, France, a small rural commune nestled in the horseshoe between the scenic Rhine and Soane Rivers that lay below the foothills of the gently sloping Vosges Mountains. Here sheep and cattle grazed in high pastures near fields of blueberries that gave the mountains their distinctive bluish hue.

His mother died the year after he was born, and he went to live with grandparents Pierre Laurent and Jeanne Baptiste Taiclet Mathey. When Joseph was seventeen, his grandfather died, followed soon by his grandmother. Many other family members, fearful of war, fled their quaint stone houses and the land they'd worked for generations for new lives in Paris, Belgium, and the United States. Only the Vosges Mountains, Alsace, and the Rhine River separated the Mathey homestead from Prussia, a distance about as far as New York from Philadelphia.

Prussian chancellor Otto von Bismarck was at war, determined to unify Germany and settle scores with France, which had conquered parts of Prussia during the Napoleonic wars. He had defeated Austria. Eastern France appeared to be his next target.

Soon after Joseph's grandparents died, an American uncle heard about the tragedy and arranged for the teenage boy to join him. Joseph set sail in 1869 from LeHavre, France, bound for New York. After landing in the U.S., he made his way to Vienna, Ohio, to join his extended family.

The home they chose was alive with opportunity and blessed with what seemed to be an endless supply of natural resources. Glaciers ripped through this part of Ohio thousands of years before, carving out gentle hills, green valleys, a labyrinth of rivers, deep lakes, and rich soil that was superior for planting. Limestone deposits lay under the surface, disintegrating in the rain and frost to repair crop waste and enrich the soil so it was perfect for growing wheat, corn, oats, and potatoes. Sheep grazed on the bluegrass grown in the limestone soil and produced a finer quality of wool.

The area offered more than rich farmland. Colonel Edwin Drake struck oil northeast of Vienna in Titusville, Pennsylvania, a decade earlier. Oil derricks rose, boomtowns erupted, and speculators, financiers, and fortune seekers headed to the region from all corners of the country and abroad.

Farther south, along the Ohio-Pennsylvania line, more natural resources were discovered—coal deposits and iron ore in Poland and Youngstown, Ohio; iron ore, tin, and limestone on the Pennsylvania side. Mines and factories lined both sides of the state border. The post–Civil War Industrial Revolution in America had begun, and all the ingredients for manufacturing were centered along the eastern Ohio and western Pennsylvania border.

Joseph first found work as a coal miner in nearby Shenango, Pennsylvania. Also nearby, he met the young Elizabeth Butler, who lived in Hickory. Elizabeth's father, Messach Butler, was also an immigrant, a coal miner who'd come to the United States from Glamorgan, South Wales—a place where rich veins of coal had been mined since the time of the Romans. He arrived in New York on October 24, 1854, on the ship *Kataholm* with his wife Anna and their young children, Caradoc, Talieson, and

Gomer—ages three, two, and a few months. After settling here, they would have eight more children, including Elizabeth, who was born in 1857.

Coal miners in the United States could get $1 to $1.50 a day, double what they could make in Wales, luring over eighty-four thousand Welsh to Pennsylvania between 1850 and 1930. For Messach, the wages in the new country were too attractive to refuse, especially with his family growing so quickly. He soon became a mine foreman.

Josephine's father Joseph and her maternal grandfather Messach had both left Europe for a better life in the U.S., but they came from different cultures and backgrounds. Messach was Welsh; Joseph was French. Messach was Protestant. Joseph was Catholic. Joseph wanted to marry Elizabeth, but the Butlers were adamantly opposed. The cultural differences were a big factor, but there was more. She was only sixteen. Her parents believed she was too young to be married—and they thought he was too old for her at twenty-two. Yet, despite her family's objections, Elizabeth and Joseph were married. Messach Butler promptly disowned his daughter.

With his new bride by his side, Joseph wanted to replicate the idyllic farm life he'd known in France, and left coal mining to work on the Vienna, Ohio, farm of the uncle who brought him to America, Constant Taiclet. It wasn't long before the ever-ambitious young man began looking for new opportunities. Soon he found a nearby farm in Vienna he could lease and run on his own.

Joseph worked from early morning until late at night, organizing, managing, plowing, seeding, harvesting, shearing, making certain nothing was overlooked. He was scrupulously honest and expected everyone else to be as well.

A year after they married, in 1874, Elizabeth had her first child, Anne. The family lived in a simple two-story frame farmhouse that burst with the ever-growing number of children. Nearly every year after that for the next twenty-five years, a new Mathey child arrived. After Anne there were Sarah, Joseph Felix, John, Mary, Emma, Flora, Ellen, Albert, Edna—then Josephine—followed by Henry, Alice, Joseph William, Ethel May, Hazel, and, finally, Eugene. Five died shortly after birth or in early childhood.

Perhaps as a consequence of the rapidly expanding family, Josephine never knew exactly when she was born. The family celebrated her birthday on January 19, but the official Mahoning County record shows that Josephine Clementine Mathey entered life on February 20, 1891.

The first five Mathey children's birth dates were recorded in their Catholic church. That changed when Emma came along in 1881.

The family called their priest as they always did after a new baby was born, but this time, the priest grumbled that the family never came to church, never contributed, and the only time he saw any of them was when they were having a baby or burying one. When they did call on him, he complained they never paid him anything.

Joseph was furious. Priests were supposed to be godly, to baptize and bury children to assure their place in heaven. Priests should care for their congregations, not squabble over money. Joseph wondered if the priest had any idea how much it took to house and feed all these children. He vowed he would never call on the priest—any priest—again, for anything. And he didn't. That was the end of the Catholic Church for the family and the end of the babies' records the priest had so carefully documented.

There would be no more Mathey children's births documented in the church records. Counties were just beginning to keep records, but the process was haphazard and the state of Ohio didn't mandate birth registration until 1908, so, with all their children and so much to do, Joseph and Elizabeth were careless about recording the later children's birth dates. It was a low priority. It would get done when it got done, if it got done. It's likely Josephine was born in January, but her parents neglected to record it until later.

As was typical in his generation, Joseph Mathey expected his sons to work in the fields, grow the crops, and raise the livestock. His wife and daughters would care for the home and the younger children. Unfortunately, only three of the surviving Mathey children were boys, so Joseph hired farmhands for the heavy work. Before he hired them, he gave them a test. He offered a drink of moonshine. If they took more than one drink, they wouldn't get the job. But it wasn't long before Joseph discovered how deeply the cost of employing farmhands cut into profits, so he decided to let the girls do some of the arduous work, choosing practicality over tradition. That meant the girls did double duty, also helping Elizabeth run the house and care for the younger children.

All the children had duties corresponding to their ages: the older ones plowed the fields and planted and harvested crops; the younger ones fed the livestock, cleaned the stalls, collected the eggs, and cared for the chickens, pigs, and sheep. Josephine wanted to help with nearly everything. She didn't mind the hard work or long hours and insisted on doing all the things the boys did, even the rough farm work. She bristled if she was told she couldn't do something just because she was a girl. Or because she was too young. Her family called her a tomboy, but she thought the word *independent* suited her better.

She begged her father to let her plow the fields like the older boys, but she was too small to follow the harrow, so her father inserted a board between the two sides where she could sit. Then she'd be off—her bright hazel eyes fastened on her task, her little arms proudly yanking the reins so the lines she plowed were straight, her brown hair gleaming with the red highlights you could only see in the sun.

She loved to work outside where the sun warmed her skin and the breeze caressed her cheeks, to be free and alone, not simply one of a crowd of noisy brothers and sisters, and her father trusted her and counted on her. Once he told her what needed to be done, he left her alone.

In the early morning, as soon as the first hint of light appeared through window of the bedroom she shared with her sisters, Josephine bounded down the stairs, gulped a quick breakfast, and headed toward the open field. Her father hitched the harrow to the horse and she went to work, eagerly perched on her specially crafted seat. No one needed to remind her or check on her. She was where she wanted to be, happily singing as she worked, still singing when she came back to the farmhouse in the evening, earning another nickname "Singing Josie."

CHAPTER TWO
The Early Years

Josephine's early life on the farm wasn't just work. Nature had crafted her playground. She loved to explore the woods and streams.

She'd run down to the creek where the fields met the trees and feel the cool water tickling her toes. She'd hopscotch over rocks that looked like giant turtle shells splashed by the rippling water that slithered over them on its way to the Mahoning River. She'd watch the frogs pop into the water from their hiding places in the tall grass along the bank and try to catch them, dipping her hands in the water quietly and forming them into a cup, then snapping them shut, even though the frogs' springlike legs were so quick, they got away most of the time.

She was always happy then, whether she was working or playing. But her adventurous, independent spirit often landed her in trouble. She was Tom Sawyer in a dress and pantaloons, always coming up with imaginative ideas that didn't turn out quite right.

On her fourth birthday, Josephine got a little red wagon. She loved it more than anything. It was the one thing that was just hers. She didn't need to share it with her houseful of brothers and sisters—or anybody else. The red wagon was Josephine's treasure. Whenever she had an extra minute, she'd grab her wagon and run to the shed where her father kept the pigs and pull the wagon around and around and around the shed, past the pigs that were lolling and squealing nearby.

In the late fall, after the harvest was over and the weather turned colder, Josephine's father put a stack of straw close to the shed so the little pigs and their mothers and fathers could crawl under it or nestle beside it to keep warm. It was good for the pigs, but when Josephine made her daily trek to the shed with her wagon, she was frustrated to see the straw in her way. She grasped the handle of the little red wagon and tried to yank it through the straw, but the straw didn't budge. Now she was angry—and she was dead set on moving the obstacle out of her way, so she reached into the stack, grabbed the biggest bunch of straw her little arms could hold, and tugged it out. With that, a near avalanche of straw tumbled down from above, landing on her head and nearly burying her little wagon.

She shook off the straw and flopped on the ground to figure out a way to get rid of the straw so she could play with her wagon. She had an idea. She ran into the house, opened the kitchen cabinet, grabbed some matches from their usual place, and headed back to the shed. She struck the matches and lit the straw, listening to it crackle as it started to burn and watching the yellowish flames shoot up like magic from different places in the straw. It was fun to watch, but she was impatient. She was determined to play in the shed, she still couldn't get around the straw, and now the fire was in her way. Her idea wasn't working, so she left to find a new place to play and headed toward the field near the road, now empty of the re-cently harvested wheat.

The fire quickly consumed the straw pile and started to spread. Joseph and the farmhands began pumping water from the well to quell the fire. Little Josephine brought her wagon and sat down calmly by the side of the road with her brothers and sisters to watch the bright yellow, red, and orange flames leap upward, their black smoke spewing high into the clouds as burning shards of wood snapped to the ground. She was en-grossed. It was better than fireworks on the Fourth of July. Farmers from nearby and miles away heaved metal pails of water on the raging flames, trying to save the farmhouse and the barn. There were people everywhere. It was the most excit-ing thing she'd ever seen!

Josephine had set her family's farm ablaze! The fire now

was burning the sheds where the pigs were kept. It was spreading to the horse barn. But she saw only the pretty colors dancing toward the sky and bigger crowds than she'd ever seen.

In her excitement, she momentarily forgot how the fire started—or perhaps she didn't want to remember. But after it was over, she realized what she had done. The shed was a pile of black timbers, and about a hundred little pigs and their mothers and fathers burned and died. Josephine cried and cried and cried. No one could console her. How could she have hurt those little animals?

Within a few weeks, her father rebuilt the shed, added a bigger outside pen, and stocked more pigs, hundreds of them—some pink, some black, some spotted. Josephine liked to stand outside the pen and tickle their pink snouts as they pushed against the fence, their ears pointing in different directions like leaf-shaped road signs.

One day, as winter approached, Josephine was near the pen when she heard a plaintive squeal that sounded like an animal in distress. She looked around, but the sound was coming from farther away. She headed toward the shed. Inside, she spotted a baby pig, struggling to shake off a tin can that had somehow attached to its head. The little pig was frantically jerking its head from side to side, and letting out muffled birdlike sounds.

Josephine leaned down and grasped the can with both hands, trying with all her might to pull it off. She tried and tried, but it wouldn't budge. The piggy squealed louder with each yank. She didn't want to hurt the pig and didn't know what else to do, so she ran outside and called one of the farmhands to help her.

The farmhand gently rotated the can from side to side until finally it came off. The tiny pig was shaking and so thin you could see the outline of his bones under his pale pink skin. Josephine picked him up, snuggled him in her arms, and, holding him close, headed past the barn to the adjacent milk house where the cows' milk was cooled. She poured out a cupful, warmed it up, and patiently dribbled the milk into the pig's mouth with a spoon until all the milk was gone. She wanted to make certain the piggy would be safe and away from the other animals, so she brought the piggy to a quiet corner of the barn and stayed with him until dinnertime. When it was time to go back to the farmhouse, she found an old woolen blanket and wrapped the piggy tightly so he wouldn't be cold during the night.

Josephine told her father all about the pig and pleaded with him to let her have it for a pet. Her father took a look. The pig was scrawny and not much use to him, so he told her she could have it if she could save its life.

All through dinner, she thought about the little piggy, all by himself in the barn, thin and probably hungry. After everyone had gone to bed, she tiptoed carefully down the stairs so the creaking floorboards wouldn't alert her parents and went to the barn. It was really cold there, so she brought the piggy into the house, sat down with him in the dining room, and fed him more warm milk, then rocked him like her mother rocked her little sister. By four o'clock in the morning, Josephine was so tired her eyes kept closing. She couldn't stay awake any longer, so she reluctantly wrapped the piggy in the old blanket and left him in the dining room for the rest of the night while she went upstairs to get some sleep.

Josephine's mother came down early to start breakfast and nearly tripped over the happy piggy, who was running around the house on its undersized legs, wagging its corkscrew tail furiously. She shrieked, horrified to find a pig in the house. She was sure she knew the culprit. "Josephine!" she called. Her daughter, still groggy from her lack of sleep, stumbled her way down the stairs. Elizabeth asked Josephine why on earth she'd brought a pig in the house and demanded that it be put back in the shed.

Josephine protested, begging her mother to let the poor little piggy stay, but the answer was an unconditional "no." Grudgingly, Josephine picked up the piggy and headed outside toward the shed. On the way, she passed Rover's doghouse. Rover was gone, out running in the field, and the doghouse was empty. It was the perfect place for her piggy. She placed the old blanket, a saucer of milk, and the piggy inside, evicting Rover and disobeying her mother.

Every morning, before doing her chores, she'd stop at the doghouse to see her piggy. She scrubbed him and kept him nice and clean, but she thought he was still too thin. He needed to get bigger and stronger. As usual, she went to the milk house, but this time she skimmed the cream off the top and gave that to him. It worked. Thanks in part to his cream diet, the pig became huge. It was hard to keep him hidden in the doghouse—and soon, Josephine's father discovered the pig and put a quick end to its pampered lifestyle. Piggy had to join the hundreds of other pigs slopping around in the pen. Josephine ran out to see him every day. She'd call, and he'd come waddling over to the fence, where Josephine would greet him happily, stroking his smooth skin and rubbing her nose against his snout.

Finally, it was time for the pigs to be butchered. Josephine begged and pleaded with her father to save him, but he said no.

She kept badgering, but he wouldn't change his mind. Josephine was devastated. Seeing how upset she was, Joseph said he'd give her the money he got for the pig. She stomped into the farmhouse, realizing it was useless to argue further. She was angry and sad at the same time. But there was an up-side. She could use the money to pay the general store, where she'd run up a bill of five dollars buying penny candy.

The terrain in southeastern Ohio was nothing like the flat farm-land of much of the Midwest. Here, densely forested hills cra-dled billowing rows of corn and wheat that stretched for miles, then merged like an optical illusion, dotted occasionally with white clapboard farmhouses situated close to the road in front of the red or white barns, sheds, and silos that identified the dwellers' occupations.

For the young Josephine, the hills and valleys were enchant-ing. The Matheys' sheep grazed on nearby slopes that spilled into the acres of golden wheat fields she happily plowed. Where the fields met the trees, cool streams rippled across rounded boulders on their way to join the Beaver or Shenango Rivers, ignoring the artificial lines that separated Ohio from Pennsylvania. Where the forests deepened, Josephine found leafy hidden trails she could explore on horseback.

More than the other animals on the farm, except maybe the pigs, she loved the horses and learned to ride not long after she learned to walk. Riding came as naturally to her as catching frogs or running through the fields. She'd ride like she was rid-ing the wind—free, wild, and unrestrained. She was fearless and determined, possibly because she had to find her own way as one of the youngest children. Or perhaps it was simply in her genes.

While she was still very young, a colt on the farm caught her eye. He was black as midnight with a coat that glistened like the stars. And he was spunky, not like the other horses that lolled around, chomping on the grass. He'd prance around the pasture like it was his alone, his muzzle lifted toward the sky, his legs barely touching the ground. She called him "Star." He had spirit, her father said, just like Josephine. She liked that. She felt a kinship to the colt, whose independent streak seemed to mirror her own.

Whenever she had the chance, Josephine headed for the field where he grazed. She looked up at the long-lashed brown eyes that were nearly as big as her hands. She wanted to stroke his neck and brush his coat like she did the other horses, but he'd rear up and let out a menacing whinny.

She knew he was unruly, but that didn't matter. She wanted to ride him. Oh, how she wanted to ride him! But even though she was still a young girl, she understood he was too wild. He needed to be broken. She'd watched her father break some of the other horses and asked her father to do it, but he was too busy. It could wait. Josephine, as usual, could not. Maybe she could do it. Maybe she could break Star. She remembered how her father would put on the bridle, attach the lunge lines, and have the horses walk, trot, or cantor around him in a large circle. It didn't look very hard. If she broke Star, she could ride him, and maybe her father would even let him be her horse.

She stared at Star for a while, her eyes dancing with anticipation. She was going to do it, to break him in, even though she barely came up to his elbow. Her father had warned her to stay away from the frisky young colts, telling her she could get hurt, and she knew he wouldn't approve. If the farmhands saw her, they'd probably tell him, so she waited until they were away from the barn, then she made her move. She stepped toward Star. The young colt tossed his head from side to side, snorted, and stamped his hoof on the ground. He wasn't going to make it easy, but Josephine was confident she knew what to do. She strode to the barn, got some oats, and placed the pail strategically next to the fence. Star moved toward it and began eating. While he was distracted, she quietly climbed on the fence in back of him. When he lifted his head, she slipped on his bridle and attached the extra-long reins she'd seen her father use, so if he kicked high, he would not kick her.

She climbed down, got on the colt, waited until he finished eating, then started him on an easy gait. Just as she was feeling proud of herself for her fine horsemanship, Star suddenly thrashed his head and began to run faster and faster.

She held the lines as tight as she could, but she was no match for him. Her little arms weren't strong enough to stop him. Soon her feet were off the ground, and the colt was dragging her around and around with him. She clung on for dear life, terrified.

The colt dragged her along the ground, bumped her up and down with each step, until she finally let go of the reins and fell onto the ground. Then he stopped. Josephine lay in the pasture, unconscious. A farmhand saw her, ran to her, and screamed for help, fearing she was dead. Men ran in from the nearby wheat fields. They carried her back to the house and her horrified mother Elizabeth.

When Josephine opened her eyes, her mother was sitting in the chair next to her bed, stroking her forehead. Her father was standing over her, his eyes glaring with fear and anger. He told her to never, ever do anything like that again. Then he grabbed his riding whip and thrashed her already bruised and sore backside, once, twice, three times. Josephine refused to cry.

That experience wasn't enough to make Josephine give up on horses. She drove horses for the farmhands who gathered sap from metal pails that hung from the maple trees that covered the hills. The farm had a large sugar camp, where the sap was boiled and transformed into the maple syrup her father sold and Josephine drenched on her breakfast pancakes.

Even though her job was simply to drive the horses, her father had been giving her more and more responsibility on the farm, and she felt like she was in charge. She didn't like the way the farmhands were gathering the sap and told them so. She had a better idea and insisted the farmhands do it her way. They paid no attention. They weren't about to take orders from a little girl just because she was their boss's daughter.

That made her mad.

She threw down the reins, leaped off the wagon, and stomped into the woods. The farmhands continued working, happy to be freed from her meddling. Josephine kept walking, going farther and farther into the woods, watching the robins and chipmunks and squirrels, picking wildflowers, and gradually forgetting how angry she'd been. She was enjoying being by herself.

When the farmhands finished collecting the sap, they told Joseph what had happened. He assumed Josephine had gone back to the sugar camp. When he found she was missing, he panicked and quickly alerted the authorities.

Bells rang, whistles blew, people were called from far and near to hunt for her. Darkness approached, and still they'd found no sign of Josephine. They dragged the wells and searched the forest with oil lanterns until deep into the night. Finally, they gave up the search in despair.

Her parents were frantic. They stayed awake—still watching, waiting, and hoping for some sign of Josephine. In the early morning hours, they heard a shuffling noise outside and hustled to open the front door. It was Josephine. She ambled into the farmhouse acting like nothing unusual had happened but looking like a wounded soldier returning from the war. Her arms and legs were scratched and bleeding, her dress torn where it caught on branches and wire fences.

Her parents were so happy to see her, they omitted the usual whipping.

Being lost hadn't scared Josephine. She was proud of herself. She'd found her way home.

Josephine's father let her do work on the farm that only the older children usually did. But there was one thing he and Elizabeth didn't allow her to do and that was go to school. From the time she was four years old, Josephine had wanted to go to school like her older brothers and sisters. Now, even though she was almost five, her parents insisted she wasn't old enough. Josephine begged to go, arguing that she could do everything the older children did—she could ride a horse and plow a field—so she should be able to go to school. Besides, she knew she was smart and learned quickly. But her parents insisted she needed to wait until she was six like everyone else.

"But I'm not like everyone else," Josephine would say to

her parents. Her father didn't think about her age when he trusted her to drive the horses and do farm chores on her own. She wanted to go to school, and she was determined to find a way. If they didn't let her participate, she'd just go along with her brothers and sisters and watch. And she did. She was there so much, the teacher decided she might as well enroll her.

With that, her parents gave in.

Because children were needed on the farms, most rural schools had two sessions—a winter term that began after the harvest in November and continued through April, and a summer term from May to August. Older boys attended school only in the winter so they could help their fathers during the growing and harvesting seasons. Lucky Josephine started school in November 1896, two months before her sixth birthday and six months before she normally would have entered school for the next term, which began in May.

Like the other children, Josephine needed to finish her chores before school. On the first morning before school, she got up at 5:00 a.m., ate breakfast, cleaned up her dishes, and headed to the barn and sheds to feed the horses and pigs and collect the eggs. Then, she stopped by the doghouse where Rover greeted her, his tail wagging furiously, his huge black ears flopping in her face as she bent down to leave his food.

She rushed back to the farmhouse to change into the long dress that had been an older sister's, pulled on her heavy woolen socks, and laced up her ankle-high shoes so her feet would keep warm. She knew the classroom would be chilly since its only heat came from a potbellied stove, and the weather could be cold and drafty in late autumn.

Josephine joined her other school-bound siblings, juggling her lunch pail and finding it hard to keep her shoes from getting tangled in her ankle-length dress. Her round bonnet sat crookedly atop a cascade of Shirley Temple curls held together by a big bow. She was happy, her eyes dancing with excitement as they passed the sameness of the fields that had recently been stripped of their wheat and corn.

The school sat near the crest of a hill, framed by a scattering of graceful maple trees that had mostly shed their brilliant autumn reds and golds. A gabled bell tower topped the small building. It looked like a lighthouse, beckoning Josephine to discover the secrets of the world beyond the farm.

She was no longer a visitor. She'd learn to read and write like her siblings. She'd discover wondrous cities like New York where electrified streetcars rumbled through streets dwarfed by buildings ten times taller than any she'd ever seen—and where thousands of people arrived every day on huge ocean steamers that passed the towering new statue of a lady holding a torch. She'd find out about other faraway places, like France where her father was born.

Josephine had made so many trips to the school she knew the routine. The school bell rang at 8:00 a.m., and the students formed two lines—one for the boys, one for the girls. The girls entered the long cloakroom first, hanging their coats and caps on nails and placing their lunch pails on the shelf above. There were two doors into the classroom. The girls went through the girls' door and stood at their desks while the boys entered through the second door. As the children walked in, they "made their manners" by curtsying or bowing to the teacher.

They'd sit down on wooden seats connected to desks—boys and girls on opposite sides of the classroom. In front of the desks were two long, wooden recitation benches that looked like church pews and were nearly as wide as the classroom. A potbellied stove sat on one side. A blackboard, made of wood and painted black, covered the walls in the front of the room, with chalk trays running along the bottom.

The children stood up straight to recite the Pledge of Allegiance with their hands over their hearts. Next they recited the Lord's Prayer or had a "moral" lesson, usually from the Bible, before splitting into small groups based on their progress rather than their age.

Josephine sat near the front with the younger children and practiced her letters in her copybook and her numbers on a slate board. The older children took turns coming to the recitation bench to recite or read from a textbook. Morning lessons were devoted to the "three R's"—reading, 'riting, and 'rithmetic. The children used the *McGuffey Reader,* which taught the three R's plus rules of conduct and religion and had its roots in Poland, Ohio, where William Holmes McGuffey taught in a schoolhouse in 1820, giving the children lessons on how to lead a good, wholesome life as well as how to read. His inspiration for the *Reader* came from his early teaching days.

The classroom was noisy. Thirteen different lessons could go on at the same time. Students read aloud; practiced; memorized; recited speeches, poems, and lessons; or listened to the teacher. Josephine wasn't bothered by the noise. She had so many brothers and sisters, the clatter didn't matter.

At noon, the children ate lunch, then ran outside to play tag, leapfrog, or fox and geese. In the afternoon, they studied spelling, grammar, history, and geography. Between subjects, the teacher read stories with morals. Each child practiced speaking by standing in front of the class and discussing the story.

Josephine was bright, and she worked as hard on her schoolwork as she did on the farm. She was polite and reverential in class, but she had a mind of her own, and her actions often astonished her teacher who expected her to be ladylike and demure like her female classmates. Josephine had a hard time staying still or quiet. Being ladylike was impossible.

One day, she spied a squirrel up in a large maple tree, and decided to climb the tree and bring the squirrel down for the other schoolchildren. Josephine made it up to a high branch and was about to grab the squirrel when the teacher came outside. She was shocked to see a girl up in a tree, her petticoats showing for everyone to see. She demanded that Josephine come down immediately, reprimanding her and saying, "It's bad enough for boys to climb trees, let alone girls!"

Josephine scrambled down, the squirrel tumbling with her and ending up tangled inside her dress. Josephine felt it squirming and started to scream, running around the school, trying to shake it off, fearing it might bite her. The squirrel scampered away and the excitement died down, but Josephine soon felt the smack of the teacher's hickory stick.

Like the other children, Josephine was expected to sit quietly, listen, and be respectful. Children were admonished to speak the truth, be honest, be punctual, and be kind. Any infraction was met with swift discipline—whipping with a rod or ruler, spanking with a hickory stick, standing in a corner, or sitting on a stool with a dunce cap on their heads.

When she did get in trouble, which wasn't often, it was usually because of her curiosity or because she was used to doing things her own way. She was eager to learn—but she could be as untamed as the horse she once tried to break, with an indestructible free spirit and an optimism that convinced her there was nothing she couldn't do if she put her mind to it.

Josephine was in the cocoon of her large family, but the world beyond the farm and the little schoolhouse was changing. It was change that would affect the farm, her family—and would eventually change her.

Josephine's father had come to America to pursue the dream of becoming a farmer in the fertile lands of northeastern Ohio. But now, Thomas Jefferson's ideal of an agrarian society was being eclipsed by the Industrial Revolution.

The late nineteenth century had blossomed into an era of limitless progress, breaking down barriers that had stifled growth and discovery and unleashing an unparalleled surge of creativity. The Modern Age burst forth like a tornado, shattering the constraints of the Victorian era and leaving economic, political, scientific, social, and cultural turmoil in its wake.

The 1893 Chicago World's Fair dazzled the world with wondrous new technologies—the telephone, telegraph, phonograph, lightbulb, and the marvels of electricity. Darwin's theory of evolution was upending the scientific and religious communities. Ernst Mach and Sigmund Freud were unleashing secrets from the depths of the human mind. Impressionist painters were dabbing their canvasses with visual effects instead of realistic depictions.

People began to move from farms to cities to seize the new opportunities. Immigrants from all over the globe rushed to America's shores. Mushrooming numbers poured into newly built Ellis Island in New York Harbor. By 1897, the nation's population topped 72.2 million, double what it had been thirty years before, with two-thirds now living in the industrialized northern states.

The family farm was under duress. Many farmers went bankrupt. Mechanization of farm equipment created new reapers and threshers that rapidly increased agricultural output. Farmers could produce more crops at less expense. By the end of the decade, prices for farm products had declined by 50 percent.

Like many small farmers, Joseph Mathey was barely holding on. Large-scale farm production had become the norm. Farms like his seemed to be relics of the past. Over one-third of U.S. farmers leased their farms and couldn't afford to purchase property, especially the sizable farmland needed to make a profit in this new era. Joseph faced this dilemma and wondered how much longer he could survive.

He loved farming. It had sustained his family and taught his children the useful skills he'd learned from his grandfather. He was determined not to fail. He would find a way.

Joseph had always fixed his own machinery when it had broken, so he decided to start a business repairing other farmers' machinery for a fee. He rented a small space across the Ohio-Pennsylvania state line in Bessemer, Pennsylvania, and opened a blacksmith shop.

Every Monday morning, very early, Josephine would hitch the horses to the wagon and drive him the six miles from the farm to his shop in Bessemer. On Saturday morning, she'd drive back to Bessemer to pick him up. In good weather, each trip would take nearly an hour. In winter, much longer as they trotted their way down narrow roads through the mounting snow.

Joseph's blacksmith business did well. In addition to servicing farm equipment, he began shoeing horses and doing other small jobs for new customers at the Bessemer limestone mines. He was spending so much time at the blacksmith shop, he wanted to find a closer farm, one that was larger and would give him the opportunity to be more successful in the changing economic environment. He also wanted his large family to have a bigger and more comfortable farmhouse. He could afford it now, and he found just the right place.

He leased a farm with some 230 acres of land and a nice house, and the family moved to Bessemer. Ponds, creeks, and limestone quarries peppered the landscape. The town had been farmland until 1887, when a group of blast furnace operators from Youngstown, Ohio, discovered the limestone needed for their steel furnaces. They formed the Bessemer Limestone

Company, named after the English inventor of the Bessemer smelting process, Sir Henry Bessemer. Workers from Sweden, Finland, Austria, and later Italy descended on the tiny town to work in the new industry, settling in small, close together, company-owned, company-furnished houses. Limestone mining was hard work, done by hand. The workers blasted holes in the rock using dynamite, then drilled and crushed the rock with a sledgehammer before shoveling it onto ore cars pulled by mules. They were paid 50 cents for a four-ton carload.

The Mathey farm was south of the town's tiny center where Josephine's new school stood. Its land sloped slightly, rising to the edge of the tree-covered hills, reminding Joseph of his boyhood home. A rock-strewn creek meandered past the limestone ledges and clusters of tall trees that hovered over leaf-covered carriage and horse trails. It wound its way farther through grassy banks where cows grazed, then fanned out into a perfect swimming hole before streaming on.

The children loved their new home. Josephine and her siblings especially liked to go to the swimming hole, pull off their clothes, and jump in. One of them stood guard to make sure no one was coming. If someone did show up, they'd jump out of the water and quickly scramble to get dressed.

Josephine liked to fish there, too, or in one of the ponds upstream. One hot, sweaty afternoon she decided to take her younger brother Joseph fishing. It would be cool, and she could almost taste the fish they were going to catch. After they finished their chores, they gathered their fishing poles and headed down to the creek. They watched for the telltale ripples that let them know where the fish were, baited their fishhooks, and threw their lines into the water. Then they waited for the fish to jerk their lines. And waited. They sat down on the creek bank and waited some more. There wasn't a single bite.

The two of them moved to another spot. After an hour, they hooked a couple of small fish—too small to take home for a family dinner—so they threw them back. Josephine was frustrated. She had no patience waiting around for things to happen.

There must be a better way to catch fish, she thought, a way that doesn't take so long. Maybe she should get a net. No, she had a better idea.

The two would-be fishermen trudged to the limestone quarry on the farm. Josephine gathered a few sticks of dynamite and some of the fuse the miners used to extract the limestone. They were going to catch fish her way. With her little brother following closely behind, she headed back through the fields and woods to the creek. Josephine expected a big haul, so she and Joseph broke off branches from a nearby willow tree, then picked off all the leaves so they'd have a place to string the fish.

Now everything was ready. She lit the fuse and threw the dynamite into the creek. It exploded with a boom so loud the ground shook and they had to cover their ears! Fish started popping up everywhere, floating on top of the water. Quickly the two of them waded in, hoisting their branches and stringing up the fish.

Josephine figured she'd thought of everything. But she hadn't considered one thing. The blast could be heard miles away, and suddenly the game warden appeared at the top of the hill, a shotgun on his shoulder. Terrified, the two fishing entrepreneurs grabbed the fish-filled branches and ran as fast as they could into the woods. Because they were young and faster on their feet than the much older game warden, he soon was far behind. When they reached a branch of the creek mostly hidden by trees, they stopped to catch their breath. They looked around. There was no sign of the warden. The only noise came from the birds in the trees. Believing they made a clean getaway, they moved on, following the creek until it widened again. It looked like another good place to get fish. They broke off more willow branches, stripped them, pulled out the dynamite, lit it, threw it in the water, and strung another batch of fish on the branches.

There was still no sign of the warden, and the two fishermen headed home with their enormous haul. Joseph and Elizabeth were shocked to see the two children coming toward the farmhouse with dozens of fish hanging from their backs. They stared, amazed at what they were seeing. Now, everything made sense. The game warden had come by earlier, telling them about the blast and looking for the two children.

They scolded the budding fishermen, reminding them that the dynamite could have killed them, and warning them that the game warden had been there looking for them and was planning to come back.

Terrified, the two of them handed the branches with the hanging fish to Joseph, flew up the stairs two steps at a time, and hid in a closet, fearfully awaiting the game warden's arrival. But the game warden never came back. And that evening, the fresh fish tasted really good.

CHAPTER THREE

Making a Decision

1902, Bessemer, Pennsylvania

The Sears Roebuck catalog arrived, and Josephine ran to grab it from the postman. It was heavy, as thick as her hand was wide. She sat on the steps and opened it near the back where she knew she'd find the ladies' fashions—dresses, waists, capes, and bathing suits. Unlike her clothes, these were already made. You didn't need to sew them yourself.

She lingered awhile on one page, singling out a delicate "white lawn" shirtwaist with an elegant high collar and strips of lace from the shoulder to the waist. It looked cool and pretty. Just right for spring. Many of the new dresses had ruffles that sprouted from the shoulders like rippled wings edged in lace. She pictured how she might look in the ladies' fashions, even though she couldn't yet wear them, and wondered if it hurt when the corsets scrunched your waist. All the ladies' clothes showed waists so teeny she wondered how they held up the plentiful bosoms that blossomed above them. The corsets must be pretty strong.

She flipped the pages back to the corset section, holding the catalog upright and turning it toward her so no one passing by, especially her brothers, would see what she was looking at. There were "flexibone" corsets, hook corsets, high bust corsets, and "perfect form" corsets made of lace and ribbons and satiny fabric. They'd likely turn anyone's body into a figure eight.

The catalog had more ladies' hats than clothes. Pages and

pages of them—huge Cuban hats, wider than a woman's shoulders, topped with colorful feathers that towered over the wearer's head and were meant to perch on upswept hair.

Josephine was eleven going on twelve, and her body was gradually reshaping itself from the stick figure of childhood to the voluptuous curves that were to mark her teens. Her face was longer and more defined, accented by a thin aquiline nose and electric green eyes flecked with brown and fringed in black—eyes that commanded you to look at them and always let you know what she was feeling. Her loose ringlets of brownish-auburn hair seemed to defy her attempts at ladylike control, letting out stray hairs that wanted to go their own way. She was less than five feet tall but walked with a confidence that belied her short stature.

The catalog opened her eyes to the wondrous flood of consumer goods soon to become equated with happiness and status for American families. She wished her family could have incandescent lights, sewing machines, and fans that were powered by electricity—but electricity hadn't yet come to Bessemer. There were "wonder cook stoves" and heaters that ran on oil or gas instead of wood or coal. They were all there, in this one catalog. You could order them in the mail and they'd be delivered right to your home, all these wonderful items that could ease the burdens of everyday work and home life, burdens she was beginning to feel she carried more than her share of.

Change was coming to Bessemer more slowly than to cities like Pittsburgh and Cleveland, but it was coming, thanks in part to the rash of inventions and discoveries—electricity, oil, steel, horseless carriages—that were revolutionizing every aspect of American life and affecting people in profound ways. The safe, comfortable Victorian-era order was breaking apart, accompanied by a new spirit of reform and a growing desire of the populace for more control of their lives.

The young, like Josephine, began to resist the constraints and taboos of their elders. A growing link between romantic love and courtship transformed sexual and moral values. No longer were adolescents and young adults limited to old-fashioned courtship rituals like tea parties. They could go on buggy rides and hold hands. They could even be alone.

Josephine watched her older sisters and brothers closely.

One by one, she saw them leave the farm, heading off to get married or make a life of their own. Many had given up the farming life. Her oldest sister Anne had married William Sweeney nine years earlier, and their home across the Ohio line in Poland Village was bursting with five children—all under seven years old. Sarah married a farmer from Scotland, John Heaps Jr., had a four-year-old daughter, Sarah, and lived in Vienna, Ohio. Ellen married engineer Mark Gillam and lived nearby in Bessemer. Their first child, Cyrus, was now three.

John Thomas Mathey was a machinist and engaged. Flora was studying to be a nurse. Emma was now twenty. Albert and Edna were in their teens, and Josephine's three younger siblings—Alice, Joseph Jr., and Ethel—were nine, eight, and six years old.

Her father counted on her to handle more than her share of the arduous farm work. Her mother kept her busy in her free hours caring for the younger children. With the oldest children gone and his own time consumed by the blacksmith shop, Joseph relied on Josephine to convey daily responsibilities to the farmhands and work alongside them. Of all the children, she was the most capable. And she was the one who most loved working on the farm. When school was not in session, her father would go to Josephine's bedroom at five o'clock in the morning, before going to his place of business, and give her orders to be carried out by the several farmhands. At seven o'clock in the morning, the teams set out to work in the fields, Josephine along with them. They worked from seven in the morning until noon, and from one in the afternoon to six at night.

Josephine followed the plow, reaped, harrowed, mowed, raked, and planted corn, wheat, and potatoes. She cared for the sheep. She brought them down to the swimming hole. One by one, she eased them out of the wagon and washed them until their coats were sparkling clean. She sheared their wool, then piled it into a wagon and took it to town to be sold.

She helped with everything that was needed on the farm and took pride in her work. The house was set back three-quarters of a mile from the main road, and Josephine refused to let anyone else work the fields in front because everyone could see them and the rows needed to be straight, perfect. She was sure no one else would do it well enough. She would be defined by her work, whatever the cost to herself.

That became clear one spring day while she was working. Josephine scalded her leg almost to the bone. She dropped to the ground, her leg screaming with the stinging pain, her nerves driving the pain through her body, her face scrunching so all you could see were her clenched teeth. She dug her fingernails into the palm of her hand, dragged herself to her feet, and hobbled to the farmhouse where her alarmed mother dressed the wound.

Before her mother could stop her, Josephine ran back out to the fields. Heavy showers had been forecast and she needed to get her work done before the rains came.

She did get it done, but the price was high. Her leg became badly infected. For weeks afterward, she was bedridden, but she was content because she had completed the job. When she was asked why she'd gone back to the fields with such a terrible injury, she said she was worried that if she didn't do it herself, the rows wouldn't be straight when the wheat came up, and if they looked bad, people would think she'd done it.

But over time, as the months and years passed, the hard work began to wear on her. Josephine, the young girl who wanted to do anything and everything on the farm, was becoming weary of a life of planting and plowing and threshing and harvesting and feeding and housework and caring for her younger brother and sisters.

She was growing up. She was changing. Her world was changing. And the change was coming with lightning speed. It was all very confusing.

Josephine saw a handsome young man drive by regularly when she plowed the fields in front of the farmhouse. He had a fine-looking carriage with a beautiful black horse and was dressed like he was headed for church in a neatly pressed suit and top hat. She wondered who he was and where he was going.

She soon found out.

She was on her way to pick up supplies for the farm, riding her horse along the main road that led from the farm to the center of town, when her stirrup broke. The horse began galloping at full speed and she couldn't stop him. She couldn't slow him down. Josephine clung to the horse's neck, fighting to hold on, bouncing up and down. With each stride, her grip loosened a little more.

The young man happened to be driving his carriage in the opposite direction, coming toward her when he saw her struggling. Instantaneously, he darted from his carriage, ran toward the horse, stopped it, and lifted her off.

Josephine stared at the stranger, mesmerized. He had saved her life; he was her hero.

She learned he was from New Castle, a fast-growing city of twenty-eight thousand located in a valley between the Shenango and Mahoning Rivers, a few miles east of Bessemer, and that for almost a year, he'd been coming to Bessemer twice a week to take orders for a liquor company.

Josephine was twelve but looked like a teenager. He was in his early twenties, nearly twice her age. But apparently he was just as taken with Josephine, and from that day on, they saw each other whenever they could.

On the days he came to town, she met him after school. They sat close together in the shade of a big oak tree at the end of a secluded lane three-quarters of a mile from the farmhouse. He told her about New Castle: the beautiful homes on hills overlooking the city; the meandering park with lakes and rides and a baseball field; and the steel, tin, and ceramic mills that brought in thousands of immigrants from the British Isles, Germany, Italy, and all over eastern Europe. Electricity illuminated homes and businesses and powered streetcars that transported people throughout the city. The lights, more than anything, intrigued Josephine.

He took her for short rides in his carriage and let her drive.

Josephine knew her parents would never approve, so she devised a scheme to keep their meetings secret. On the days the young man came to town, her younger sister Ethel would go straight home after school to keep an eye on their mother and make sure she didn't suspect anything. If her mother went looking for Josephine, Ethel took the shortcut up the lane to alert Josephine, who immediately sprinted home, aiming to get there first.

The plan seemed to be working. If her mother asked why

Josephine was late coming home from school, she'd say she was just talking to a friend, which wasn't entirely untrue.

On Josephine's birthday, the young man gave her a diamond and garnet ring that had belonged to his late mother. Josephine treasured it but knew she needed to hide it from her parents. She found a tiny box, placed the ring inside, and buried it in a special place under a tree in the backyard. When no one was nearby, she'd dig up the box, open it, and stare at it like it was a crystal ball that would summon his image.

She was happier than she'd ever been.

But Bessemer was a small town, and secrets were difficult to keep. One day, Josephine's mother went to a Ladies' Aid Society meeting. She enjoyed spending time with the women, but usually, she was too busy on the farm. However, this day she could attend, and she got an earful! One of the ladies asked her if she knew her daughter was going with an older man who worked for a liquor company. That was all her mother needed to hear. Elizabeth thought anyone who worked for a liquor company surely belonged in hell. She was livid and so was Joseph. They confronted Josephine and she admitted everything. She told them he'd saved her life and that he was wonderful. But her honesty didn't quell their anger. They asked her to hand over the ring he had given her, but she refused, and they got even angrier. Out came the riding whip. Josephine was severely punished and not permitted to leave the farm on the days he came to town.

But when Josephine wanted to do something, no punishment could stop her. She would see him, no matter what her parents did. And she had a plan. Some of the fields she plowed were close to the main road in Bessemer, the road the young man regularly traveled. When she knew he'd be coming, she'd manage to work in those fields or fish by a nearby bridge. To deflect suspicion, she made sure she always had a brother or sister with her. She knew they'd never tell.

Despite her precautions, her parents discovered she was still seeing the young man. They insisted on meeting with him at the farmhouse. He complied, explaining that he loved and wanted to marry Josephine. Her aghast parents reminded him she was much too young. They ordered him to stay away until Josephine was eighteen. They told him if at that time they still cared about each other, they would give their consent to their marriage.

Josephine was defeated, but she held on to the glimmer of hope they could be together when she was old enough. She never tried to see him after that; she would obey her parents' wishes and wait for her time to come.

Several weeks later, he stopped by the farmhouse to tell her and her parents that he had joined the navy and would be gone four years. That evening, her mother allowed her to see him alone, and they said good-bye.

Several days a week, Josephine got a letter from him. They came from all over the world. She read them over and over and tucked them in a box under her bed. She wanted to make sure no one else got her letters, so she asked the postmaster to hold her mail. Every day she went to the post office to see if she had a letter. If she did, she stopped at the meadow on the way back to read it. She'd then search for a four-leaf clover. She thought if she found one, the letters would keep coming.

With each letter she learned more about life beyond the farm. She ached to see new sights, to have experiences like he was having. The tasks she'd loved became burdensome. A desire to be free of the shackles of farm life fermented inside her. She wanted to be on her own.

Josephine lay motionless in her narrow metal bed, afraid to move for fear she'd make a sound and rouse her father or mother or siblings. Her eyes felt pasted open, frozen by excitement and fear. Her ears strained to listen for the chimes from the grandfather clock in the downstairs hallway.

Even though she was only twelve, she was going to leave the farm.

Her father was placing too many demands on her. She was always exhausted. But until now, leaving home was just an idea.

The day before, Josephine had come home from school late, smiling and singing as she walked into the farmhouse. She and her friends had stopped at the store for some penny candy. Her parents, stung by her deception with the young man, were suspicious. They didn't believe her, and her father gave her one of the worst whippings of her young life.

Her backside seared with pain and she'd done nothing wrong. She worked longer and harder than anyone else on the farm. Evenings, she helped her mother with the house and the younger children. What *her parents* did was wrong.

She was angry, really angry. She wanted to be free, get away, go out into the world and earn her own money.

Her mother and father had gone to bed dog-tired, and she knew they'd be up again before dawn. She'd gone to bed, too, and pulled her covers up over her shoulders so no one could see she had clothes on. Then she waited for everyone to fall asleep. She listened for sounds. All she heard was the wind whistling through the trees. When the clock struck twelve she'd make her move.

She waited and listened, and on the twelfth chime, she eased herself out of the bed and slipped on the shoes she'd carefully placed next to it. Earlier, she had rolled a few items of clothing in an old baby blanket, tying it so it would be easy to carry, and tucked it under her bed; now she picked up the bundle and began to creep down the stairs toward the front door. The wooden floorboards of the old farmhouse groaned as her feet pressed against them. She stopped for a few seconds, wondering if anyone heard.

Slowly, quietly, she made her way down the stairs and past the hall clock.

She turned toward the front door . . . and gasped.

Her father stood there, blocking the door. In the dim light, his eyes looked as black as the devil's. He was holding a riding whip in his right hand. She knew what was coming.

A few weeks passed, and Josephine went back to her normal routine.

It was harvest time. She'd been in the cornfields since dawn, plucking ears of corn from their stalks with a metal husking hook strapped to her mitten and throwing them into the wagon her team of horses pulled through the rows. She loved this time of year, but she was becoming more and more weary of what she thought was her slave-like existence. The glimmer of being free, of going off on her own, burned fresh in her mind.

She'd seen how her father had gone from leasing just a few acres of farmland to bigger and bigger farms, how he'd taken advantage of the changing farm environment to begin his own blacksmith business. She hated him right now, but she admired his smart business sense. He started with nothing. Josephine knew she was smart like her father. She could make it on her own too.

As the sky darkened, she headed back to the farmhouse. It was dinnertime. She was exhausted, but, as usual, she helped her mother set out the meal.

After dinner, her mother asked her to help her younger sister Ethel with the dishes. Josephine would wash them; Ethel would dry. Josephine washed the first batch and waited for Ethel to dry them, but Ethel was stalling. She remained in the living room playing, and when Josephine called her, she said she wanted to wash instead of dry. Josephine, though irritated, decided to be a good sport. She agreed to dry if Ethel would wash the rest.

Again she called her younger sister. Ethel said she changed her mind. She wanted to dry them, and Josephine should do the washing. Josephine was furious. She was going to end up doing all the dishes herself. She refused and Ethel started crying.

Her mother heard the argument and hurried into the kitchen. Not knowing what had transpired, she ordered Josephine to do the dishes. Josephine tried to explain to her mother what Ethel was doing, but Elizabeth was tired and had no patience for petty squabbling. She told Josephine to just finish the dishes. Again Josephine refused, saying "no" as loud as she could. It wasn't fair. She'd been working all day while her sister just played.

Out came the whip. Again and again, Josephine felt the stinging lash on her backside.

That night, she again decided to leave home. This time she really meant it.

Josephine knew her mother was going to town the next day. She waited until her mother left, bundled up her clothes as she had before, and said good-bye to her brothers and sisters. Penniless, she walked away from the farm and the family she had loved so much.

II: STRUGGLES

I wanted to be free, get away, to go out into the world and earn my own money, like my father did.
—JOSEPHINE MATHEY MORHARD

CHAPTER FOUR
On Her Own

Josephine scurried down the familiar road, looking back only long enough to make certain no one had seen her. Surges of adrenaline pulsed through her veins. Her heart thumped against her chest. Every breath felt fresh, new, as if it were her first. She was a vagabond on an adventure—free, unencumbered. No one could give her orders or punish her. Nothing could hold her back.

She barely glanced at the harvested rows of wheat she had painstakingly plowed, the dense, forested trails she loved to explore, the sheds of squealing pigs she lovingly cared for, the placid sheep grazing on the hill, and the big oak tree where she often met her sweetheart. The old farmhouse grew more distant.

Her eyes focused solely on the course ahead, on the tiny center of Bessemer where she'd make her own way. She would wait for her sailor boyfriend, and until she was old enough to marry him, she would find a job. But not on a farm. Never again on a farm.

But what would she do? Where would she live? Her mind was racing faster than the feet that propelled her toward Bessemer's Main Street. She'd ask around. She'd find something.

As she neared her destination, Bessemer's scattering of one- and two-story brick and frame buildings came into view—the storefront shops for farm supplies and groceries, the fire station, school, post office, the few businesses, and a small hotel.

Here, just a few miles from the Ohio line, East Poland Avenue met North and South Main Streets. It was a crossroads that separated two distinct neighborhoods.

South of the center was the life Josephine had known—the miles of farmland where manicured fields of golden wheat, hay, and corn met rippling clear blue streams and the green expanse of the gently rolling hills. This was where farm entrepreneurs raised and sold their crops and livestock and took their chances on the market, where neighboring farmhouses were distanced by acres of fertile land, and where large families toiled to keep their way of life.

One the other side of the borough, up North Main and past Churchill Road, steep ridges of dynamited rock carved the terrain, creating a vast gray moonscape of cratered pits, hollowed out to feed the furnaces that melted iron into steel. This was Hillsville, the enclave ruled by the Bessemer Limestone Company. Here bold, hardy immigrants from Sweden, Finland, Austria, and southern Italy sweated in quarries—blasting, drilling, crushing the stone, and loading it on ore cars—all by hand. A day's work netted them $1.65. They lived in tiny copycat houses, owned by the company and jammed together like the layers of limestone.

The differing cultures and ways of life converged in the center of Bessemer, where trouble exploded as regularly as the dynamite in the quarries. Many farmers resented the limestone company's intrusion on their way of life, though they happily leased portions of their land to the company for generous fees. Most feared the immigrants. The limestone workers were becoming a larger and larger proportion of the population. They looked different, acted different, wore different clothes, spoke different languages, and had different religious beliefs. Longtime residents believed they threatened their way of life. And their daughters.

The atmosphere was volatile. Trouble between the two sides was inevitable. There were clashes, shouting, fights.

Josephine had heard a little of this from her father, but she was not worried. She was free. As she made her way up Main Street, she decided to find a place to stay, with a family that didn't have a farm, in a quiet part of town—a family with an extra room to spare. She could take care of their children in exchange for the room.

She stopped at the store where her family bought supplies for the farm. She told the owner she needed a job. He stared at the not-yet-teen figure before him and suggested she head back home.

She wandered down South Main Street and up Poland Avenue, asking everyone she saw if they needed help caring for children or doing housework. No one did. Did they know of anyone who did? she asked. Again and again the answer was no. She plopped on the grass at the side of the road near the school.

A horse and buggy was parked nearby. A man dressed in a dark suit soon approached it. She hopped to her feet, asking if he knew anyone who needed help caring for children.

"As a matter of fact, I do," he replied, and wrote down the name of a lady who lived outside of town. "She has a little girl who is quite ill," he told Josephine.

Josephine trudged to the lady's house and told her she had experience caring for her younger siblings. Could she have a job? And did they have a room where she could stay? The lady was desperate for help. She didn't even ask why such a young girl was on her own. She hired Josephine and gave her a closet-size room with a single bed where she could sleep. She could take time off to go to school as long as she got her chores done. Josephine laid her bundle of clothes on the bed and went to work.

A few days later, she heard a knock on the door. She looked out of the front-room window and saw the familiar face—the tired wide-set eyes, the lips that used to smile but now turned down slightly at the corners, and the salt-and-pepper hair parted in the middle and pulled back in a severe knot.

It was her mother. She'd found out where Josephine was and came after her.

Josephine heard the door open and her name called. Her heart pounded. As her eyes met her mother's, she felt a quick twinge of guilt. She wanted to melt in her mother's arms. Elizabeth Mathey, her cheeks moistened with tears, begged Josephine to come back home. But as much as she loved her mother, Josephine would not. Her mother pleaded. Josephine was firm. She was tired of working in the fields. She wanted to be part of the world beyond their farm. She would never go home again.

Josephine's wandering life had begun. She was about to learn what life could be like for a young girl away from the farm and her family and on her own.

The colorful posters were everywhere in Bessemer. Pasted on store windows. Nailed to trees. Tacked on the doors of buildings. The Medicine Show was coming. Josephine was excited. In small rural towns like this, the Medicine Show was *the* entertainment of the year. There were circus routines, morality plays, and vaudeville skits. There were contests for prizes like pens, knickknacks, and china.

Bessemer had no theaters or large gathering places for plays or musical performances—the only choice for entertainment in town was the Medicine Show.

It was called a Medicine Show for an obvious reason. It was there to sell medicine. Like an early version of today's television commercials, the medical companies concocted entertainment and contests to draw crowds. Then they made their pitch for products like Hamlin's Wizard Oil Liniment, which offered "soothing counter-irritant relief in muscular aches, pains, stiffness of neck, shoulders, backs, sides and limbs due to overexertion or exposure"—and supposedly, it could cure pneumonia and cancer. Or Lefty LeClaire's Nonpareil Rubbing Oil, which the pitchmen claimed could restore hearing to a deaf person.

There were bands, performers, plays, auctions, and contests of all kinds to lure the customers. The Fabulous Kelley (Thomas P. Kelley) brought his Big Free Fun Show to parks and fairgrounds throughout the Midwest and eastern Canada, setting down a tent that seated six thousand and featured an eighteen-square-foot platform, lit by gas torches, which served as the stage for well-known vaudeville acts performing songs and skits like *Dollar for a Kiss* and *Widow Bedot*. Between acts, the medicine pitchmen would come on.

The pitchmen, too, were entertainers, using gimmicks to lure the crowds to buy their medicines. Lefty LeClaire would invite older people with limited hearing from embedded earwax to come onstage. He'd put some of his oil in the person's ear, rub it, and claim the "deaf" person could now hear.

Amateur Nights let housewives, farmers, mineworkers, and other would-be entertainers try their hand at comedy or show off their professed singing or instrumental talents, often to comic effect. And Strong Men, Most Popular Baby, Log Sawing, and other contests attracted burly farm workers and families by offering trinkets to the winners as prizes.

Josephine liked the contests best, and she was confident she could win. She considered herself lucky and she knew she could saw a log and ride a horse as well as any man.

She corralled a school chum to go with her after she finished her chores. Hundreds of people were there already, standing behind the white fences to watch the horse riding and jumping contests and gathering in tents for other attractions. The two girls made their way through the crowd, clomping through the mud and jumping over plops of manure. There were contests for plowing, horse jumping, riding, racing, log sawing, and just about every other farm skill. Josephine entered as many as she could. As she expected, she did well. Her arms bulged with prizes.

People began following her, watching to see how she'd fare. One was a dark-haired man with a deep tan who seemed to be watching every contest she entered. Her friend from school said she knew him. He was a newcomer to Bessemer and lived on the other side of town, near the limestone company. Between contests, he'd come over and talk to them, mostly to Josephine. He seemed like a nice man, she thought.

When it was time for the last contest of the night, Josephine went to the sign-up table to enter. A man in the crowd yelled out that Josephine shouldn't be allowed in the contest because she'd already won prizes; other people deserved a chance. The dark-haired man from the other side of town pushed through the crowd, pointed his finger at the man accusingly, and insisted she'd won every prize fair and square. Others joined in and took sides. People began pushing and shouting. The arguments grew heated. Then the man in charge held up his hands to quiet the crowd and declared that "unless she was allowed to enter, there would be no show."

Josephine was embarrassed. She didn't want to be the center of attention, and she didn't need any more prizes, so she refused to enter. She'd had enough excitement for one day. Besides, it was getting late. Josephine and her school friend decided to leave. The dark-haired man said he'd escort the two of them home. Josephine was thankful he'd stood up for her, and she was still a bit shaken by the near riot, plus it was dark and she lived about a mile away on the outskirts of town.

Josephine's friend lived closest so they dropped her off first. Then, the two of them had to walk another half mile to get to Josephine's home. The walk was pleasant and the conversation flowed easily. Josephine talked about working on the farm and how she loved to ride horses, and the stranger listened quietly. As they neared the home where Josephine was staying, the man stopped, turned, and edged toward her. His eyes, barely visible in the darkness, glowed with determination.

Before Josephine knew what had happened, the man lunged and pushed her to the ground. He thrust his body over hers, nearly smothering her small frame. She felt his thick, rough hands grab at her. She could barely breathe and she thought she would vomit. She kicked. She pushed. She hit. She fought. She had to stop him. But he was so big. So strong.

When she felt she had little fight left, she offered a silent prayer, asking God to help her. Then, like lightning, an idea struck. Her hat! It was held in place by a hat pin! She grabbed it, and before the man knew what was happening, she plunged it into his face, again and again, leaving it full of tiny holes.

The man sprang off her, blood dripping down his face. He looked at Josephine as if he couldn't believe what this young girl had done to him. She quickly jumped up, still fearful but furious, holding the hatpin like a sword. She saw the man's demeanor change. He became contrite and apologized, begging her for forgiveness. But Josephine was in no mood to forgive. She ran toward the house, then stopped at the door and looked back. She lowered her head, aimed her cold, unblinking eyes squarely at his, and told him he'd better be out of town by daybreak. If he wasn't, she said she would have him tarred and feathered and ridden out on a rail. And she likely would have done it too.

*   *   *

The next morning, as the first hint of light touched her face, Josephine slipped out of bed, once again gathered up her clothes, prizes, and a few belongings, tied them together, and walked away from the lady's home, headed for Main Street in Bessemer Center.

She needed to get away and had an idea where she could go. She knew one of her father's wagons would come by on its way to Poland, Ohio, where he'd bought another farm. She sat down on the grass and waited. Something inside her had changed. The dark-haired man had seen to that. She didn't know who to trust anymore. She wanted to find a place where she felt safe, protected, where she could have a real home, where she felt like part of a family, not just a servant with a tiny room.

Bessemer had changed. Josephine knew that now. She'd seen the anger and violence erupt, disrupting the quiet community she'd known. It wasn't just at the Medicine Show. Quarrels between the farmers and the immigrant quarry workers escalated. Work in the quarries paid poorly, so the workers relied on hunting to provide meat for their families. They looked for groundhogs to make a nice stew, or rabbits or anything that flew. Many of the Italian workers hunted songbirds—a delicacy in their native land. But here, hunting them was against the law. The only place the limestone workers had to hunt was on privately owned farmland. When they did, the farmers claimed the immigrants were trespassing and poaching their livestock. They felt under siege as the armed foreigners roamed their fields. The farmers came together and successfully pressured the government to pass new laws against poaching and mandate costly licenses for anyone wanting to hunt. Game wardens enforced the new laws relentlessly.

The Italians were especially angry. All they wanted to do was hunt for food to eat. They retaliated by forming a secret society known as the Black Hand. Threatening messages, extortion demands, and ransom notes went to the farmers—all imprinted with a nefarious "black hand." They committed vandalism, theft, and intimidation. Eventually the Black Hand was accused of murder.

Josephine had seen the vandalism in town and heard rumors of crimes, but she hadn't been fearful before. Now she saw danger in the face of every man she didn't know.

She was going to see a family named Kerr. People in town had been talking about them for days. They'd suffered a terrible tragedy. Their only daughter, Lizzie, had passed away. Josephine had heard the Kerrs were good people, always helping others, and they were wealthy. They lived in a beautiful home in Boardman, Ohio, a community not far from the Pennsylvania–Ohio state line with acres of apple orchards, farms, and almost no industry except in the small northeast corner that bordered Youngstown.

Josephine felt sad for them. Maybe they'd like to have a young girl around as much as she wanted a good home. Maybe the Kerrs would be her answer, as much as she could be theirs.

Boardman was about six miles from Bessemer, just past Poland. Her father's wagon would take her about a mile from their place.

Soon she saw the familiar horse and wagon heading toward her. One of her father's farm workers was driving and he recognized her. She told him she was going to see a friend not far from her father's farm, and jumped in the back. She rode as far as the road that led from Poland to Boardman. When the driver turned toward her father's farm, she jumped off and started to walk the extra mile toward the Kerr home.

The family lived in a freshly painted three-story farmhouse with shutters and a porch that extended the length of the house. Surrounding it were acres of pristine fields and barns.

Josephine stood quietly for a moment, looking at the small group of horses grazing behind wooden fences painted the same white as the house—their coats glistening, their manes and tails smoothly brushed. She soaked in the comforting farm smells, sounds, and sights. Here everything looked fresh, perfect, like a picture—even the barns and sheds. It was unlike her family's farm—no faded or curling paint or patched-up barn doors or gaggles of kids running around. The house commanded a spot set back from the road just enough for the family's privacy while still allowing admiring glances from passers-by.

Josephine slowly walked toward the house, convinced she'd found a home and could, in turn, help ease the sorrow of the family inside. She stepped to the front door and rang the bell. Mrs. Kerr opened the door. Her eyes looked kind, Josephine thought, warm but with a lingering sadness—a little like her mother's eyes looked when she'd begged Josephine to come back home.

Sure she'd come to the right place, Josephine boldly introduced herself.

"I understand you lost your daughter, and I wondered if I could fill her place."

The woman stood there, stunned, at the impudence of this brash young girl who was bringing her back to the pain of losing her only daughter and dared to think she could replace her. No one could ever replace Lizzie.

The warmth Josephine had seen in Mrs. Kerr's eyes hardened into a chilly stare. The woman couldn't speak for a moment, then barked at Josephine, "Who are you? Where are you from? How did you get here?"

Josephine backed away. This was not the reaction she expected. She started to answer, but more words wouldn't come out.

Josephine wanted to disappear. Mrs. Kerr didn't want her. She'd come here desperate to find a place where she'd be safe, comfortable, cared for, and not need to work so hard to get enough food to eat or a bed to sleep on. She thought she could help a family whose distress was even worse than her own, but now she realized she'd done the wrong thing. She made the lady feel worse.

She lowered her head and turned toward the road, trying to contain her tears. Where was she going to go? She couldn't go back to the lady's house in Bessemer. She'd sneaked out without telling her. She wouldn't go back home. She just wouldn't. She was way out in Boardman and her father's buggy wouldn't be coming near for another day.

Suddenly Mrs. Kerr called to her. "Wait," she said in a shaky but no longer harsh voice. "Please. Come in."

Josephine reluctantly obeyed, entering slowly, uncertainly, while Mrs. Kerr directed her into the living room and motioned her to a velvety-soft chair with a rounded back. Mrs. Kerr sat down across from her in a matching chair, her posture erect, her hands folded in her lap, her head tilted toward Josephine, eyeing her with a mixture of curiosity and wariness. Josephine waited for the questions she knew would be coming.

Again, Mrs. Kerr asked her name, this time more softly, now sensing the young girl's vulnerability. Josephine mumbled her reply, and as she did, she began sobbing, no longer the presumptuous young girl who first appeared on the Kerrs' doorstep.

Mrs. Kerr offered her a handkerchief and, once again, asked where she was from and what prompted her to come to their home. Her chest now heaving with sobs, Josephine blurted out her story, telling the woman about her overflowing family, the backbreaking work on the farm, the whippings, running away, caring for the lady's sick child, and finally, what the dark-haired man tried to do to her.

Josephine told Mrs. Kerr she'd just wanted a place where she'd be safe and where someone would care about her, and that she'd heard about the Kerrs' daughter and that the family was nice, and she thought maybe they'd like to have a girl like her with their own daughter gone. But now she knew she'd made a mistake, and she was sorry, really sorry.

Mrs. Kerr listened intently, leaning in toward Josephine more closely with each word of Josephine's tortured story. She looked at Josephine's rough, callused hands. She believed her. She moved her chair closer and placed her hand in Josephine's, then gently asked if she'd thought about going back home. Josephine said she'd never, ever, go home to live again.

Mrs. Kerr then asked Josephine if she'd like some tea and introduced her to the rest of the family. Mr. Kerr's first name was Irwin, he'd served in the Civil War and had been given a generous plot of farmland for his military service. He'd made the most of it and became a successful farmer. Mrs. Kerr's first name was Sarah. Her older sister, Louisa—a warm, friendly lady everyone called Aunt Lou—and the Kerrs' son Walter, who helped on the farm, also lived there.

Josephine brightened as she met the family, and she brushed the tears from her face. But, as brash as she'd been in presenting herself to the Kerrs as a substitute daughter, she felt awkward in this beautiful home, with these refined people. She was the tomboy who plowed fields, split logs, and drove horses. They sipped tea out of tiny china cups and had furniture that looked like it came from a European palace—at least she thought it looked like that even though she'd never seen what furniture from palaces looked like.

Finally, Mrs. Kerr told Josephine the family would consider her request, but they were going to need to talk to her mother. She told Josephine she would come and see her in the coming week, but for now, she suggested Josephine go back to her family. She'd take her there.

Josephine was quick to give her usual answer, "no," she wouldn't go back. If she went home, even for a while, they'd insist she stay and make it more difficult for her to go elsewhere. She needed them to understand that she was never, ever coming back. Mrs. Kerr then asked if she'd go back to the lady's house where she'd been staying. No, she couldn't do that either. The lady would be mad she left without telling her. Finally, Josephine said she'd go stay with her sister Sarah, called Sadie, who lived nearby on a farm in Coalburg, but just temporarily.

The following week, Mrs. Kerr called for her at school as she said she would. Josephine excitedly hopped in her carriage, and they headed for the farm to talk to her mother.

Josephine cried when she walked into the farmhouse and saw her mother. She would later write, "My dear, beautiful mother, with so many children—and so little to do with. Bless her. I was determined to relieve her of her burden, at least of me. I made it clear that I wouldn't stay on the farm, so she let me go to my new home."

Torn between love for her family and the new life she yearned for, she left with Mrs. Kerr, again brushing away tears as she rode away in the fine carriage.

The Kerrs treated her like she was their missing daughter. Her room was near a staircase that swirled its way down into the foyer. Paintings of mountains and trees and rivers were on the walls, and her bed was soft with blankets and quilts and soft pillows. The Kerrs let her have their daughter Lizzie's riding horse and any of her things that she wanted. She had riding lessons and nice clothes. She had a chaperone wherever she went. The Kerrs were a second family to her, and Aunt Lou was the doting aunt she never had. She could talk to her about anything, even her sailor boyfriend, whose letters were still arriving regularly.

*   *   *

Josephine quickly flipped through the day's mail, looking for the next letter from her sweetheart. It had been two years since they parted at her family's insistence, and he'd been all over the world since he joined the navy. His letters were full of tales of the war in Haiti and exotic lands in the Far East, of the wonders of cities and the pink sands and turquoise waters of ocean-side beaches.

Once in a while he'd send a gift—often a small glass animal with the name of a place he'd visited colorfully painted on the side—and she'd hold it in her hand like a magical orb, picturing the two of them catching a train in New York's Grand Central Terminal or riding horses through a rain forest on a distant island.

Josephine was fourteen now, living in Boardman with the Kerr family but thinking of the day when the two of them could be together. As the months passed, that day was beginning to seem more than a far-off dream. They were making plans. He told her he'd saved nearly all of his pay so they could have a home. In four more years, they could be married with her family's consent. She imagined her mother and father, sisters and brothers, and the Kerrs at the wedding—smiling, telling her how lovely she looked in her white gown.

She saw the familiar handwriting, the white envelope addressed to "Miss Josephine Mathey." From the stamp she knew her sailor was back in the United States. Excited, she tore open the envelope and began to read: *"Dear Josephine. I didn't want to write this letter, but I need to tell you . . ."*

She froze, almost afraid to read more. He went on to write that his ship had come into port after months at sea. He was so happy to be back in the U.S. that he went out with his sailor friends to celebrate. But he did something terrible. The letter didn't elaborate on what it was. He wrote only that all his money was gone, everything he saved for their future together. He promised he'd start over. He'd make it up to her.

Josephine was devastated. She read the letter over and over, somehow hoping she hadn't read it right, that the words didn't say what she knew they did. She tried to hold back the tears, but they rolled down her cheeks anyway. Her brain was a jumble of thoughts, of questions. What had he done? Where had the money gone? How could he have lost everything? Had someone stolen the money? Could he have spent it on a woman? Or women?

She remembered one time when she saw him driving by her school with a lady in his carriage, a pretty lady who was closer to his age. Josephine was in the schoolyard with her friends. She remembered his carriage galloping by, the two of them talking and laughing, looking happy together, looking like lovers. She remembered her anger, her tears. The same feelings consumed her now.

Then, he'd shrugged off her concerns, saying the lady was an old friend. She relented. But now, those old feelings came back and reached a crescendo. Her brain raced through imagined scenes of him with other women. And worse, much worse. The money for their future was gone, and she was convinced she knew why.

The tears stopped. Her eyes began to glow with the hatred only love can spark.

It was finished. She was angry at what he had done, angry that he could be so weak. Somehow, all the love she had ever had for him was gone. He was dead to her.

As she lay in her warm, comfortable bed that night, the thought of moving on festered in her brain. Now everything had changed. She loved the Kerrs. They were wonderful to her and had given her a life she'd only dreamed of. Life there had been very different from anything she'd known before. It was still not the life of freedom she craved, but, under the Kerrs' tutelage, she'd learned to act and dress like a lady, develop refined tastes, and transform her love of horses into becoming an expert horsewoman. The Kerrs had time to give her that her own mother did not. They were proud of her and encouraged her, but even the comfort and love of this new family didn't quell Josephine's defining lust for freedom.

She was restless, no longer content to stay, no longer willing to wait for her sailor. She wanted to get away, and once again make her own way. She yearned to be on her own.

The bright lights of Youngstown beckoned. The city was right next to Boardman, but it was as different as a field of corn from a blazing trough of molten steel.

Youngstown had long been luring young people away from farm towns like Boardman, Poland, and Bessemer—places where commercial agricultural enterprises were sucking the life out of family farms and where trouble between farmers and miners was constantly brewing. Industrialization had changed everything. Little opportunity remained in the rural areas.

Youngstown was where Josephine wanted to be, and she had a plan.

All the time she was living with the Kerrs, Josephine had kept in close touch with her family, and the Kerrs made it possible for her to see them often, especially her sister Sadie, who was fifteen years older than Josephine and had been married since she was nineteen. Josephine looked to her like a mother, and as independent and strong-minded as Josephine was, she still turned to Sadie when she needed help. This was one of those times. Sadie had often asked Josephine to come and live with them at her home in nearby Coalburg, believing she should live with family not with strangers, but Josephine always refused. Josephine knew she'd be welcome to stay with them while she looked for work in Youngstown.

Sadie usually came into Boardman on Saturdays to get supplies, so Josephine would make an excuse to go into town, find Sadie, and tell her what she was planning. She said nothing to the Kerrs about what had happened with her sailor boyfriend or that she was going to leave. She knew they'd be unhappy, and she didn't know what to say to them. So Josephine did what she had always done when she was in an uncomfortable situation.

She silently disappeared, again.

CHAPTER FIVE

Bright Lights

Youngstown bustled with energy, unlike the sleepy farm towns of Bessemer, Poland, and Boardman. Here clusters of white-columned buildings rose high above the red brick streets as if to match the height of the surrounding hills. Finely dressed people puffed along Federal Street in Stanley Steamers or motored in elegant new Oldsmobile Broughams that boasted gold-colored fixtures, white-spoked bicycle-style wheels, and double rows of black pincushion leather seats that lifted the occupants high above the ground so they looked like royalty next to the horse-drawn buggies that shared the street.

The city, founded in 1797 as part of the original Western Reserve of Connecticut, had become one of the great steelmaking districts of the world thanks to the rich veins of iron ore and coal deposits discovered nearby and its many water and rail transportation options. The population, now over one hundred thousand, made it one of the largest cities in the country.

Just west of downtown's pristine atmosphere was the machinery that churned out the city's success. Here, clouds of black smoke smothered the sky, spewing regularly out of the slender black smokestacks that lined the Mahoning River as it snaked its way through the city. At night, red, yellow, and orange flames flared into the blackness, igniting a fireworks display that rivaled the Fourth of July.

Chugging alongside the mills were the steam locomotives that transported raw materials to the blast furnaces and hauled the finished steel to the factories that turned it into the cars, bridges, skyscraper girders, machinery, and appliances that were transforming the country. Youngstown was a place where people made things—things that changed lives.

Josephine was sure her own life would change for the better in Youngstown. She'd visited the city often when she was living in Boardman with the Kerrs. There was more opportunity there and many more things to do. But her sister Sadie wasn't convinced. Sadie thought something terrible was certain to happen to Josephine, on her own in a big city like Youngstown. She pleaded with Josephine to stay with them, but Josephine wasn't worried; on the contrary, she craved the excitement. She told Sadie she'd stay with her only until she found a job in Youngstown.

Josephine jumped into her job search as soon as she settled in at her sister's home. She was willing to do anything—anything except farm work. Day after day, she searched through the want ads. She thought maybe she could find work in one of the many factories in the city, but the only factory openings listed at the time were for men. There wasn't much for a girl like her with few skills, just the usual jobs: caring for children or working as a domestic. She set her sights lower. She responded to one ad.

Wanted. Someone to care for two children.

Josephine had plenty of experience looking after children; she had cared for her younger siblings and the sick child when she first left home. She was sure she'd get the job. She got out her best frock and headed for the home of the family that placed the ad. Their name was Metzger, and they owned a drugstore. Best of all, they lived in Youngstown. Both husband and wife worked long hours in the store and were desperate for help. They were impressed with Josephine, and she got the job.

Josephine worked hard, aiming to please the Metzgers and take good care of the children, and in return they treated her like she was one of the family. She was so diligent, Mrs. Metzger soon began to rely on her for other household duties, and, before long, she was not only looking after the children, she was washing, ironing, and scrubbing. It was hard work, but nowhere near as hard as farm work, and Josephine didn't care as long as she was able to be in Youngstown.

But the years of hard work were beginning to show.

One evening Mr. Metzger's brother, who lived with the family, looked at her callused hands, then stared at her and asked, "How did you get these?"

Embarrassed, Josephine lied and told him, "I was born this way."

Josephine's sister Flora stopped in one day to visit her at the Metzgers. Josephine leaned in, listening closely to catch every word as Flora excitedly told her about all the job opportunities now available for women with skills. At twenty-three, Flora was eight years older than Josephine, and unlike her other older sisters—who married and were raising children—Flora was single and had a career. She was one of the "new" women of the early twentieth century—women who wanted more than husbands and double-digit numbers of children. They saw possibilities beyond those of their mothers and grandmothers.

In their grandmother's generation, girls—if they had any education at all—received it in charitable or religious institutions, learning domestic skills, reading, and sometimes writing. They had no access to public education. Even wealthy girls' education was limited to private finishing schools where they could study painting, play the harpsichord, and practice sewing skills like embroidery. Women weren't allowed to own property until the mid-1800s.

The common belief among many men was that women's brains were inferior, that they were incapable of doing more than caring for husbands, children, and homes. One noted philosopher of the time theorized, "The whole education of women should be relative to men. To please them, to be useful to them, honored by them, to educate them when young, to care for them when grown, to counsel them, to console them and to make life sweet and agreeable for them—these are the duties for women at all times and what should be taught to them from their infancy."

Further, he noted, women needed to be constrained or they would tyrannize men, "given the ease with which women arouse men's senses . . . men would finally be their victims."

A few brave women defied their generation's logic. By the time Josephine and Flora's mother Elizabeth was born, there had been progress. Women had access to public education.

More teachers were needed and so-called normal schools began training women to fill those positions. Women's colleges were created in New England and New York. Still, the curricula at these colleges lagged far behind that of men's colleges like Harvard. Oberlin College in Ohio, which admitted women in 1839, was the first to offer women an education equal to men. And yet, only a tiny minority of women took advantage of these educational opportunities. The vast number of women in Elizabeth Mathey's generation continued to opt for domestic life.

Flora, Josephine, and women like them who came of age in the early twentieth century benefited from a rare convergence of economic, political, and social factors that uprooted societal norms. Women began to see the tiniest light of opportunity.

Youngstown's steel, Pennsylvania's oil, and the harnessing of electricity had created new technologies—sewing machines, washers, ready-to-wear clothing—that made it easier for women to handle household duties. With the new appliances, women could escape some of the domestic drudgery. Life became easier.

At the same time, companies that manufactured these goods found women's talents and abilities ideally suited to many of the new jobs manufacturing created. Women who knew how to sew and weave could be hired to run new power-driven looms. By the time Josephine was born, women in some cities worked in industries that produced clothing, textiles, containers, boxes, tobacco, printing, carpets, rugs, and hats. However, this progress was tempered by the deplorable conditions these women were often subjected to—sweatshops where temperatures often topped 100 degrees—and the extremely low wages they earned for their labor.

Slaves had been emancipated, but only men were granted a Constitutional right to vote. Women were excluded, still second-class citizens. Ohio's women hadn't felt as much discrimination as others, but suffrage was a hot topic in women's groups that sprang up in villages and cities alike. As if awakening from a deep sleep, women demanded the vote with a passion that would forever change the image they would have of themselves.

Josephine hadn't paid much attention to the issue at first. It was unfair, she thought, and she had a fierce belief in fairness. But it wasn't just about the vote. It was everything. She'd always been able to do what the boys did on the farm, but it was different on the outside. In that world, she was relegated to "women's work."

Flora was a nurse. She'd been out in the world too. She understood Josephine's desire to be on her own and make something of herself, but she believed her young sister had better options than caring for children. Flora had come to the Metzger home that day to convince Josephine to get an education.

Flora explained there were courses Josephine could take to become a practical nurse, or she could get a diploma from a Nightingale nursing school, like the one affiliated with Youngstown's St. Elizabeth Hospital where Flora worked. If Josephine preferred to teach, she could go to a normal school.

Josephine thought for a minute. She wasn't interested in nursing or teaching. She wanted to go into business like their father. In that case, Flora said, she could go to a business school. Ever since the typewriter was invented in 1867, women had been hired as bookkeepers, accountants, cashiers, typists, and stenographers. Business schools taught those skills. Flora knew of a school in Youngstown that trained people for office work. Josephine's eyes brightened, then faded. She couldn't afford it. Flora was quick to assure her sister that the family would help her. Josephine knew everyone in her family was concerned about her. They'd begged her to come back to the farm, but Josephine had always stubbornly refused. She wanted to do things on her own, in her own way. But getting an education where she could learn business skills . . . that was intriguing. She wondered if there was a way she could accept their help and still keep her independence.

Josephine eventually decided she would take them up on their offer to help with the cost of school, but she wouldn't go back to the farm. And she would work to pay for her board. Josephine approached the Metzgers, and made them a proposition: if she could take time off to go to school, she'd like to continue working for them. They gave their support. Soon she was on her way to Youngstown-Brown Business College on W. Federal Street where she would study to become a bookkeeper.

Josephine was excited, but it didn't take very long for her to realize that her limited schooling in math wasn't good enough to be a bookkeeper. She kept at it for five months but was slowly falling behind. Discouraged but still determined to make a place for herself in the business world, she went to the administration and asked to change to stenography. The answer was a firm "no." Never one to be deterred, Josephine quietly entered the stenography class, took a seat, and went to work. Surprisingly, the school let her stay.

Josephine liked stenography and excelled in school, but she was finding it difficult to handle the schoolwork and everything the Metzgers expected her to do. She'd get up at 4:00 a.m. to do chores before school, and after school she had children to look after, dinner to prepare, cleaning, and scrubbing. It was just too much, and again, Josephine felt she needed to move on. She put an ad in the Youngstown paper saying she'd care for children after school in exchange for meals and a place to stay. There would be no more cooking, cleaning, and scrubbing—and no more pay. She said good-bye to the Metzgers and was off to a new family. But she hadn't considered the consequences. She had a room, and her tuition was covered, but she had no money for anything else. Her clothes became threadbare. She tore one of her few shirtwaists. One morning as she walked along Federal Avenue on the way to school, she looked down at the fraying hemlines of her ankle-length skirts. Nubby stones on the road burst through the worn soles of her shoes, rubbing against the bottoms of her feet. She stuffed her shoes with paper, but that didn't really help. Just when she was feeling she couldn't walk a step farther, she saw a man kick what looked like a crunched up brown paper bag out of his way. She was curious. It looked like there might be something in it. She thought to herself, *If he doesn't pick it up I will.*

He didn't, so she did. Inside was a tiny package. Josephine tore it open. To her amazement, she found sixteen dollars, which to her was a fortune. She couldn't believe her good luck. Shirtwaists cost less than one dollar. So did skirts and underskirts and stockings. She could buy a dress and enough new clothes to last for months!

Then she stopped herself. Her conscience intervened. She couldn't keep it. This money belonged to someone else.

Reluctantly, believing she was doing the right thing, Josephine took the money to the head of the business college and asked him to post an ad to see if anyone would claim it. He peered at her shabby clothing and told her she found it and should keep it, adding that anyone could claim the money, whether or not it was theirs.

But Josephine couldn't take it without trying to find the owner. She checked every day to see if anyone claimed the money. After a couple of weeks, when no one did, she finally felt she could take the badly needed money.

Life was getting better for Josephine. She was happy. She could see a future for herself. She'd been studying stenography for four months, and everything was going well. She was sure she was ready for a job.

She no longer looked or felt like the little twelve-year-old girl who left home with her few clothes tied in a baby blanket. She was in her mid-teens now, still a bit under five feet tall, but she walked with confidence—head held high, eyes focused straight ahead, posture erect.

She was not conventionally pretty—her aquiline nose a bit too rounded and long—but somehow her features melded together to give her a distinct beauty all her own. She had a slender face and electric green eyes flecked with brown and fringed in black—eyes that dared you to look at them and always let you know if she was happy or angry. Her brownish-auburn hair seemed to make the color of her eyes even more intense. Her bright coloring seemed to reflect her feisty nature.

Perhaps the biggest change was the blossoming of her figure. She had slender arms and legs and a tiny waist—even without the boned corsets of the day—that encircled hourglass curves, the kind other women envied and men lusted after. But Josephine wasn't one to display these attributes. She hid them as much as she could, wearing modest dresses or white shirt-waists with high collars and flowing dark skirts, aiming for a refinement that now seemed natural despite her tomboy past.

One day, as she was walking out of Youngstown's new post office building after mailing a letter, she was suddenly stopped by a man who asked her if she was Joe Mathey's daughter.

She said she was, confident anyone who knew her father

must be a fine man. He saw her book and steno pad and wanted
to know how much schooling she'd had. She told him she'd
been in the steno department for four months and had learned a
lot. She was eager to put her training to work.

He seemed interested and asked her if she thought she was
good enough to take a position as a stenographer. Quickly, she
answered, "Yes." She was sure she'd learned enough to go to
work. And she could use the money. He said he needed someone like her to work in his office on Federal Street and told her
to stop by the next day after school, writing the address down
for her on a piece of paper.

As soon as school was out the next day, she hurried down
the street to the address he'd given her, excited that she might
actually get a job in the business world. The address was a wholesale coffee business. She knocked on the door. The man, smiling
broadly, opened the door, welcomed her, and she stepped inside.
But as soon as she did, she heard the lock turn in the door behind
her. She was uneasy. Something didn't feel right. Her excitement
turned to dread.

She remembered the dark-haired man from the Medicine
Show. Her mind raced, and her body stiffened. She needed to
get out of there. She walked toward one of the coffee displays
set up around the room while she figured out what to do. She
stepped slowly from display to display, feigning curiosity about
the different kinds of coffee, picking up the bags, examining
them, asking questions and commenting that she'd never seen
coffees like these. She needed to make her way back to the
front door and get out of there. The man, perhaps charmed that
she was so interested in his coffee business, smiled and made
no move to stop her. When she reached the door, she quickly
turned the lock and swung open the door.

The man, finally aware of what she was doing, lunged toward her and grabbed her arm, but Josephine, already halfway
out the door, screamed, slammed the door against him, yanked
her arm away from the astonished man, and ran.

Josephine wanted a job, but not at that price. The experience
made her wiser and more cautious, but not discouraged about
the business world.

Josephine took odd jobs to earn money as she once again
scoured the classified ads in the Youngstown newspapers.

When she came across an ad that said the Lyric Theater needed a stenographer, she applied for the job.

Theaters abounded in Youngstown. In 1901 the cavernous Park Theater opened, presenting movies, vaudeville, and live theater to huge audiences—shows like *Big-Hearted Jim* and *To Die at Dawn.* Sam Warner, one of Youngstown's now-famous Warner Brothers, and a local partner had taken over the city's Old Grand Opera House where they presented vaudeville shows and plays. Josephine hadn't heard of the Lyric Theater, but she quickly answered the ad.

The Lyric Theater was on W. Federal Street. It was a small theater, not far from the school, that presented live stage plays. She told the manager she had been studying stenography and was good at it. He offered her the job, explaining that the theater was just starting out, so they couldn't pay much. He could give her $4 a week to take dictation and type. She gladly accepted.

When she reported for work the next day, she saw a sign of the theater's limited finances. Her typewriter was on a soap box that acted as her desk. She didn't care. She sat down, put in a piece of paper, and tested the machine, pressing the round metal-edged buttons against the carbon ribbon to imprint the letters and pulling the carriage return to move the paper to the next line.

Finally, she had a job as a stenographer even if the workspace was a bit rough. With a job and an income, she no longer needed to barter her child care services for a room. She could pay for one. She found a room in a house about three miles from her new job. Rent was $2 a week and included breakfast. That left a modest $2 for everything else—far from enough to sustain herself. Once again she was struggling. She decided to walk the three miles to and from work instead of paying for the streetcar. Many days, breakfast was her only real meal of the day. She would often buy a bag of peanuts for lunch or gingersnaps for supper. Some nights were so bad that she would kneel at her bedside and pray to God to take her home. She was tired, weary, and hungry, but she never showed it. On her worst nights, she would just go to sleep and wake ready for another day's battle.

As she always did, she worked tirelessly at her job, fulfilling her employers' needs if not her own, and earning the respect and admiration of the theater managers. She also learned about theater.

After a few months, she had an opportunity to do readings from plays on Sunday afternoons and evenings. That added a much-needed $5 to her weekly earnings. She was building a reputation among the theatergoers, who occasionally asked her to give readings to groups like the Ohio G.A.R.—a Civil War group named after the Grand Army of the Republic.

From its shaky beginning, the theater began to draw enough people to make a small profit, and the manager replaced the soapbox with a real desk and bought Josephine a new typewriter.

Josephine liked the theater job and the people she worked with and met, but the theater faced considerable competition and the audiences remained modest. When she saw an ad for a higher-paying stenography job, she applied for it and was hired.

She promptly resigned from her position at the theater and reported to her new job the following morning. However, when she arrived, the manager told her he'd decided she was not experienced enough to handle the work. Josephine was dumbfounded. How could they fire her before she even had a chance to start? She'd given up her job for nothing. Now she had no job and no income.

She desperately knocked on the doors of every business she could find, but she couldn't find work as a stenographer or a typist or even a receptionist. Finally, she got a break—a job as assistant to the cashier of the Mohegan Market, which had about fifty employees. She would work in a cashier's booth and take over for the head cashier when the store was busy.

After Josephine had been on the job for a few days, the manager asked her out to dinner. He was much older. Worse, he was married. She said no, believing he'd understand that a teenage girl couldn't go out with an older, married man. But he was persistent, scheming in every possible way to get Josephine to go out with him. She kept saying no.

One day the manager came to her and told her he wanted to keep her cashier's cage open during her lunch hour and that he'd take care of the cashiering then so she could go to lunch. Josephine thought nothing of it; it made good business sense to keep it open at lunchtime. But a few days later she would question his motives.

He called her into his office and told her that her register was $50 short. Fifty dollars was missing, and someone must have stolen it; he said that someone must be Josephine.

She was taken aback. She would never steal. How could he accuse her of such a thing?

And then it became clear: he told her there were ways she could pay back the sum, and they didn't involve money. He told her how much he liked her, and he really didn't want to have to report it. He smirked and walked out of the office, telling her to think about it and he'd be back to hear her decision.

Once he left, furiously, impulsively, she locked the office door, took the key, went to a phone and called the Burns Detective Agency, which was well known for uncovering criminal wrongdoing. She asked the agency to send a detective to the market. Her call completed, she went up to the manager and told him what she'd done. He stared, incredulous at the young girl's audacity, his eyes bulging, his arm positioned to strike a blow.

The detective arrived just in time. The manager, so angry he was barely able to speak, pointed his finger repeatedly, accusingly at Josephine, then finally stuttered that she had stolen $50 from the market. The detective asked her to tell her side.

Josephine spelled out every detail of what had happened in the cashier's booth—how she handled the money, recounted it to make sure everything was correct, how there was never a shortage when she was working in the cashier's cage by herself. She didn't say anything about the manager's repeated attempts to seduce her.

The detective listened attentively, looked back at the manager, then at Josephine. He then asked her if she was Joe Mathey's daughter. That was a strange question, she thought, but she answered yes.

"We don't even need to search you. Joe Mathey's daughter would never steal money. He's the most honest man I know."

To Josephine's surprise, the manager didn't fire her. With jobs in scarce supply, she needed to stay, but she made sure she wouldn't be accused of stealing again. Before lunchtime when the manager took over her spot, she asked the assistant manager to count the money in the cage. She asked him to count it again when she returned. As she suspected, each day $5 to $7 was missing from her cage during the time she was gone.

This time, in her most defiant voice, now unafraid of losing her job, she told the manager what she had discovered—and, in front of everyone, called him a thief.

This time she was fired.

The pattern of her life was emerging.

Josephine was now nineteen. After years of cleaning other people's floors, watching their kids, and typing their letters, Josephine finally had a good job in the field she wanted. She was a stenographer for an iron manufacturing company. To make up for her lack of early education, she kept a dictionary by her side, checking to make certain her spelling was correct and looking up words she didn't know. She was fast and accurate.

She had a room in a three-story clapboard house on Falls Road in Youngstown, a working-class neighborhood of English and Welsh immigrants and their descendants, much like her mother's family. Fifty-four-year-old Anna Hopes was head of a household that included her daughter Alice, her son-in-law Walter Rudge Jr., a train conductor who'd come to the United States in 1888 from England on the *British King*, and eleven-year-old granddaughter Mildred.

Despite her insistence on being independent, Josephine had always remained in close touch with her family. Her parents and most of her siblings lived nearby—in the towns bordering southeast Ohio and western Pennsylvania—and she visited regularly.

Anne, Sadie, John, Ellen, Emma, and Albert were all married. They had fifteen children between them—still less than their parents' original brood. Anne and her husband William Sweeney had eight, ranging in age from four to fifteen. Joseph, Ethel, and Alice were still at home. Only Flora had moved away from the area. She was living in Cleveland and was a nurse at City Hospital, a city-run facility that cared primarily for poor people suffering from contagious diseases like cholera, smallpox, and tuberculosis.

Josephine was intrigued with her sister's life. Cleveland was thriving. It was the fifth largest city in the country—behind only New York, Chicago, Philadelphia, and Detroit—and it was thirteen times larger than Youngstown, with a population around seven hundred thousand. Cleveland had become a center of industry, propelled originally by the demand for Civil War materials and boosted by the expansion of railroads, telegraphs, coal mines, iron mills, and the mammoth oil-refining business begun by John D. Rockefeller.

Cleveland was also a key transportation hub. Here, the Erie and Ohio Canals flowed into Lake Erie, creating a web of shipping lines that brought raw materials and finished products to and from the Eastern seaboard through the Great Lakes and down the Ohio River to the Mississippi. Railroads, too, converged here, bringing the region's oil and steel to the rest of the country.

In Cleveland, barons, shipping magnates, inventors, and political leaders made deals, then retreated to grand mansions on "Millionaire's Row," which peered over Lake Erie, one of the Great Lakes. Euclid Avenue was known as the "Showplace of America." The elm tree–lined boulevard was internationally admired, often compared to the Champs-Elysees in Paris.

No greater concentration of wealth, no mansions with a higher valuation, existed in America, not even on New York's Fifth Avenue. At one time or another, John D. Rockefeller, arc light inventor Charles Brush, U.S. Secretary of State John Hay, and Western Union founder Jeptha Wade lived here along with scores of other industrialists and politicians. Their turreted estates rose from acres of parklike surroundings set far back from the wide sandstone avenue.

Josephine was determined to make something of herself, as determined as her father had been. She wanted to be successful in business like he was, and like he did, she moved from place to place, each time looking for a better opportunity. She had good business experience now, and in Cleveland, a city so full of promise and excitement, she was certain to find an even better stenography job, one that would pay more. Maybe she'd even find romance.

Each time Josephine visited Flora in Cleveland, she checked the classifieds, searching for the right position, one in a good company where she'd make more money. It didn't take long before she found one and came to Cleveland to live. It was

1915 and she was twenty-four. She soon impressed her new employer with her strong work ethic and outgoing personality. People liked her, and she went out of her way to be helpful. She was determined to do her job to perfection.

She loved working in Cleveland's vigorous business climate, associating with interesting people and developing her organizational skills. She'd achieved exactly what she wanted—she was financially secure and independent. But something was missing from her life. She still yearned for male companionship.

Homer Prentice was a chiropractor. He'd moved to Cleveland in 1914 to open a practice. Like Josephine, he was from the Youngstown area, growing up in Beaver Township, a small community bordering Boardman, where Josephine lived with the Kerrs and where her sisters Anne and Edna now lived.

When Homer was in his late teens, he married a woman and they had two children, but he moved to Cleveland alone. In 1915, a year after relocating, Homer was divorced. The same year he moved his practice to 8313 Euclid Avenue, up the avenue from the fabled mansions but near enough to attract wealthy customers.

Around the same time, Josephine was living on East 80th Street, boarding in a home that was several blocks southwest of Homer's office. It wasn't long before the two met and began seeing each other. Homer was six years older than Josephine— tall, with blue eyes and brown hair—and Josephine was in love for the first time since she'd said good-bye to her sailor sweetheart. She'd had boyfriends, but none of her relationships had been serious. Homer was the one, she thought. She was sure he felt the same way about her. However, as the months went on, he became more and more distant. Finally, he told her their romance was over.

Josephine was heartbroken.

Her relationships with men never seemed to work out, but she was making her own money, good money for a woman, and without a romantic relationship, no one could hurt her.

Not long afterward, Josephine's twenty-year-old sister Ethel came to Cleveland. She'd followed in Josephine's footsteps and become a stenographer. Josephine and Ethel moved in together in a roomy apartment building at 7114 Carnegie Avenue. Now three of the sisters were living in Cleveland.

CHAPTER SIX

The Promoter

Josephine walked toward the soaring red brick towers of Cleveland's Carter Hotel, looking fetching in a stylish hat that framed her face and a long dress that showed her abundant curves.

The Carter was one of the buildings reshaping the face of downtown Cleveland. A new City Hall now overlooked Cleveland Municipal Stadium and Lake Erie at the north end of East 9th Street—an imposing, classically inspired gray granite building with a three-story Grand Hall that looked like an indoor Parthenon with its Doric columns of Boticini marble.

City Hall and its architectural twin, the Cuyahoga County Court House, bookended a park named for Wellington, Ohio, native and famed *Spirit of '76* painter, Archibald Willard. They formed the northern portion of Cleveland's master downtown plan, directed by famed architect Daniel Burnham who designed Chicago's "White City" and refined and implemented L'Enfant's plan for the Washington, D.C., Mall. The new Cleveland Public Library and Public Auditorium were also underway.

Twenty miles east of downtown, an arts and education mecca known as University Circle was rising on land donated by Western Union founder Jeptha Wade. Western Reserve University and Case Institute of Technology stood next to one another, educating students in the liberal arts, science, and technology. The Cleveland Museum of Art had opened, the Cleveland Orchestra was being formed, and the Cleveland

Playhouse and Playhouse Settlement (later Karamu House) were presenting live theater.

The city was alive with the innovation and transformation that marked the Progressive Era; and World War I had upped the demand for the weapons, munitions, cars, and trucks Cleveland produced.

Thanks to its thriving industry, Josephine flourished in Cleveland. She was certain her battles were behind her. She worked hard, like she always had, aiming to be the best stenographer she could be. When an opening became available as an executive secretary, she was hired. Still, she wanted her own business. She had good experience, and she'd made many contacts in her years working for Cleveland companies. There was no reason she couldn't open her own stenography business, so she did. She had no trouble getting clients.

Josephine was on her way to see the Carter Hotel's display of new typewriters. The Carter was the newest hotel in Cleveland—a showplace, with six hundred rooms for guests and twenty-six meeting rooms that could seat up to two thousand. Its five restaurants boasted head chef Hector Boiardi (later famous as Chef Boyardee) who'd come from the famed Greenbrier Resort where he'd supervised catering for both of President Woodrow Wilson's marriages.

Josephine passed the yellow-and-black-striped awnings and flower-filled window boxes that graced the outer windows of the hotel coffee shop and headed through the grand lobby to the side room with the typewriters.

As she ran her fingers along a typewriter's round button-like keys, she noticed an unusual-looking gentleman approaching her. Josephine thought he was quite handsome with fine features, even though he was short, about five feet two inches, only a couple of inches taller than she was. But he was dressed differently in a light-colored militaristic bush jacket usually worn by adventurers, its two outsize pockets looking like they could hold anything from binoculars to a day's lunch. His dark brown hair was sculpted into sideburns that curved to a point on his cheeks.

He said his name was George Gerau, but he was called Jerry. He said he was of French descent and proudly claimed Napoleon as one of his ancestors. He regaled her with a snapshot of his many business ventures in the first few minutes. He was an attorney and real estate investor from New York. Besides his legal work, he'd invented an internal combustion engine, had several businesses in California, and was now developing a hotel in Miami Beach, Florida. He was in Cleveland to talk to investors.

Josephine had never met anyone like Jerry Gerau. He was exciting. Smart, sophisticated, wealthy. He had ambition like she did. She was dazzled. Sparks flew, and Josephine's usual apprehension began to melt.

Apparently, he was taken with her too. Soon they were a couple. Finally, she thought, she'd found a kindred spirit, someone to build a life with.

Most people who knew him agreed that George Baldwin (Jerry) Gerau was indeed smart, sophisticated, and, well, sometimes wealthy. But there was more to his story. Much more.

He was born in Brooklyn. His father was also named George—George Lemont Gerau. His mother's maiden name was Nettie Harriett Porter. From an early age, Gerau had big ideas. He grew up in a world where manufacturing had come of age and new machines were transforming American life. Among them was the first practical Singer sewing machine. In 1899, Jerry, still in his late teens, and a colleague named Charles Hodsdon, received a patent for a simple and improved way to thread sewing machine needles.

Like his alleged ancestor, Gerau was restless and wanted to conquer new territories. While on the lookout, he worked as a broker in a Brooklyn office with his father and brother Lemont. In 1901, the right opportunity came. *The New York Times* blazed the headline BIG DEAL IN COAL MINES: FAIRMONT COAL, A NEW CORPORATION, ACQUIRES 36 PLANTS IN THE WEST VIRGINIA DISTRICT. Fairmont, West Virginia, was home to one hundred millionaires who'd made their money largely from the plentiful coalfields.

Gerau left Brooklyn to tap the potential riches of West Virginia coal. Based on his history as a broker, it's likely he was involved in buying and selling land. He also got his license as an attorney.

While in Fairmont, he married a young local woman and fathered a son, George, and a daughter, Nettie—carrying on the Gerau family names. But soon, he was gone—gone from the town and from his young family. What happened isn't clear. What is clear is that Gerau had a very short attention span. He was always chasing the next big thing and began collecting wives with the same enthusiasm he embraced in his business ventures.

By 1910, he was in Los Angeles, gaining acclaim and well-placed contacts as an attorney, apparently with another wife. A May *Los Angeles Herald* article reported that "George B. Gerau, a well-known attorney of Los Angeles, accompanied by Mrs. Gerau, is registered at the Hotel Del Coronado," where they were "passing a few weeks."

The newspaper also detailed his myriad business ventures. He was the chief organizer of the Protective Labor Union Insurance Company of the United States and Canada, created solely for members of the American Federation of Labor (AFL), then under the legendary union leader Samuel L. Gompers. The company, capitalized at $2,500,000, offered one million shares of its stock at union meetings all over the country. Gerau was an effective pitchman, claiming the major U.S. insurance companies were anti-union.

In July 1910, the Geraus headed for Lake Arrowhead in the San Bernardino Mountains on a combination pleasure and business venture. California was then the largest oil-producing state in the nation. Speculators clamored to cash in on the oil boom. In 1910, a score of oil derricks went up. Gerau was never one to overlook a chance to make money. He posted ads in the *Los Angeles Herald* under the headline GOOD OIL OP-PORTUNITY. He offered, "in Ten Acre Lots . . . at $25 an acre," an "undivided part of my patented oil land, which is located in the Barstow-Hiawatha field, destined to be one of the Greatest Oil Fields in the State of California."

George and Dorothy P. Gerau sold deeds for acres of land— the average price, $250 for ten acres. In August 1911, George Gerau licensed a considerable portion of twenty acres of land owned by Coulson Oil Lands Company. He planned to drill there for oil. He told the *Petaluma Argus Courier* that the esti-mated cost of drilling in the oil sands was "$16,000 to $20,000."

Unfortunately, none of the oil wells in the Barstow Hiawatha field produced oil.

By March 1912, Gerau was off to New Mexico where he was selling alfalfa land for $10 an acre.

Many of his business ventures worked. Others did not. He made a fortune. He lost a fortune. No matter. He rose like a phoenix to start again.

At one of his many low points, his name made the newspapers again. On May 10, 1913, Jerry and a friend named Edward Crane spent the night in jail after defrauding the Arrowhead Hot Springs Hotel out of a $220 hotel room and board bill. Bail was set at $150.

In attempting to spring himself out of jail, Gerau bragged to the bail bondsman about his relationship to Samuel Gompers and claimed other noted friends—Job Harriman (who ran for vice president of the United States on the Socialist ticket in 1900 and later ran for Los Angeles mayor), Launcy Butler, secretary of the Central Labor Council, and a Dr. Severenson at the Auditorium Hotel—would vouch for him and say he was "good for the amount." Crane was released on $150 bail. Jerry remained. None of his well-placed friends came to Gerau's aid.

It wasn't long before he bounced back again in a big way. He moved his law practice to San Francisco and become part owner of the Hotel Carlton on Turk Street. In December 1913, he held a dinner party to reveal a life-changing announcement. He was engaged to Miss Sadie Julia Gompers, the only daughter of AFL head Samuel Gompers. Miss Gompers was described as a "handsome brunette" who was "educated in New York and is an accomplished musician." The Gompers family and several noted friends attended the engagement party. The news made papers across the country. The wedding was to take place at the Gompers's home in Washington, D.C.

A couple of weeks later, the *Salt Lake Telegram* in Salt Lake City, Utah, printed a large photo of Gerau and reported he was in Salt Lake City with his private secretary en route to New York. He had been scheduled to arrive earlier when Miss Gompers and her mother were visiting the city, but "owing to business interests that caused his delay, he was unable to join his fiancée."

He was quoted as saying, "I intend going to Butte to look over some mining interests I have there and in New York. I will later meet Miss Gompers in Washington, where on March 21, my birthday, I will marry the dearest and only woman in the world, an event that I will mark as the greatest in my career."

Miss Gompers, meanwhile, declared herself a suffragette and was quoted as saying she was in favor of "eugenic" marriages, following an unfortunate trend of the time that advocated marriage only between "fit" individuals with traits deemed desirable, which reached its ghastly apex in World War II with Hitler's advocacy of Aryan supremacy.

Gerau's life and career were on high. Everywhere he went—and he went everywhere—reporters followed. George B. Gerau was happy to oblige. In one article featuring a multiple column photo, he was quoted as saying, "I'm just a plain corporation lawyer . . . I have practiced in the Superior and Federal Courts of fourteen states and I think I have a dream of the future. Because I am a corporation lawyer I am not necessarily prevented from being able to recognize the great onmarch of labor that Samuel Gompers has fathered in this country. Gompers was a dreamer along his line, as I am a dreamer along mine."

In February, Gerau awoke from his dream. Miss Sadie Gompers announced "the breaking of her engagement to George B. Gerau, well known in Oakland and San Francisco. The reason for the broken engagement was not made public." She said only "there were good reasons for ending the engagement but absolutely declined to discuss the matter further." Later, in Washington, she added, "I did it for good and sufficient reasons."

On May 5, 1914, Jerry Gerau married yet another woman, a twenty-two-year-old from British Columbia. The marriage registration listed his father correctly as George L. Gerau but instead of his mother's real name—Nettie Harriett Porter—he gave her name as Antoinette Harriett Bonaparte—highlighting his alleged ancestry to the French emperor. He called himself a "bachelor," apparently forgetting his prior marriages.

In 1918, a notice appeared in the *San Francisco Chronicle*. "Destitute Girl Seeks Location of Father. Nettie Harriett Gerau, a thirteen-year-old girl of Fairmont, W. Va., has written to the police asking them to find her father, George B. Gerau, believed to be connected with the hotel business here. The girl says she is destitute."

By that time, her father was on the other side of the continent, near another ocean—in Miami, Florida. Florida was the latest land of opportunity. It was being advertised as a "vision of Paradise" with its sandy beaches, swaying palm trees, and tropical climate. Railroads and a highway from Jacksonville to Miami now made it easy to travel down the Florida coast. Warm weather vacations were no longer just for the rich. Middle-class Americans owned automobiles, could get credit, and enjoyed time off with pay for vacations. Tourism was born, and Florida was the biggest beneficiary.

In Miami Beach, Gerau managed the Casa Grande Hotel Company, again promoting it with half-page newspaper ads: "The hotel property will include 506 acres with an ocean beach frontage of 3200 feet. It will be located on the Ocean Beach Highway."

He was selling shares in the company—"$1 million of 7 percent cumulative preferred stock." The prospectus noted that "George H. Burrows, a prominent attorney of Cleveland, is president and secretary of the hotel company; I. R. Davies, president of the Ideal Rubber Co. of Cleveland is treasurer . . ."

George B. (Jerry) Gerau was headed for Cleveland.

Josephine knew nothing of his past, only that he was the most exciting man she'd ever met. He was always a gentleman with her. He was charming. He expounded on the untapped potential in Florida. He brought her to fine restaurants and introduced her to his Cleveland investors, men whose names she recognized from the newspapers.

The day before Independence Day, July 3, 1919, Josephine gave up her own hard-fought independence. She married Jerry Gerau in New York.

At the beginning, Josephine had a life she'd only imagined. She traveled with Gerau to New York City and Miami in his private rail car or his large black Packard. The couple had all the luxuries the time afforded. Jerry Gerau opened a law office in Cleveland and quickly ingratiated himself with the powers-that-be.

World War I was over, and the Roaring Twenties burst out of its restraints. Opportunity seemed boundless. Times were good, the country was prospering and so were its people. Americans could buy cars and just about anything they wanted on the installment plan. They had creature comforts like refrigerators and washing machines they purchased for $5 down and $8–$10 a month or vacuum cleaners for $2 down and $2 a month.

Excess was the norm. Opulent movie theaters reminiscent of European palaces rose in city after city, enticing men and women with silent moving picture royalty—the adorable Mary Pickford, "It" girl Clara Bow, and darkly handsome Rudolph Valentino—in kingly trappings like grand marble staircases, crystal chandeliers, massive pipe organs, tapestries, and murals.

Competing with movie theaters were new steel-and-concrete ballparks that ushered in a new era for baseball. Babe Ruth was a sensation—pitching and hitting home runs for the Boston Red Sox. In Cleveland, the Indians were on their way to the World Series.

The flamboyant times had a darker side. Moneymaking became almost as big a sport as baseball. Schemes abounded, luring people to part with savings in pursuit of easy riches. Despite Prohibition, speakeasies flourished, bootleggers stole liquor, made their own, or smuggled it in. Big time crime erupted.

In December 1919, five months after their marriage, Josephine found she was pregnant. Jerry insisted she go to the best obstetrician in New York City—so every few weeks she'd take their railroad car to New York.

On September 15, 1920, Geraldine Elizabeth Gerau was born, weighing seven and a half pounds. Now a beautiful hazel-eyed, dark-haired little girl would share their outwardly idyllic life. Just a few weeks later, on October 12, the Cleveland Indians won the World Series over the Brooklyn Dodgers. It was a good sign!

Jerry was busy with new clients in Cleveland and his ventures in Miami. Cleveland's automobile and steel industries were thriving. As usual, he smelled opportunity. He got to know the industry's chief executives, became involved with the International Speedway Association, and launched his own auto parts company. In 1922, the *Trenton Evening Times* listed him as president of a shuttle valve company and one of several "men prominently identified with the automobile industry in this country" who were endorsing a new $3,500,000 motor speedway in Atlantic City. International Speedway Association president C. H. Berlekamp and the Osbourne Engineering Company, builders of the Polo Grounds in New York City— both of Cleveland—were behind the project.

Gerau applied for a patent on an internal combustion engine he invented and began working on a prototype in a shop in Chagrin Falls, a pretty town east of Cleveland. Josephine contacted her brother Joseph W. Mathey, now with Youngstown Sheet and Tube and in a position to help Jerry market the idea. Joseph was intrigued and came up to see it, promising to do what he could to help.

The heady times soon gave way to a crumbling marriage. Jerry Gerau began staying out late and coming home smelling of liquor. Sometimes he wouldn't come home until morning. In May 1922, he choked Josephine by the throat until she was rescued by one of the neighbors. Afterward he left for several days.

For Josephine, divorce was taboo, so she gave him another chance.

Jerry, Josephine, and Geraldine took their train car to New York City, heading for a convention to showcase his engine concept. While Jerry headed for the convention, Josephine and Geraldine explored the city. Back in their hotel, they waited for Jerry to return so they could go to dinner. Five o'clock came, then six, then seven. Jerry didn't return. Josephine bundled Geraldine up and headed toward the convention site to look for him. She didn't need to look far. In an alleyway near the hotel, she saw the familiar figure, blacked out and lying on the ground, an empty whiskey bottle by his side.

Furious, she left him there. Holding Geraldine in her arms, she stormed to the railroad station. They were going back to Cleveland.

Jerry Gerau followed her, and Josephine again felt she had no choice but to take him back.

It wasn't long before Jerry had another moneymaking scheme. The land boom in Florida was heating up. Hundreds of thousands of middle-class people streamed into the Sunshine State—some of them vacationers or "snowbirds" seeking relief from the harsh winters of the north; others, speculators who craved "instant wealth" or ordinary people who heard they could double their money buying Florida properties.

The state of Florida, eager to attract new investors to its abundance of land, helped the boom times by relaxing its regulation of Realtors. Cities like Tampa spent enormous sums building roads and improving their infrastructure. There were a few warnings, but they were trampled by the frenzied stampede toward instant wealth. *Forbes* magazine worried that land prices were based on high expectations rather than any accurate assessment of the land's value.

Seduced again by possible riches and not heeding the warnings, Jerry, Josephine, and Geraldine packed up for Tampa in the winter of 1923. Tampa land was cheap and easy to flip for a big profit. Gerau began speculating in Florida land full time, investing in properties all down the Gulf Coast and making more money than ever. He was a charter member of the appropriately named Optimists Club of Tampa, a who's who of Tampa leaders who believed in the city's future.

At one gathering, Optimist Club International vice president J. Bailey Wray stirred the crowd with his stunning oratory. "Optimism is the beacon of a stormy sea and the hope of a sick room. It was optimism that brought Columbus to these rugged shores . . . led the Duke of Wellington on to victory in Waterloo and brought the Pilgrims to New England. . . . Optimism is the fuel which keeps our business institutions going." This became Gerau's mantra.

He and Josephine were socially prominent. They bought property in Sarasota and became friends with John A. Ringling, one of the Ringling brothers of traveling circus fame. Ringling had come to Sarasota in 1912 and was heavily involved in developing the city and its islands as resort destinations.

Huge ads and articles began to appear in the *Tampa Times,* offering property owned by George B. Gerau: "Here's a Real Opportunity: Sarasota Gulf Front Property. Fifteen acres fronting on the Gulf of Mexico . . . located on Siesta Key, aptly termed

'America's Loveliest Gems' on the Gulf of Mexico . . . near developments underway by the Ringlings . . . and a score of other big developers who are building what is termed America's Greatest Winter Resort on Sarasota's incomparable beach. Adjoining Mr. Gerau's fifteen acres is the famed Whittemore estate."

The ad went on to say, "With millionaires carrying out extensive development, with resorts being built nearby, and with vivid memories of Miami Beach and Daytona Beach developments and fortunes, those now purchasing in and about Sarasota have implicit confidence in the soundness of their investments and the speedy realization of large returns."

When Geraldine turned five, her parents enrolled her in a private kindergarten in Tampa. Her early childhood was idyllic. In middle school, Geraldine wrote a paper she called *My Biography*. In it she wrote that living in Florida was "the adventure of my life . . . there are many children that would envy some of the adventures I've had, but the one most thrilling is the one I remember best. My ambition was to ride a camel . . . I had an advantage because my mother and daddy knew Mr. Ringling of Ringling Brothers Circus very well. I was quite a favorite of Uncle Tugg, as I called him. He used to tell me about the lands where he got his camels, elephants, etc."

Geraldine wanted him to tell her the stories about camels over and over. He was enchanted. He promised to give her a ride on a camel, and one day he did. The circus was having a parade in Sarasota, with many of the animals. He helped Geraldine up on the camel's back.

"How proud I was to sit on Uncle Tugg's camel and go clump, bump down the street in Sarasota, Florida," she wrote. "After a few minutes of riding, it was rather hard sitting and swaying from side to side. In fact I rocked so much I began to slide. Down I went 'plop' right down on the ground. It was a hard landing but not half as hard as riding Pruger, the camel."

Josephine and Geraldine were living lives many only dreamed of, but the costs were steep. Outsiders thought Jerry was brilliant and charming. He could be that with his family, too, sometimes. Other times, he was quarrelsome, belittling, abu-

sive. They lived in luxury, but bills went unpaid. He'd entertain his new friends and be out all night. Sometimes Josephine
didn't know where he was for days.

In Tampa, Jerry was investing and reinvesting and reinvesting again in Florida land, ballooning the family's wealth. Land
prices kept rising and rising in what appeared to be a never-
ending ascent. Investors were certain the boom times would
continue indefinitely.

Realtors, eager to cash in, began selling Florida land sight
unseen. Young "binder boys" were hired to represent Realtors,
getting down payments (or binders) and thirty-day financing
by doing nothing more than demonstrating their tennis skills
on properties that had nothing more than a tennis court and an
empty field. There was talk of properties being sold three times
in a day.

In less than two years after Jerry, Josephine, and Geraldine
arrived in Tampa, the price of land had risen to the point where
few people could afford to buy it. The number of customers
trickled down. Investors sold their land. Northern bankers lost
money on Florida investments. Construction companies laid
off workers.

Tampa had borrowed heavily to finance the city's growth.
Now it was suffocating in debt. Neighboring St. Petersburg
had become the most indebted city in the United States, per citizen. Realtors closed down. Investors headed back north. The
Florida land boom turned into the Florida land bust. Wary
tourists no longer visited. Investors, speculators, home and
land buyers looked elsewhere. Even John Ringling cut back.
He'd developed much of Sarasota and next planned a Ritz
Carlton resort at the southern tip of Longboat Key, one of the
barrier islands off Sarasota, but it never materialized.

Jerry Gerau lost everything. Napoleon's alleged descendant
had met his Waterloo. Defeated, he brought his family back
north, but no longer in a private railroad car. They camped
along the way. A 1924 photo shows the family at a campsite in
Wilkes Barre, Pennsylvania, on their way back to Cleveland.
Gerau claimed to be there for discussions with local businessmen about acquiring a motor speedway that could be used as a
stadium to host national sporting events.

Still selling himself. Still pretending. But he was no longer the supremely self-confident lawyer/investor with the high-profile friends and big ideas. His core had been broken and he fell into a deep depression that only eased when he drank. They came back to Cleveland, and he spent most of his time drinking. He'd quarrel, become physically abusive, threaten Josephine, and use profane language in front of Geraldine. He'd come home late at night or not until morning—or not at all. The husband who'd once given Josephine a fantasy life disgusted her.

As Gerau's alcoholism, abusive behavior, and disappearances worsened, Josephine started to have what she called nervous attacks. They culminated in what people then referred to as a nervous breakdown. She lapsed into a catatonic state of mental and physical exhaustion that left her barely able to function. Hopelessness replaced hope. The simplest tasks—getting dressed, brushing teeth, eating—became overwhelming. She lingered in bed for days, unlike the confident, fearless woman she'd been.

In July 1926, Jerry Gerau took off "for parts unknown."

On August 5, Josephine Mathey Gerau filed for divorce. She gave her husband's last known address as 2126 Fairmount Boulevard in Cleveland Heights. Jerry Gerau couldn't be located. Josephine's lawyer put a notice in the *Daily Legal News* notifying Gerau, whose place of residence was unknown, that Josephine had petitioned for a divorce.

She cited "gross neglect of duty" and that "he has failed to properly support said plaintiff and provide for the support and maintenance of the minor child such as food and clothing for herself and child . . . despite being well able to do so." She also cited "cruel and abusive treatment suffered at his hands," which was endangering her health. "The defendant comes home late at night or early in the morning under influence of liquor. He has threatened to do bodily harm."

The sheriff finally found him, but he never appeared for the hearing. Once again he had disappeared.

Josephine was awarded an uncontested divorce in Cuyahoga County Common Pleas Court on September 25, 1926.

Josephine could feel the hours of pounding the concrete in the soles of her feet. She'd been traipsing down the gritty streets of Tonawanda, New York, lugging samples of mending fluid, while six-year-old Geraldine waited in the car. Tonawanda, about two hundred miles northeast of Cleveland, was north of Buffalo on the Erie Canal and was part of her territory. Desperate to make money, she'd taken a sales job promising above-average earnings but requiring her to travel far from home.

Despite his grandiose financial schemes, Gerau had left Josephine and Geraldine destitute. The court had ordered him to pay Josephine $5 a week and given him visitation rights to see Geraldine, but he'd vanished. Josephine had to deal with the piles of bills he left behind and support her daughter and herself.

She'd seen ads seeking women to sell transparent mending fluid, a hot new item for repairing silk stockings and other fabrics: "Salein wanted . . . Easy seller. Large profits. Guaranteed to launder . . . darns stockings in 30 seconds . . . turns darning drudgery into agreeable task . . . Our agents are making $9 a day."

She'd given up her stenography business when she married Gerau and now her skills were rusty. This looked like a good opportunity to make enough money to catch up on her bills. The $9 a day the mending fluid job offered was $45 a week, much better than the invisible $5 a week in support she wasn't getting from Gerau, and double the average weekly pay for women, which hovered around $24. Mending fluid sounded like the answer. She was sure she could sell the 25- or 50-cent tubes even if it meant going to Tonawanda. She had few other choices.

Sunny Florida and the high life she'd once lived were a distant memory. Tonawanda, New York, where winters brought brutal lake effect snow in from Lake Erie on the west and Lake Ontario to the north, was her reality. And she had a daughter now. Life was much more complicated than it had been when she was on her own as a single woman with responsibility for no one but herself.

The divorce had given her some relief from the day-to-day angst of her marriage, but the emotional and financial burdens were unrelenting. The lingering memories of her dream-to-nightmare marriage consumed her like a raging cancer, festering and erupting into nighttime panic. Even in the light of day, it seemed like she was at the bottom of a deep, dark well. She'd been ripped of her self-confidence. She needed to find some of her old Josephine determination and spirit. For herself and for her daughter.

She turned to her religious faith, which had often comforted her in rough times and, she believed, helped her do what was right. Her family had remained deeply religious despite their falling out with the Catholic Church, especially her mother Elizabeth who often used biblical lessons to communicate the values she wanted to instill in her children.

Josephine had discovered the Christian Science Church when she first came back to Cleveland from Florida, after her marriage to Jerry Gerau had become intolerable.

Christian Science had become a phenomenon in the mid-1920s with over a thousand churches in the U.S., Canada, and England. For Josephine, the attraction was more than its popularity. It was personal.

Mary Baker Eddy had founded the church. Like Josephine, Baker Eddy's life had been difficult. She'd also been raised on a farm. Her first husband died three months after their child was born. Her second husband deserted her, and she struggled with chronic illnesses.

When conventional medicine failed to help, Baker Eddy looked for alternative treatments. She experimented with placebos and came to believe that a patient's belief had much to do with healing. She also sought comfort in the Bible. Believing her approach helped her recover from a severe fall, she began to study both the Scriptures and healing methods and published her beliefs in the book *Science and Health*. In 1879, she founded the Church of Christ, Scientist.

Josephine felt a kinship to her, and reading Eddy's book seemed to offer her some comfort. Some passages seemed to have been written just for her: "'Let there be light,' is the perpetual demand of Truth and Love, changing chaos into order and discord into the music of the spheres."

"Home is the dearest spot on earth, and it should be the centre, though not the boundary, of the affections."

She thought often about home. When she was Geraldine's age, home was the farm, with her dear mother and ambitious father, her noisy gaggle of siblings; it was driving the family's horse-drawn carriage as it clopped down the dusty roads to and from her father's farm; it was sunny days plowing the fields, riding the horses, playing with piggies, and washing the sheep. She'd walked away when she was just a child, wanting her independence, but what had that independence gained? Mostly, her life had been an up-and-down struggle. Her childhood on the farm seemed idyllic compared to what she was giving her own daughter, who waited in a stuffy car while Josephine lugged her supplies from house to house—her daughter whose father was gone and no one knew where.

She wanted Geraldine to have a better life. She needed to find a way.

CHAPTER SEVEN

The Butcher

April 28, 1913, New York Harbor

The SS *Rochambeau* bellowed its guttural, ear-splitting whistle as it entered the tight channel called the Narrows. Passenger #100615010289 strained to see the shadowy tops of New York's tall buildings over the sliver of Brooklyn that obstructed his view. Brooding clouds filled the sky. Rain splattered against the deck and portholes. He had his German army helmet and sharpshooter medals packed carefully in the bottom of his suitcase, and now he was just waiting to depart.

According to the ship's manifest, he was Albert Herbert Morhard, age twenty-six, height five feet five inches, and brown haired. It stated he had the required $50 to start life in his new country and was headed for Chicago to join his older brother Alfred. Like Albert, nearly 95 percent of immigrants who came to the United States at that time planned to join family or friends; often a father, brother, or husband who'd arrived earlier.

His nine-day voyage began in LeHavre, France. He was one of more than two thousand passengers on the *Rochambeau*, most of them hopeful émigrés from Italy, Germany, and France who'd spent days, sometimes weeks, getting to the port, taking multiple trains, driving wagons and on rare occasions, even proceeding on foot. Most of them were escaping poverty. Albert was escaping his past.

The *Rochambeau* was one of three French Line ships in service. It had been built in 1911, mainly to carry the growing streams of immigrants to the United States. Because of this, it only had two kinds of accommodations—second-class cabins and third-class or steerage. The ship was white with a black hull, masts fore and aft, and two imposing red funnels that looked top-heavy, not symmetrical, like they were meant for a larger ship and had been plunked down on an upper deck that didn't look much deeper than a black piece of cardboard.

Before boarding, each passenger was asked dozens of questions, among them his or her name, age, gender, marital status, occupation, nationality, ability to read or write, race, physical and mental health, last residence, destination, and the name and address of anyone they were planning to meet in the U.S. They needed to vow that they'd never been in prison or an almshouse and that they were not polygamists or anarchists. Then it was on to vaccinations and their first medical exam. They'd receive a second upon entry to New York.

The 428 second-class passengers paid $177 each for serviceable if not luxurious quarters. The 1,700 in steerage bought $77 tickets that stuffed them in dungeon-like third berths in the bowels of the ship. Round-trip tickets went for $135.50, but few of the passengers would be making the return trip.

On approaching New York, the *Rochambeau* anchored in the quarantine zone in New York's Lower Harbor. Here U.S. Public Health medical inspectors came aboard to conduct a rough inspection, but only of the more privileged cabin class passengers—asking them to remove any headgear so they could check for smallpox and looking each one over quickly to detect signs of insanity or diseases like cholera, plague, and typhoid fever.

Infectious diseases, it was believed, were nearly always transmitted by those in steerage—so steerage passengers weren't allowed the brief onboard inspection. Instead, they were crammed into barges headed for Ellis Island. There, eleven doctors were tasked with examining all incoming passengers. At the time, two thousand to five thousand people passed through Ellis Island daily.

Immigrants who failed either the onboard or Ellis Island exam could be sent to "quarantine" hospitals on nearby Swinburn or Hoffman Island—or they could be deported. Albert was grateful that the exam was so cursory and that his arrival would not be delayed.

As the ship slowly navigated the watery passageway, Albert saw the welcoming Statue of Liberty lifting her lamp "beside the golden door." Just beyond the statue, an endless flow of European wives, husbands, fathers, mothers, and children plodded onto the dock from the teeming barges and made their way to the multiple lines, ready to be processed at the fortress-like brick buildings of Ellis Island.

The majestic Manhattan skyline loomed straight ahead.

The crew secured the ropes at Pier 15, where French Line ships docked. After many weeks on the road and on the water, Albert was finally in New York. Through the slight drizzle, he trudged down the gangplank to the gritty city of nearly five million. Here, everything was bigger, faster, a kaleidoscope of sights, sounds, and smells. The people he saw seemed like a microcosm of the Europe he'd left behind.

New York City at the turn of the twentieth century was a bustling metropolis. Jet-colored automobiles buzzed through streets where horses had recently roamed. Trains clattered overhead and under the ground. Pushcarts hawked pickles, knishes, and sausages. Suffragettes marched in the streets. Longshoremen sweated as they hauled in ships' cargo while nearby fishermen brought in their catch. The city's buildings appeared to be competing to see if any could top the Woolworth Building, whose sixty stories made it the tallest in the world.

The city wasn't only about industry. New York was also home to three professional baseball teams. Brooklyn Dodger fans gloated about brand-new Ebbets Field. The Highlanders had changed their name to the New York Yankees and were alternating game days at the Polo Grounds with the New York Giants while waiting for the new Yankee Stadium to be completed in the Bronx. There was, if only briefly, a women's baseball team, the New York Female Giants.

Underlying the glitz was a world of corruption. Reformers attempted to rid Tammany Hall of the shady politicians who ruled the city, but they proved to be no better. The Mafia was gaining a stronghold in Little Italy. Feuds between mobsters often ended in the killing of rivals like "Nine-fingered" Charlie Lombardi. A future mob head named Vito Genovese would soon arrive in New York from his native Sicily. Prostitution, white slavery, and venereal diseases were rampant. At the Fulton Theater on West 46th Street, the play *Damaged Goods* depicted the plight of women in the midst of the moral depravity of the times.

This was the new world Albert Herbert Morhard entered. It was very different from his birthplace in Germany. He pulled out his train ticket to Chicago and headed for the dazzling new Grand Central Station.

Anything and everything seemed possible in the United States—an immigrant could leave everything behind. Even killing a man.

Albert Herbert Morhard was born on February 22, 1887, in Mülhausen, Alsace, Germany, a city of around one hundred thousand residents nestled between the blue-tinged Vosges Mountains and the scenic Rhine River. Frequent wars between the French and Germans had made Alsace an ongoing bargaining chip. For eight hundred years, much of Alsace was part of the German Kingdom of the Holy Roman Empire. Mülhausen, located close to the border with Switzerland, broke off to join the Swiss Confederation in 1515. In 1648, Alsace became part of France as a reward for services in the 30 Years' War. Following the Franco-Prussian War in 1870, Alsace returned to the newly unified Germany under Chancellor Otto von Bismarck.

Once Alsace became part of Germany, French residents, the majority of the population, were allowed to emigrate to France. About sixty thousand did. To take their place, Germany recruited immigrants from various parts of the German Empire. Among them were Albert's parents, Christian and Marie Madeleine, or as she'd been known in Germany, Magdalena. They came from Bamberg.

Christian opened a meat market in Mülhausen, and the couple had five children—Alfred, Eugene, Albert, Camille, Marie Madeleine, and Arthur. When Albert was six years old, Christian Morhard passed away. Two years later, his mother married Frenchman Henri Hammes who took over the meat market and trained his stepsons to be butchers.

When he was a boy, Albert joined the *Turnverein* (meaning "gymnastics" in German) or Turner Club, a German nationalist gymnastics association of athletes formed to build a "united" nation of physically strong, well-rounded men. The Turners sponsored national competitions that brought athletes from all over Germany to compete against each other. It was similar to the Olympics, but with political underpinnings. The Turn-verein had played a significant role in German unification in 1871. By the time Albert joined, the focus had turned exclusively to promoting physical sports—gymnastics, boxing, diving, and swimming. Albert was skilled at them all.

His athletic pursuits gave him the defined muscles of a body-builder. Even though he was short, he was physically powerful. He had balanced features, a firm square chin, and an engaging smile that echoed in his blue eyes when things were going his way. When he was challenged, his eyes turned stone gray and his temper exploded.

Albert worked in the family meat market until he was in his mid-twenties. Sometime around 1911, he was conscripted into the Imperial German Army, the largest in the world at the time. There, his physical strength was an asset. But it would also be his undoing. Whenever he was confronted, Albert's boxer-trained hands settled the clashes, until his hands got him into trouble. It is said that he killed a man in the army and was told to either leave the country or be arrested.

In America he had a chance for a fresh start. He had ambition. America was the land of opportunity, and he was going to take advantage of every possibility the country offered. His brother told him about the good-paying jobs in the Chicago stockyards. That was where he was headed.

The New York Central train pulled into the eleven-track shed that marked the entrance to Chicago's LaSalle Street Station. After a twenty-hour overnight trip along the Great Lakes, Albert had reached his destination. He headed down the broad marble staircase to retrieve his belongings in the baggage room. It was morning, but the sun was nearly eclipsed by the thick residue of soot and coal dust floating in the air and into his lungs from the smokestacks that lined the horizon. Albert found it hard to draw a breath.

Chicago was the railroad hub of the nation. Train tracks weaved above and through neighborhoods to factories that shipped goods to all parts of the country—and to and from the Chicago stockyards.

His brother Fred had come to the United States for a job in the stockyards four years earlier. Fred's wife, Marietta, joined him later, traveling from Alsace via Cherbourg on the SS *Amerika*. Albert arrived in the middle of the week, and Fred was at work so Albert boarded the L Train for the stockyards.

As far as he could see, pigs and cattle crammed into pens awaited their fate in the connected slaughterhouses and packing plants. The stench made him cover his mouth and nose with his hands. He could smell it from six miles away—the animal manure wafting from the pens, garbage rotting in open city dumps, streets muddied by overflowing cesspools. Decomposing waste floated down the Chicago River, which the packing plants used as their "sewer," releasing gaseous bubbles that often caught fire and gave it the name "Bubble Creek." Smoke was everywhere.

The stockyards covered over five hundred acres of former swampland owned by railroads, including the Vanderbilts' New York Central. There were thirteen thousand pens, and three hundred miles of railroad tracks. With his meat market experience, Albert quickly got a job at the Armour plant, the largest factory in the world, joining over twenty-five thousand other men, women, and children. He was a skilled butcher, but to save costs and speed efficiency, Armour split up the usual butcher job and instituted a line of workers doing various jobs—a concept that helped inspire Henry Ford's automobile assembly line.

Armour was known for paying low wages and the rooms were dirty and foul smelling, but most immigrant workers were happy to have a job. Albert worked ten to sixteen hours a day, standing at a wooden table in a long line of workers, clad in a white apron, wielding a meat cleaver with a blade longer than his forearm.

Before long, Albert met a young Polish woman named Frances Verner. On September 26, 1914, they married. Frances soon became pregnant and the next year, on August 6, 1915, their son Albert was stillborn. He was buried two days later.

Back in Mühlhausen, Albert's family was in danger. On August 7, 1914, the French Army attacked the city, seeking to regain Alsace from Germany in one of the opening attacks of World War I. Albert's loyalties were divided. His mother and father were German; his stepfather, who'd raised him, was French.

In the U.S., the Armour Company was feeling the effects of the war. The company had relied on European workers, but since the war began, immigration had declined 80 percent, decimating recruiting. In response, the company began bringing in African-Americans from southern states. Around the same time, the Europeans protested the inhumane conditions at the plant. They formed a Stockyards Labor Council (SLC) demanding substantial wage increases, equal pay for women, and an eight-hour day. That caused the company to up its recruitment of southern blacks by 300 to 500 percent. When the SLC tried work stoppages, the company hired more blacks to fill their places. Racial tensions escalated. Europeans were losing their jobs to blacks or leaving for better jobs.

In 1917, Albert was living with his wife on Sedgwick Street in Chicago. The situation at Armour had become unbearable. The U.S. was now in World War I. His new country had entered the war on the side of the French, who were fighting the Germans. Many German-Americans were being ostracized in this country, but, as required, he completed the mandatory registration for the U.S. Army on June 5, 1917, noting that he deserved an exemption because he had a sick wife.

In the midst of the turmoil, Albert and his brother Alfred fled Chicago, apparently leaving their wives behind. By 1918, his brother Alfred was working as a butcher in Manhattan and living on West 21st Street. Albert went east to another city, Cleveland. He'd had enough of life in the stockyards. He wanted to be a real butcher and have his own meat market like his father and stepfather. Soon he did; he opened a shop on Cedar Avenue in Cleveland. He had visions of opening a chain of markets.

In 1923, Albert married again. His second wife was Ida Baker. Their marriage license stated that Albert had never been married before. Meanwhile, records show that in 1928, his first wife Frances was alive, living in a rooming house in Chicago, and working as a hotel maid.

Soon, yet another woman would enter his life.

CHAPTER EIGHT

Another Try, and Another

With Geraldine in hand, Josephine headed past the storefronts on Cleveland's busy Euclid Avenue toward the neighborhood meat market. The market, at 15648 Euclid, was just a short walk from the brick apartment at 15800 Euclid where Josephine and Geraldine lived.

Josephine thought the friendly butcher, Albert Morhard, was good-looking—built like heavyweight boxing champ Gene Tunney with broad shoulders, the muscled arms of an athlete, and thick hands that looked like Albert might have been a boxer himself.

She'd shied away from romantic relationships since her divorce from George Gerau, but she found herself drawn to the smart and witty meat market owner. The customers loved him. He had a great personality. He made her laugh. His eyes penetrated hers in a way that told her he was attracted to her too. He reminded her a little of her father—the heavy accent, the constant search for new opportunities, and the same fierce drive to be successful. Mühlhausen, where Albert was from, was right across the Vosges Mountains from Champagney, where her father was born. She felt at home with him.

Albert seemed safe. She saw no sign that he had bad habits like those of her former husband.

They soon became a couple.

Albert told her he'd been married before but his wife, Ida, had died in childbirth. Josephine felt sorry for him—the poor man must be suffering. She didn't know Ida was still quite alive and living in Cleveland or that he'd had another wife before her. It's likely Albert was still married when Josephine met him in early 1927. Cuyahoga County Common Pleas Court records show Albert and Ida were divorced on January 29 of that year.

Josephine and Albert married on March 7, 1927, a little more than a month after his divorce from Ida was final. Finally, she thought, she had an attentive, successful husband and seven-year-old Geraldine had a father. She was blissful.

As the Twenties roared on, the economy continued to boom. In the 1928 presidential election, the Republicans, who had claimed the presidency since 1921, advertised, "Republican prosperity has reduced hours and increased earning capacity, silenced discontent, put the proverbial 'chicken in every pot.' And a car in every backyard, to boot."

The erupting economy bolstered Albert's meat market. His customers ordered filet mignon, tenderloin, strip steak, and other expensive, profitable cuts of beef as well as the usual ground beef, pork, and chicken. Josephine helped in the market when Geraldine was in school, and he taught her the business. They complemented each other. He did the butchering, ordered the meats, and handled the finances; she took care of the customers, displays, made stews, and ground the hamburger meat.

The market was flourishing. Albert had seen the influx of Clevelanders into the inner-ring suburbs and decided to open another market at 14623 Woodworth Avenue in East Cleveland. He hired another butcher to run the new market, and Josephine would often drop in to see how they were faring.

Geraldine was now eight years old. Josephine wanted a place with a yard where her daughter could play and where there were neighborhood children her own age. She found a two-family rental in Cleveland Heights, a growing suburb set high on a ridge above Cleveland where developers had carved out tree-lined streets and built spacious homes.

In the 1920s, the city's Euclid Heights and Fairmount neighborhoods sported Tudor and Victorian mansions that rivaled those on Cleveland's famed "Millionaire's Row." In other neighborhoods, middle-income residents could choose between newer and more modern Craftsman bungalows, two-story Victorian homes, two-family homes, and apartment buildings.

Streetcars rambled down the main thoroughfares, conveniently connecting the suburb with Cleveland's businesses and industries. It seemed the perfect place for a young family.

Three of her sisters lived just a few miles away. Flora was still single. Alice had been married to Frank Payne for thirteen years and had three children—Alice, Virginia, and Howard. Ethel was married to George Reardon and had a daughter Ruth, who was the same age as Geraldine. Geraldine was happy to have her cousins nearby.

Albert decided to find a better location for his Cleveland market, one that was also closer to their new home. He rented a storefront on East 93rd Street and Hough Avenue, a popular area a short trip down Cedar Hill and close to the streetcar line. As business grew in the city, he saw opportunity in the suburbs bordering Cleveland, where growth was exploding. In 1928 the Woodworth Avenue market opened, and Albert planned to keep expanding.

As he became more successful, Josephine began to see changes in Albert. He had always been meticulous about the quality of the meat he sold, but he began using preservatives to keep the meat from going bad. This was against the Meat Inspection Act. Customers complained to the Health Department. A city chemist obtained samples of meat from two of his markets. In October 1928, Cleveland municipal judge Mary Grossman fined him $5 for using preservatives. He denied using the fluid on meat. He said he only used it for cleaning.

Josephine was beginning to see how much different Albert was from her father who, despite his hard-driving nature, was known for his honesty and ethics.

It wasn't just in his business. Albert began drinking more than the occasional German beer and would have unexpected outbursts that affected the family. He had a terrible temper, especially when he'd been drinking. One day, Geraldine was in the backseat of the car and started to cry. Albert screamed, "Can't you keep that brat quiet? I'll give you ten thousand dollars if you get rid of that child."

Josephine was horrified. The next day he apologized and brought home a toy for Geraldine. Josephine forgave him.

In January 1929, the family got the news that Josephine, now almost thirty-nine, was pregnant. On October 6, their tiny son was born at home on Desota Road in Cleveland Heights. His given name was Albert Joseph Morhard—the first name for his father, the middle name for his mother. They called him Junior. It was three weeks before the stock market crash.

The Morhard marriage would be as up and down as the market—and like the market, it was beginning to sink, but their tiny son seemed to bring new life to the marriage.

With a new member of the family, Josephine and Albert wanted a larger home, so they moved a few streets over to a two-story frame house on Cedarbrook Road with a front porch as wide as the house and roses climbing a lattice along the side. Josephine busied herself caring for the children and making a nice home for the family. She doted on the children and was determined to give them the best childhood experiences she could.

She remembered all she loved about her family's farm—the piggies, horses, bunnies, and the dog Rover. She remembered the kindness of the Kerrs, their lovely home, how they taught a tomboy to be ladylike and gave her riding lessons and fine clothes.

She got the children an English sheepdog they named Rags for the feathery gray hair covering his face and eyes, and two white bunnies who munched on carrots in their backyard coop and sometimes snuggled in the kids' laps.

Josephine loved horses; Geraldine did too. She took Geraldine horseback riding and made sure her daughter had riding lessons. She tried to involve Junior in the horses she loved, but he wasn't interested.

Every Sunday, she'd bring the children to the Christian Science Church for Sunday school, hoping the teachings that had helped her would also help them.

She perfectly prepared the steaks, pork, and chicken Albert would bring from the market; she fixed the medium rare hamburgers that were Junior's favorites and the lima beans he hated but she insisted he eat. She baked extra rich brownies that rose as high as an inch and were topped with a huge heaping of moist chocolate frosting that melted deliciously on the children's tongues.

Geraldine seemed to have overcome her bruised past. Junior was the happy, healthy boy Josephine wanted him to be. He loved animals as much as Josephine did, and he'd sprawl on the living room couch cradling the two bunnies with Rags sitting beside him.

In 1931, still doing well despite the onset of the Depression, the Morhards rented a lovely three-story Colonial with a wide porch and a big yard on Sycamore Road, where there were dozens of kids for Geraldine and Junior to play with and family-friendly neighborhood events, like a Fourth of July celebration that lasted all day, with flags flying, a parade, games, and prizes for the best-decorated houses.

On the Fourth of July, Albert took Junior to buy firecrackers at the stand on the corner—bottle rockets, TNTs, cherry bombs—and they set them off in the backyard. Little Junior watched in awe as the brilliant lights and crackling sounds of the fireworks burst into the air.

Most evenings Albert came home from work laughing and joking in his heavily accented English. As the night progressed, he'd start talking in French, break out into German, then Polish, then Hungarian to entertain them. They listened to Cleveland Rams football games and boxing matches on the radio.

Albert showed his love for the children. He would throw Junior up in the air and catch him like a football. Junior loved it and would laugh and laugh. Albert would walk around the living room on his hands with his feet ramrod straight in the air to amuse the kids. He was short and stocky, but he was all muscle, built like a fullback. Everything about him was big except his height. He had huge hands and thick fingers, except for the little finger on his left hand, which had been permanently bent from an accident with a meat cleaver.

In the summer, Albert took Junior and Geraldine to Cumberland Pool in Cleveland Heights, a huge pool with a high diving board that intimidated most would-be divers and sent others flailing into the water. Albert awed the two children and the onlookers with perfect double somersaults that landed with barely a splash and swan dives where he floated down as gracefully as a bird into the water. He taught Geraldine to dive off the high board, and she, too, soon became an expert diver.

Everyone in the family loved to go swimming on hot summer days, especially on Lake Erie beaches, where all you could see beyond the dirtlike sand was blue water and white sails. Across the vast expanse of water, Canada's beaches were invisible. Lake Erie looked just like the ocean, except the fresh water didn't stick to your skin like saltwater, and no one had to worry about sharks. There were none.

Albert often drove the family to Josephine's sister Ethel's cottage in Willoughby, but one sweaty summer day he took them on a long ride east to Blackstone Beach in Perry. The beach lay below a steep cliff. They walked down a long wooden stairway to get to the water. Junior rushed into the lake to catch a wave and ride it back to the shore.

Lake Erie is the warmest of the Great Lakes. It's also the shallowest, which means the wind can whip up waves in an instant that surge as high as ten or fifteen feet.

Junior stayed in the water, riding the waves again and again. He saw a huge wave coming. He jumped into it; but this time the wave rippled and pulled him under. He tried to fight his way out, but the wave was stronger than his small body. He was terrified—sure he was going to drown. In a flash, his father headed for the water, grabbed the small boy with his strong arms, and pulled him out.

Unfortunately, the happy, serene times didn't last. As time went on, it wasn't big waves that terrified Junior. It was his father. Whether success was changing him or his true personality was emerging, Albert began staying out late and drinking. When he drank, he became brutal. For Junior, the memories flashed in nightmarish spurts.

They lived on Sycamore Street. He was only three years old. He was pulling his wooden train around the overstuffed armchair in the living room. His father had come in the kitchen door. His parents started arguing. Junior heard his mother shriek. He crouched behind the chair to peer at what he really didn't want to see. His father held a meat cleaver in his hand, high, like he was ready to chop a side of beef. Only it wasn't a side of beef. It was his mother. Albert was chasing Josephine around the dining room table, threatening her with the meat cleaver.

Junior smelled the cheap whiskey on his father's breath. The small boy let out a piercing cry and began shaking, terrified that his father was going to kill his mother. His father stopped, perhaps warned by his son's cry or realizing the gravity of what he was doing.

Josephine raced to grab Junior and get away.

The harrowing scene burned in Junior's memory.

The next day, Albert was overcome with guilt over what he'd done. He told Josephine he was sorry. Drinking made him that way. He was going to stop drinking. He'd never do anything like that to her again. For the next few days, he turned on his considerable charm and brought home gifts to ease his conscience. A bunch of red roses. A pretty pin.

Josephine took a long while to warm up to him again, but eventually she forgave him, thinking he really meant what he said, that he would change. He seemed to be trying. She wanted to believe him. So did Junior and Geraldine.

In 1934, Albert got an inheritance of $10,000 from a relative in Alsace. He decided to use it to open a third market on Lakeshore Boulevard in Euclid, which had seen its population mushroom over 250 percent since the early 1920s. The Depression was underway, but people still needed food.

Josephine wanted to use the money to buy a house. Even though the Sycamore house was lovely, it wasn't theirs. They'd always rented. Owning a house would be an investment. She'd seen a new development in a hilly, forested area of University Heights, named for its proximity to Jesuit-run John Carroll University.

Albert agreed to give her $1,000 of the inheritance for a down payment. On August 15, 1934, she became the owner of a house at 2499 Traymore Road in University Heights, Ohio. The deed was in her name—Josephine C. Morhard—only. Perhaps she had an inkling of what was to come.

It was a pretty red brick house with white shutters and blocks of gray stone framing the white front door. It was one of only three houses on a lovely winding street that crossed over busy Warrensville Center Road on one end and ended up close to the large homes being built in the neighboring community of Shaker Heights on the other. Like Sycamore, it was a wonderful place for the kids. They'd slide down the Traymore Road hill in the snowy wintertime, climb the trees and explore the woods around the house in summer, and play in the yard that was often full of Geraldine and Albert's neighborhood friends and their Mathey cousins.

There were three floors: the first floor with a living room, dining room, kitchen, and bath; three bedrooms and a bath on the second floor; a large unfinished suite on the third floor; and a full basement. Junior and Geraldine would each have their own room.

Albert liked the new house, but he was beginning to enjoy drinking more. Whenever he drank he became abusive and violent with Josephine—shaking her, hitting her. Junior saw it all, and it had a lasting effect.

Junior would hear his father's brown Essex pull into the drive and waited to see if he smelled of liquor. If he did, Junior got out of the way, for he knew there was going to be trouble. He knew his mother wouldn't tolerate the drinking. She saw it in her first marriage, and she was seeing it again in her second. She couldn't stand what it did to people, especially the people she loved. When Albert came home that way, she'd start shouting at him. They'd have terrible fights. Junior would cover his ears, but he didn't want to leave the house. He never knew what his father might do to his mother.

In just one of the many harrowing times he witnessed, he watched his father wrap his thick hands around his mother's neck and tighten his grip until she could barely breathe. He trembled so much he could barely get out the words, "Please stop. Please stop."

Albert's drinking and violent temper rippled into the meat markets. One of his longtime suppliers brought in a side of beef Albert had ordered. Albert convinced himself the man was cheating him. Before the man knew what was happening, Albert raised his right arm, clenched his thick fist, and cracked the man in his face, knocking him hard onto the wooden floor.

The more Albert drank, the more Josephine got involved in the business. She needed to. He was beginning to drive both customers and suppliers away. She looked at the books and was surprised to find out the Woodworth Avenue market was no longer making a profit. She headed there to talk to the butcher who ran it. The butcher told her the employees were sick of Albert's terrible temper and the way he treated them. They were angry and decided to retaliate by cheating him. When they made a sale, they dropped some of the money on the floor instead of putting it in the cash register. After the customers left, they picked it up and put it in their own pockets.

The butcher said he tried to stop it, but he didn't always see what they were doing. He wanted Josephine to take over the market. If she did, he said, they'd stop and the market would make money again.

Josephine told Albert what the butcher told her. She wanted a chance to turn the store around. He said no. He fired the butcher instead. They soon lost the store on Woodworth Avenue.

As Albert's drinking and outbursts became more frequent, the two remaining stores also began losing money. The man with the great personality was now belligerent, nasty, combative—to his employees, his suppliers, his customers. Many left for stores like Fisher Foods across the street from the Hough market or Heinen's on Lee Road in Shaker Heights.

Josephine tried to help. She came in, ground the meat, greeted customers with her friendliest smile, and did her best to rebuild the relationships her husband's temper had destroyed. One supplier told Josephine he'd do business with her but never again with her husband.

As the days, weeks, and months passed, there were fewer good times and more bad times. And the bad times were getting worse. Albert was coming home late more often. She'd smell liquor on his breath. They'd argue and his eyes would turn a cold gray. Often, he'd chase Josephine, grab her by the throat, choke her, crack his huge fist against her cheek, knock her to the ground, or threaten her with whatever object that happened to be nearby. She began to believe the story she'd heard from a family member that he'd killed a man in Alsace. She feared for her life. Her son feared for her even more.

One afternoon, Junior was climbing the huge maple tree that dwarfed the garage when he heard his father's light brown 1931 Hudson Essex sedan rumble up the driveway. He moved down to a sturdier branch and peered out from behind the leaves. Albert opened the car door and stepped down onto the cement pavement. Junior saw the bloodshot eyes and smelled the distinct odor he knew meant trouble. He scrambled back up the tree as quietly and as far from his father as he could and waited for the screaming to begin.

As if on cue, he heard his mother's voice rising as she saw what he'd already seen. His father was drunk. Again. He put his fingers in his ears, but he could still hear the commotion he'd heard so many times before. He hated the drinking. He hated the fighting.

Junior jumped down from the tree and opened the car door, searching for his father's whiskey bottles. He grabbed two from the car floor. He checked the bushes. He found three more in back of the garage. He picked up one, then another, then another, then another, then another and smashed, smashed, smashed them until they were in tiny pieces.

The dreaded routine continued. Albert would come home drunk. They'd argue. He'd become violent. She'd tell him to leave. He'd come back with gifts and promises. She'd take him back. But always, the other Albert would return. His volcanic temper would erupt and spew its venomous lava, devastating everything in its path. His brutal army-trained body would go on the attack.

Josephine's life was repeating itself. She'd already been divorced once, but she couldn't imagine two divorces. She pondered whether putting up with a violent alcoholic husband was her only alternative. The common wisdom of the time was that husbands and wives should stay together, however bad the situation, "for the sake of the children." She couldn't help wondering if was really best for the children to see all the violence and drinking. But Albert kept asking forgiveness, and she kept giving it.

Then one day, Josephine's sister Edna was visiting. Albert's brown Essex pulled into the driveway. The sisters were in the dining room, chatting and laughing with Geraldine. Junior heard the car and hid near the doorway that led to the kitchen, hoping it was the good father who opened the side door. He recognized the telltale odor his father thought he had masked. He shuddered.

Josephine, too, smelled the liquor on his breath. She was angry and yelled at him. He charged at them, locking Josephine and Edna together in a chokehold. Geraldine screamed and fled. Junior went with her. Their screams alerted a neighbor who called the police. Albert was handcuffed and sent to jail.

He was gone for days, but Josephine refused to press charges. When Albert finally showed up at the Traymore house, he had a beautiful bouquet of flowers in his hand. Josephine was weary of his promises, but once again she let him come back.

As 1936 came to an end, so did the marriage. Late one after-noon, Josephine walked into the Cleveland market, unexpected. Albert wasn't at the back counter or near the case where the meat was displayed. Maybe he was in the cooler. She waited. She heard strange noises in the back room. She headed for the door, turned the knob, and gasped. Her husband was there with a woman, a customer Josephine recognized, their clothes strewn on the dusty floor.

Aghast, screaming, tears gushing down her face like a water-fall, she fled. She'd been betrayed.

On November 13, 1936, Josephine C. Morhard petitioned in Cuyahoga Common Pleas Court for a "divorce, a restraining order, custody of their minor child, alimony and other relief." In the settlement, she got the meat market on 93rd and Hough; Albert kept the one on Euclid.

Josephine's two hard-drinking, high-living husbands had promised paradise but turned her life into hell.

Junior had just turned seven. Geraldine was sixteen.

Another chapter was about to begin.

Josephine picked up the family photo album sitting on her dresser. She turned to a photo of Albert, standing in front of a large storefront display window covered in white hand-painted letters advertising GROUND BEEF 21¢ LB. He's smiling engag-ingly, seductively, at the camera, his head tilted to the side, his muscular arms folded confidently across his chest. He's wear-ing a bow tie and white shirt under a white butcher's apron with a white military-style creased grocer's hat perfectly cen-tered on his head. There isn't a spot on his clothing, despite the bloody business he engaged in every day.

The next photo shows the family all together, seated on the front steps of their picture-perfect red brick Georgian house. Albert is dressed in a neatly pressed shirt and tie; his symmet-rical features only slightly marred by a too-square jaw, his thinning hair distinguished by hints of gray at the temples.

Josephine sits close to him, smiling the welcoming smile that always drew people to her. She's wearing a long dress with floral embroidery at the neckline, her dark hair in a 1930s' movie star upsweep. Her right arm cradles her young son, dressed in his Sunday best white shirt and short pants, his legs positioned for a quick getaway as soon as the dreaded picture taking is done. Pretty teenage Geraldine stands next to them.

In the pictures, life looks ideal. She stares at the photo, like she's forgotten there was a scene like this one, trying to remember if their lives ever were like that. The image of the idyllic family masked the often-harsh reality of what life had really been like inside the pretty house. The engaging, immaculately clothed butcher of the album was now out of the picture, gone, faded like the photos from their lives. However, the unsettling ghosts remained.

Albert had been busy since the divorce, but not with his remaining market. He had a twenty-six-year-old girlfriend named Fanny, twenty-two years his junior and just nine years older than Geraldine. On March 31, 1937, they applied for a marriage license.

A restraining order had kept him away from Josephine and the children, but he missed the family he'd lost. He petitioned the court to modify the order so he could see his son. He testified that he had never harmed Junior physically, even when he was drunk and at his worst. The court granted the modification and allowed him to visit Junior at his Traymore home every Wednesday between 3:30 p.m. and 5:30 p.m. as long as he paid support. The court ordered him to pay $10 a week. But he didn't pay and he was arrested. At a hearing on April 2, 1937, Albert told the judge he refused to pay more than $5 a week. He was fined $50 and threatened with a ten-day jail sentence if he didn't pay, so he paid the $50. Somehow, after that, he did an about-face. He pleaded with Josephine to let him come back home despite his promise to marry Fanny, a promise Josephine knew nothing about. She refused. He stopped drinking. He came by to see Junior, pleading again. Still she refused. He'd been sober for weeks when he finally wore Josephine down. She took him back, but she told him if he ever came home with alcohol on his breath again, that would be the end. This time she meant it.

He never went through with the marriage to Fanny. Instead, Josephine and Albert remarried in Ripley, New York, on April 25, 1937. Junior remembered them coming into his bedroom before they left, saying they'd be gone for a few days and to be good for the lady who was taking care of him.

After that, Albert seemed to be trying to be a good husband, father, and provider. The divorce shocked him into realizing how important his family was to him. He didn't want to lose them again.

Life at home was calm. Albert again became the fun father who did handstands, listened to German music on the phonograph and sports on the radio, and joked in many languages. He was attentive to Josephine and helped around the house.

But again the good times didn't last. One day, he came home from the market and Josephine again smelled liquor on his breath. That was it, the last straw. She told him to get out, for good this time. He didn't believe her. Like he always did, he came back a few days later, begging her to take him back.

They were on the porch. Junior saw the back of his father's head—the thinning, brownish hair laced with threads of gray. He watched his father drop to his knees in front of Josephine, now the supplicant, pleading, his chiseled muscles no longer inspiring fear.

He heard them arguing. Albert promised he'd change. Josephine said no. His mother finally had enough. Albert was out of the house for good.

Junior was glad he was gone. He couldn't stand the yelling, the screaming, the violence. With his father finally gone, he wouldn't freeze in fear every time the brown Essex roared into the driveway.

The good times when his father was sober, when he took him to the pool, when they cheered together for the Rams, when he told him stories about his life in Germany, when his eyes smiled, when he joked and lifted Albert in the air, were a buried memory.

Only the horror stories remained, indelibly etched on his brain—the meat cleaver, his father's hands around his mother's neck, the smell of alcohol on his father's breath. They stood out in bold primary colors, as startlingly real as the day they happened. The good times were tucked away in his mind's forgotten scrapbook.

It left Junior confused and angry. It was hard for him to reconcile the father he wanted so much to love with the father he had learned to hate.

CHAPTER NINE

Hard Times

Josephine reached her bare hand into the bloody innards of one of the chickens that had arrived earlier from State Packing, their feathers plucked but their insides intact. She kept her hand flat so her fingertips slipped easily along the breastbone—the way Albert had shown her. Slowly, she moved her fingers toward the bird's neck, feeling her way over the top of the bird's guts. When she reached as far as she could, she grasped a slimy handful and pulled them out slowly, being careful not to clasp too hard. That, she knew, might break the gallbladder and let out the green bile that could contaminate the meat.

Albert's drinking and bad temperament cost him not only his family but also his last market on Lakeshore Boulevard in Euclid. Josephine was on her own again with two children to care for. It was the Great Depression, the "the worst of times." Still, she felt lucky she had the meat market, even if it was only a ghost of what it had been.

She'd been late getting in this morning so she was rushing to get the chickens cleaned and in the display case. Thankfully, Ed—her butcher—had been there to open the store for her.

Josephine was behind for two good reasons: Albert and Geraldine. Her two children were much less predictable than the arrival of the chickens from State Packing. She rarely met her own timetable for arriving at work, but she made sure the children met theirs.

She'd sent Geraldine off early to take the green and white Cleveland Railway Company bus to Cleveland Heights High

School. Junior rode his bike to Canterbury Elementary School. Her housekeeper Leila's bus had been late, but she'd finally arrived to take care of the house and the children until Josephine got home at dinnertime. Money was tight, but Josephine knew she needed someone she trusted at the house, whether or not she could afford it.

The children, especially Junior, were constantly in her thoughts no matter how busy she was at the market. Geraldine was doing well—amazingly well considering the succession of family upheavals.

It was a different story for Junior. He'd been held back in second grade because he couldn't read. His teacher, Miss Mayes, was convinced he was smart enough and decided to figure out why. He had an October birthday; maybe the problem was that he was younger than most of the children in his class. Still, there must be another reason, she thought. She kept him late one day and had him try to read to her. She watched his eyes. He was trying to read from right to left instead of left to right. That was it. She now knew what to do.

Josephine was relieved but still concerned about Junior. When she was getting ready to leave for the market, he clung to her like he was afraid he'd never see her again. She tried to talk to him, to find out what was wrong, but he turned away and became stonily quiet. She assured him she'd be home as soon as she could after work. She hugged him and told him to have a good day at school.

Inside, she was torn. She was acutely aware of how much she needed to work, to turn the market around to keep her small family afloat. She also enjoyed the personal satisfaction she always got from working. At the same time, she desperately wanted to stay with her young son, to reassure him that everything would be all right, to give him the attention he needed. Guilt had become as much a part of her as the air she breathed.

She reached again into the chicken's cavity, this time tearing out its heart. She rinsed it over and over in the clear water of the nearby sink until she saw no sign of the chicken's blood or entrails and she was sure it was completely cleaned. She put the chicken in the display case with the others, saving the giblets for the dressing she'd make later. The stuffed chickens commanded a higher price.

It wasn't the time to think about why her life was such a mess—though during the night she'd been unable to think about anything else. Josephine had gone from high times to low before, but this was different. She'd expected the divorce to magically turn around their lives. There would be no more brutal scenes. Life would be peaceful. They would start fresh. Now, she was beginning to wonder if the chains of the past were too strong.

The market wasn't much bigger than an average living room. A refrigerated, glassed-in case dominated the right side, packed full of fresh cuts of beef, chicken, pork, ham, lamb, and turkey. Next to it, a walkway joined the meat market to the E. W. Hackenberg Grocery Store. Hackenberg's sold groceries and Josephine sold meats. It made sense for customers to have access from one to the other.

Opposite the case, an aisle brought customers to the counter in back where Josephine greeted customers and rang up sales. Two meat-cutting areas were behind the counter—the meat grinder on one, the other against the wall near the cooler where the huge two-hundred-pound sides of beef hung from hooks. The sink, as big as a washtub, connected the two.

Josephine's only employee was Ed, the butcher, who hauled and cut up the sides of beef. He handled the heavy work and covered for her when problems at home held her up. Josephine took care of everything else.

She would only offer the best quality meat, despite the un-easy economics of the Depression. She wouldn't sell inferior beef, even in ground meat, and she wouldn't add byproducts like many of her competitors did or preservatives like her former husband had, even if it meant she had to charge higher prices than her competitors.

The Hough neighborhood, where the market was located, had been one of the city's most prosperous neighborhoods, sporting many handsome Tudor, Italianate, and Victorian homes. Doan's Corner was the city's second largest shopping district. Exclusive private schools—Hathaway Brown, Laurel, Hawken, and University School—educated the scions of the still wealthy who hadn't lost their fortunes in the stock market.

Another part of Hough was nicknamed "Little Hollywood," but it wasn't because of natives like Bob Hope who grew up there. It had been infamous during Prohibition for its stretch of speakeasies and other nefarious pursuits.

The main Hough landmark was historic League Park, the pride of the neighborhood. It was smack in the middle of the city, surrounded by homes. The ballpark opened in 1891 with the legendary Cy Young pitching for the Cleveland Spiders of the National League. Now forty-plus years later, it hosted the American League Cleveland Indians, the Cleveland Buckeyes of the Negro American League, and the pro football Cleveland Rams. It was at League Park in 1920 that the Indians won their first World Series under player-manager Tris Speaker by defeating the Brooklyn Dodgers. The ballpark was about a mile from Josephine's market.

Around that time, many of Hough's wealthier residents moved farther east to newer, larger homes in Cleveland Heights and Shaker Heights. Flocks of European immigrants replaced them, living more modestly in the two-family homes and apartment buildings built to accommodate them. Many were tradesmen.

As the Depression lumbered on, the neighborhood's economy worsened. Pockets of poverty crept in. Many owners of the remaining elaborate homes no longer could afford the upkeep so they began taking in boarders and delaying maintenance. Fading, peeling paint, loose boards, and missing bricks marred formerly pristine mansions.

There were few—if any—jobs for neighborhood painters, electricians, and plumbers. Families had to choose between buying food and making rent or mortgage payments. Single-family homes were converted into apartments. Aunts, uncles, grandparents, nieces, and nephews crowded into dwellings meant for a single family. Thousands were evicted, homes boarded up, families and their possessions dumped on the sidewalk like yesterday's newspapers.

Cleveland had been hard hit by the Depression. Nearly a quarter of its population and a full half of its industrial workers were unemployed at its peak. Others kept their jobs, but their hours and wages were cut. Thousands of homeless men, women, boys, and girls congregated in shantytowns under bridges on the banks of the Cuyahoga River or huddled together on the Lake Erie waterfront. Others sought shelter in flophouses, bus terminals, and vacant buildings. The number of families receiving direct relief payments for food, clothing, and shelter was twenty times what it had been before Black Tuesday.

The U.S. government answered the crisis with a series of New Deal programs, including Works Progress Administration (WPA) work relief programs that put some people back to work on projects like building the Memorial Shoreway, a highway that ran along Lake Erie and was called "the largest WPA job in the country."

Cleveland officials added other projects to give people jobs: they began construction of mammoth Cleveland Stadium in 1931; they brought the Republican National Convention to the City in 1936; and they took on one of the most ambitious projects in the nation, the Great Lakes Exposition that brought to life 135 acres of land reclaimed from Lake Erie. It was anchored by Cleveland Municipal Stadium on the west.

The Exposition was a panorama of tall and short buildings, bright and flashing lights, stomach-churning rides, and people chatting and laughing and screaming with delight. It looked like a gigantic movie set. There was something for everyone. Futuristic exhibits introduced new inventions like television. The *Streets of the World* showcased the culture, traditions, food, music, and dance of 150 different nations. A Billy Rose Aquacade starred Olympic and movie swimming stars Eleanor Holm, Johnny Weissmuller, and a very young Esther Williams. Radioland gave fans a chance to watch broadcasts of *Fibber McGee and Molly* and other popular shows. The Globe Theatre presented fifteen of Shakespeare's plays. There was a floating stage, a floating "Showboat" nightclub; a Court of the Presidents and, of course, the Midway with its acres of amusements, carnival acts, circus, rides, and eats. It was a cotton candy world full of fun, amazement, and culture.

The Exposition lured seven million visitors and returned $70 million to the city. Still, that was not enough to satisfy city officials. The Exposition was going to close, and the buildings that brought the lakefront to life would soon be razed.

As much as Cleveland had done, it wasn't enough.

Josephine's meat market was just hanging on. The Depression played a big role, but there were other factors. Her former husband left the market with stacks of unpaid bills. Meat suppliers were hounding her. Utility companies were threatening to shut her off. She needed to pay them, or she'd lose the market—and maybe her house. Few customers were coming through the doors. Many of them had been alienated by her former husband's bursts of temper and unpredictable behavior. Josephine had to do something and quickly. She wasn't making enough money to cover the bills, but she was determined not to lose the market. It was all she had.

She knew the odds were against her. She had worked with Albert in the market, she had experience as a stenographer, but she'd never had full responsibility for managing the market. What's more, she was a woman, a divorced woman with two children—an anomaly. Men weren't used to dealing with a female business owner. As she'd discovered earlier in her life, some tried to seduce her; others attempted to cheat her, thinking she was an easy mark. Women were expected to be married, to stay home with their children. Unmarried women often were called "old maids" and mostly confined to teaching, nursing, or jobs so menial they couldn't even see a glass ceiling. There were so few mothers who worked, there were no support systems. They were on their own. It didn't matter to Josephine; she'd been on her own much of her life. She was tough and never doubted herself. She'd find a way to survive.

She plowed ahead with fierce determination. She was going to repair relationships with the customers and the suppliers, organize the books, fix up the store, and advertise specials she was sure would bring in customers. She would bring the market back to profitability. It was up to her to clean up everything if she was going to support herself, Geraldine, and Albert.

First, she had to find a way to pay the bills. No matter how hard she worked or how much she cut expenses, she wasn't making enough money to pay her suppliers, utilities, Leila, and the household bills. She got into a spiral of paying only the most critical bills—and putting off the others, including her own mortgage payments. When she couldn't hold off her creditors any longer, she began kiting checks. She opened several bank accounts and wrote checks from one account to another, then to another to give her time to cover her payments. She was buying time.

By summer's end, it looked like the Depression might soon be over. Business picked up. She got caught up on the meat market bills, and was starting to get her mortgage payments up to date. Finally, she could see an end to her financial woes.

CHAPTER TEN

The Game

Josephine and Junior were driving on Carnegie Avenue in Cleveland en route to the State Packing Company on Bolivar Road where Josephine would place her meat orders for the week.

"Ta Tat ta tata Tat. Tat ta Tat ta tatatata Tat ta."

Inside the 1936 maroon Chevrolet coupe, their first with a radio, Josephine and Junior listened for Jack Graney's staccato voice to pierce the monotonous sound of the Teletype. He and his partner, Pinky Hunter, served up an entertaining back-and-forth banter that fooled listeners into believing they were watching the game from the White Sox press box in Chicago. Really, they were hundreds of miles from the action, sitting in a tiny Cleveland studio not far from where Josephine and Junior were driving.

In one of his classic routines, Graney would pretend a ball was heading toward him and say something like, "Look out, Pinky. Here comes a foul ball." Then he'd slap the desk, making a sound like the ball had hit the press box, and say to his partner, "That was a close one, Pinky."

It was a masterful charade.

On this day—and at all the Indians' away games—a telegraph operator in the city where the game was held transmitted the plays to the Cleveland studio in Morse code. The signals spilled out on yellow paper, a ticker tape, and the local operator converted them into letters and numbers. "B1" meant first base; "S1" was strike one. With this scant information and only the white walls of the studio for visual inspiration, Graney provided play-by-play. Hunter added commentary. If there was a hit, a home run, or a pitcher got a strikeout, they would plug in crowd cheers and sometimes boos.

To Josephine and Junior, the ruse was real.

Josephine had been a Cleveland Indians fan since she moved to the city, often going to games at League Park with her sisters and friends. Later, when her life became too chaotic, leisure time was rare. But she loved baseball, and now she could listen to a game right in her own car.

The temperature was a cool 59 degrees, and the sky had become a wash of the dull gray more common to Cleveland winters. An occasional Tudor-style gas station and box-like two- to six-story buildings—most as gray as the sky—lined the avenue. They were overshadowed by towering neon signs blaring HASEROT'S, SENORA COFFEE, and HOTEL BOLTON perched high on rooftops, grasping for the community's limited dollars. Billboards preyed on unattainable dreams, depicting ultra-expensive cars like the "all-new" Cord convertible with its sleek hood, wraparound grille, and concealed headlights. (The Auburn Automobile Company, which manufactured the Cord, would be bankrupt by the year's end.)

The economy had again run into a roadblock. After a hopeful spring, another deep recession had taken hold in the fall.

The red brick headquarters of Warner & Swasey, manufacturer of telescopes and precision machine parts, interrupted the repetitive landscape near East 55th Street. Waves of black coal particles soared from its smokestacks into the clouds, flaunting its singular ability to escape the latest flare-up of the Great Depression.

In the distance, Josephine and Junior could see the top half of Cleveland's Terminal Tower, the second tallest building in the world at 708 feet, its tower capped with progressively smaller units that resembled a multi-layered wedding cake, topped with a conical cap that pointed to the sky. Junior knew the sight of the slim tower meant he would soon be seeing the converging tracks of the interurban railway and its rust-colored electric cars chugging passengers to and from the Cleveland suburbs and places as far away as Columbus, Toledo, and Erie, Pennsylvania.

Josephine took her eyes off the road long enough to cast an inquisitive glance at Junior slumped in the seat beside her, his eyes fixed on the magical black knobs that were airlifting the announcers' voices to them. He reminded her of his father—the same broad expanse of forehead, firm chin, and sturdy bone structure that gave away their shared Teutonic heritage. But Josephine was determined to make sure that was the only way Junior would be like him. She ran her hand quickly through her son's unruly black curls, unconsciously trying to smooth the disarray of their lives.

Her face showed subtle reminders of her on-and-off struggles. At forty-six, Josephine looked older than her years. A spiderweb of lines crept toward her cheek and hairline from the corners of her eyes. Well-earned creases etched her brow. Her once-shapely figure had morphed from hourglass to tumbler, spreading out everywhere except in her slender face. That was okay with her. After two disastrous marriages and a child from each of them, the only male she wanted in her life was sitting right next to her.

She'd just picked up Junior from school, and Geraldine was with friends. Josephine was in a hurry; she couldn't waste a minute. The market was struggling again. She was back in crisis mode and had much to do.

As she listened to the ball game, her latest troubles faded for the moment. It was a pleasant distraction to hear Jack Graney detail every play and chat with Hunter about the players, the weather at the ballpark, and ham it up just for fun.

Graney knew baseball better than most announcers. He'd been an Indians ballplayer himself. Nicknamed "Three-and-two Jack" for his ability to draw walks, he was a left fielder on the Indians team that won the 1920 World Series. In fourteen years with the Indians, he'd accumulated a workmanlike .250 lifetime batting average.

His fame was rooted in his many "firsts." He was the first player to face—and get a single from—the nineteen-year-old Babe Ruth in his 1914 pitching debut with the Boston Red Sox. He was the first to wear a number on his uniform—the number 1—as leadoff hitter in the June 26, 1916, Indians game against the White Sox. To complete the trilogy, he was the first former player to become a baseball broadcaster.

Graney's announcing partner, Pinky—whose given name, Cartright, was a bit too formal for the job—was a longtime radio personality who had gained early fame as a banjo player and vocalist with Emerson Gill and his Bamboo Gardens Orchestra (sometimes known as Emerson Gill and His Castle of Paris Orchestra)—the hottest dance band in Cleveland in the late 1920s.

Graney's photographic memory of the ballparks from his time as a player brought the games to life. "When he talked you could smell the resin in the dugouts, feel the clean smack of the ball against bat and see the hawkers in the stands," Bob Dolgan of the *Cleveland Plain Dealer* later wrote.

The score was 6–5 in favor of the Indians. It was the eighth inning. Indian Willis Hudlin was on the mound. He was one of the Tribe's top pitchers, earning double-digit wins nearly every year. Sadly, he was remembered more for giving up Babe Ruth's five hundredth home run in 1929. Everyone forgot Hudlin was the winner that day.

Josephine needed to get to the packinghouse, and traffic was slowing her down. Every stoplight seemed to turn red just as she approached, and she was already running late.

It was Primary Election Day in Cleveland. Voters were selecting the Republican and Democratic nominees for Cleveland mayor and city council. Over two hundred thousand people were expected to vote, and the streets were crowded. Cars moved slowly in both directions, their elongated snouts, headlight eyes, and tall silver grilles looking a bit like tigers gnashing their teeth.

People headed to the polls. Women had exchanged their plain housedresses for wide-brimmed hats, gloves, and "afternoon" frocks that widened their shoulders and flowed gracefully to a midpoint between their knees and feet. The men sported V-shaped double-breasted suits with wide lapels, fedoras artfully positioned on their heads. As Josephine drove by, she saw the usual lines of unemployed workers waiting in a soup kitchen line, likely wearing their only suit and hat.

She was sure Mayor Harold Burton would get the Republican nod and win a second term, even though Cleveland's population was decidedly Democratic. He'd made good on his promise to root out the corruption and crime that escalated dur-

Josephine Mathey as a young woman.

The Mathey family. Top row (*left to right*): John, Ellen, Emma, Flora, and Albert; middle row: Josephine, Anne, Elizabeth (mother), Joseph (father), Sarah (Sadie), and Edna; bottom row: Alice, Joseph, and Ethel

Josephine loved horses and was a skilled horsewoman.

Josphine's first husband, George B. Gerau, an attorney, land speculator, and inventor who said he was descended from Napoleon.

Josephine and George's daughter Geraldine (Gerry) on a pony ride.

Josephine's second husband, Albert H. Morhard, in front of Morhard's Meats on 93rd Street and Hough Avenue in Cleveland, the market Josephine took over after her divorce from Albert.

Josephine and Albert H. Morhard's son, Albert J. (Junior) Morhard, with his bunnies.

Josephine and Junior Morhard
at a rest area on a drive
to New York City.

The family at Niagara Falls, New York.
Front row (*left to right*): Josephine, Junior,
and Gerry; back row: Albert H. Morhard
and Lucien Hammes, a cousin from Mulhouse,
Alsace, France, where Albert was born.

The first Little Indians team at University Town Hall in their new uniforms—
just like those of the big-league Cleveland Indians (*left to right*):
Billy Myers, Jimmy Prior, Jackie Heinen, Michael Albl,
Eddie Decker, Dick Baumiller, Dave Erickson, Junior Morhard,
Buddy Myers, King Brown, Allen Koenig, and Joey Phipps.

Cleveland Indians pitching great Mel Harder was a fan of the Little Indians, often stopping by to watch the games and inviting the boys to his home for popcorn and soda. Here Allen Koenig (*left*) and Buddy Myers (*center*) show Harder their new replica Cleveland Indians uniforms.

With her Junior American League running smoothly, Mrs. Morhard decided to add a Junior National League and hold a Little World Series in League Park, weekday home of the Cleveland Indians. Here, she gives instructions to some of the boys of the new Junior National League.

The boys never forgot Josephine Morhard and what she did for them. In 1968, thirty years after the first boys' league, they held a reunion. Here, former Little Indians Dick Kusa, who pitched for the winning Little Indians team in the 1941 Little World Series in League Park, greets Mrs. Morhard, as her son Al (*right*) and John Van Thune (*center*) look on.

Mrs. Morhard's "boys" held the reunion for their baseball "mother" right before Mother's Day. Here she is with Brad Rogers, who organized the reunion, and Chet Kermode, a former Little Indian who also was on the 1947 Cleveland Heights State Championship team.

Mrs. Morhard at the reunion, surrounded by some of the professional baseball men who helped with her leagues. Front row (*left to right*): umpires Tony Pianowski and Paul Kvetko; back row: former Cleveland Indians Manager Roger Peckinpaugh and former umpire Hal Lebovitz, who went on to fame as a sportswriter and was elected to the writer's wing of the National Baseball Hall of Fame.

ing the Depression, hiring "Untouchable" Eliot Ness, who'd brought down Chicago gangster Al Capone, as his safety director.

Josephine was a storeowner, and stemming crime was important to her. She'd been a firm Republican ever since Theodore Roosevelt's presidency and supported Alf Landon in the 1936 presidential election even though President Franklin D. Roosevelt had made all-out efforts to revive the economy and put people back to work—people like many of the customers who had difficulty paying for the meat she sold. Junior was the only child in Canterbury Elementary School wearing a brown and yellow LANDON FOR PRESIDENT pin in a sea of red, white, and blue Roosevelt buttons.

From the speaker above the windshield, Jack Graney's voice grew louder, punctuating the silence between mother and son. There were cheers. It was the bottom of the ninth, and opposing catcher Luke Sewell had tied the score 6–6 with a solo homer. Josephine let out a long disapproving sigh. Junior's normally unreadable face twisted into a frown.

Graney droned in his singsong style that Cleveland manager, Steve O'Neill, was headed to the mound to replace Indians pitcher Hudlin with young hotshot Bob Feller. Feller had had an up and down year, with an injury early on.

Feller appeared unconcerned, striking out the first White Sox batter and getting the second to ground out.

There were two out, none on. Feller got his signal, took his position on the mound, and hurled a fastball. The hitter crushed a single. The runner was safe at first.

Junior banged his fist against the dash, showing his displeasure and startling Josephine. She'd taken him with her so they could spend time together. Josephine knew she'd been working too much and wondered if she was neglecting him. Junior wasn't even eight yet—nine years younger than his half sister. He needed more of her time.

Feller was up on the next batter with two strikes. He hurled another fastball. Strike three. Three outs. The game was going into overtime.

Josephine reached for the knob in the center of the dashboard and turned up the volume to better hear the raspy-voiced announcer. Next up was Indians hulking left fielder Julius "Moose" Solters, a power hitter who had been acquired in the off-season along with shortstop Lyn Lary. Solters was batting a healthy .323 since coming to the Indians.

White Sox pitcher Thornton Lee wound up. The pitch whizzed in. Graney's voice rose to a crescendo. It was a home run for Solters! The Indians were now in the lead!

The score was 7–6 in favor of the Indians. Before long, it was the bottom of the tenth, the White Sox up. Eighteen-year-old righty phenom Feller needed to keep the Sox from getting any more runs.

It was Feller's first full season in the Majors. He had come to the Indians from his family's farm in Van Meter, Iowa, signing for a dollar and an autographed baseball. His father, Bill, had encouraged him to play baseball from the time he was little, insisting it offered a better life than farming. He even built a baseball diamond on the farm.

By the time Bob Feller was nine, he could throw a ball 270 feet. He claimed he developed his massive arm strength by milking cows, picking corn, and bailing hay. He joined the Indians on summer break after his junior year in high school. In his first career start—on Sunday August 23, 1936, against the St. Louis Browns in 90-degree temperatures—he stunned fans and baseball officials by striking out fifteen batters and winning the game.

The *Cleveland Plain Dealer*'s Gordon Cobbledick said of his debut, "In what probably was the greatest major league pitching debut in all history, the farm boy from [Iowa] proved beyond the hint of a doubt his right to wear a big league uniform regardless of the fact that he never pitched so much as one ball in the minors."

After the season, he went back to Van Meter High for his senior year, rejoining the Indians after graduation. While he was still in high school, Feller's rookie feats landed him on the cover of *Time* magazine.

Early in the 1937 season, he developed a sore elbow and was out for an extended period of time. Even so, he struck out nearly 150 batters and already was one of the highest paid players on the team, earning an annual salary of $14,000, almost as much as veteran pitcher Johnny Allen and star center fielder Earl Averill.

Feller got the first two batters out. Josephine and Albert waited for the pitch. A strike. A ball. Another strike.

Junior was sitting up straighter now, his hazel eyes fastened on the source of the voices, imagining Feller's right leg raised in his signature motion and his right arm serving up the next pitch, the one that could end the game.

Feller got the signal, wound up, and hurled a blazing fastball at the outside corner. Graney called strike three. The Chicago batter was out. That was the game.

The Indians had won a nail-biter, gaining a game on the third place White Sox. Junior's head bobbed back against the light gray seat, the only outward sign the game ended the way he wanted it to.

Josephine's firm voice broke through the announcers' post-game banter. "Great game!" she declared to no one in particular, enjoying the win and momentarily distracted from her problems. She turned toward her son. "Wasn't that a great game, Junior?"

Junior didn't answer. He didn't want to miss a word Jack and Pinky said.

It was September 28, 1937, the day Junior fell in love with baseball and the Cleveland Indians. It didn't matter that his Indians were in fourth place in the American League, twenty and a half games behind the league-leading New York Yankees.

The Indians had slumped midway through the season, but they'd rallied from sixth place. It was almost the end of the season. Only a few road games remained. Cleveland fans wanted more, wishing the team had another month to play and maybe catch up.

In the morning *Plain Dealer*, Cleveland sportswriter Gordon Cobbledick echoed their feelings, lamenting that the Indians were "gone from our midst for the season," and wondering what might have been if pitchers Feller and Johnny Allen had been "on hand all season to work their particular brand of magic." Both had been out for extended periods. It was much too late for a pennant run. The Indians were twenty and a half games behind the perennial American League champs, the New York Yankees. If only they had more games.

The Yankees—the team Indians' fans and fans from cities

from Boston to Philadelphia loved to hate—had already clinched the American League pennant. Again. They led the second place Detroit Tigers by thirteen and a half games—fueled by "Iron Horse" Lou Gehrig, up-and-coming center fielder Joe DiMaggio, and twenty-game-winning pitchers Lefty Gomez and Red Ruffing.

Gehrig was having his usual stellar year, batting around .350, but Joseph Paul DiMaggio was the player grabbing the headlines. It was only his second year with the Yankees, but he'd smashed forty-six homers and piled up a batting average nearly equal to Gehrig's—a hefty .346.

Even though the Indians had no hope of overtaking the pennant winners, the scribes predicted they'd inch up in the standings next year. They had hard-hitting players on the roster like Earl Averill and first baseman Hal Trosky—along with the lights-out pitchers Feller, Mel Harder, and the talented but temperamental Johnny Allen.

Averill's career had been brilliant. Called "The Rock" for his compact, muscular build, the five-foot-nine-inch outfielder blasted enough hits to bring his batting average above .300 in six of his seven seasons with the Indians—his 1936 batting average was a whopping .378. He also led the American League with 232 hits and 15 triples.

This had been a hard luck year for him. In June, with no warning, his legs seized in a game, and he became temporarily paralyzed. Doctors discovered the thirty-five-year-old had a congenital malformation of the spine. To alleviate the pressure on his spinal column, Averill needed to alter his batting stance. The change affected both his hitting and his quickness on the field. Even so, he batted close to .300.

Like Feller, the lanky Hal Trosky (Harold Arthur Trojovsky) was a farm boy from Iowa who grew up playing baseball. He was leading the American League in runs batted in like he'd done the year before when he hit forty-two homers, was hailed as the "next Babe Ruth," posted 162 runs batted in and a .644 slugging percentage. Trosky was equally talented as a first baseman with a .993 fielding percentage, close to his amazing 1.000 in 1936.

With all his accomplishments and talent, he never made an

All Star team. His competition for All Star honors were three all-time great Hall of Fame first basemen: Lou Gehrig of the New York Yankees, Jimmy Foxx of the Boston Red Sox, and Hank Greenberg of the Detroit Tigers.

Pitcher Johnny Allen was having a record year despite being off the field for several weeks with a bout of appendicitis. He was a remarkable 15-and-0 with one game left to pitch. Fans were eager to see if he could make it through the season undefeated. If he won his last game, he'd tie Walter Johnson's record for consecutive wins.

Allen was an intense, unpredictable player who'd come to the Indians two years earlier in a trade with the Yankees. He had a sidearm heater his Yankee teammate Bill Dickey once described as the "meanest delivery in the League for a right-hander" and a "nasty" fastball many people said went with his personality. One of his trainers Earle (Doc) Painter said of him, "He expects to win every game he pitches and if he doesn't win, he may turn on anybody."

The Indians' crop of newcomers added to the team's expectations, including promising outfielders Jeff Heath and Roy Weatherly, and of course the pitcher who won the game, the teenage Feller, already on his way to superstardom. All were in their first or second years with the team.

There was good reason for fans like Josephine and Junior to be excited. The team was on the rise. Feller was Junior's first baseball hero.

In Cleveland and elsewhere, other young boys reveled in their baseball idols' exploits and antics. Cleveland had the Indians; Detroit, the Tigers; Washington, D.C., the Senators; Cincinnati, the Reds; Pittsburgh, the Pirates. In some cities, loyalties were divided and fans cheered for more than one team. Boston had the Red Sox and the Bees [In 1936, Boston's National League team changed its name from the "Braves" to the "Bees," before returning to the earlier name for the '42 season]; Chicago, the White Sox and Cubs; St. Louis, the Cardinals and Browns; Philadelphia, the Athletics and Phillies; New York, the Yankees, Giants, and the Brooklyn Dodgers.

In St. Louis, colorful Cardinals pitcher Jay Hanna "Dizzy" Dean, one of the team's famed "Gashouse Gang," delighted fans as much for his occasionally outrageous behavior, practical jokes, and predictions as for his masterful pitching. Once, after a contentious matchup with Giants' ace Carl Hubbell, he was suspended after publicly calling National League president Ford Frick and umpire George Barr, "the two greatest crooks in baseball" when a ruling didn't go his way. But he could pitch. Dizzy won an amazing thirty games in 1934, followed by twenty-eight in 1935 and twenty-four in 1936.

Dizzy's brother Paul, or "Daffy," also pitched for the Cards. When Paul joined the team in 1934, Dizzy boasted the two of them would win forty-five games that year. They won forty-nine, and the Cards went to the World Series. There, Dizzy predicted he and his brother would win two games each. Again they made good. The Cardinals beat the Detroit Tigers in seven games. Dizzy won the opener and the seventh game; Paul won the third and sixth.

In Pittsburgh, another set of baseball brothers, outfielders Paul and Lloyd Waner of the Pirates, made the sports headlines, earning the affectionate nicknames, "Big Poison" and "Little Poison." Both were prodigious batters. They remain the best-hitting brothers in Major League history, with lifetime averages of .333 and .316, respectively.

In Boston, Red Sox fans celebrated the acquisition of Jimmie "The Beast" Foxx, who was knocking the ball out of parks across the country. The Philadelphia Athletics traded him for the measly sum of $150,000 as Connie Mack dismantled his once-dominant team. Noted for his powerful swing, Foxx hit forty-one homers in his first season with the Red Sox.

Across the country, radio brought the heroics of baseball stars right into the homes and cars of millions of people, captivating other young boys like Junior. If you didn't live in a Major League city, radio made it possible to enjoy the games. If you did, you didn't need to pay admission to the ballpark. You could listen to a game, and it was free. Radio made baseball the nation's pastime.

Baseball captivated the nation. Radio wasn't the only factor. Baseball gave people an escape from the misery of joblessness, poverty, and hunger. By the time President Franklin D. Roosevelt was elected in 1932, twelve million U.S. residents were unemployed. Banks had closed. Approximately one of every four families no longer had an income. People were starving, standing in line at soup kitchens and selling their meager possessions. In city after city, thousands waited in line for a chance at three or four jobs. The homeless crowded into boxcars, docks, and "Hooverville" shanties like refugees from the horrors of war. Men rode the rails from city to city—going anywhere they might find a job. Children went to bed hungry for days at a time. Desperate mothers stole clothes off clotheslines and milk off back porches. Beggars and hoboes knocked on doors, looking for food. President Franklin D. Roosevelt famously spoke of "one-third of a nation ill-housed, ill-clad, ill nourished."

By the spring of 1937, some progress had been made in alleviating the struggles of Americans. Roosevelt's alphabet agency programs like the Civilian Conservation Corps (CCC) and Works Progress Administration (WPA) had made a dent in the consuming joblessness. Business in Cleveland and throughout the country nearly returned to pre-Depression conditions.

Unfortunately, by the fall, the country had fallen into another deep recession that was to last through most of 1938. Again, American industrial production plummeted. Unemployment skyrocketed back to 19 percent. Manufacturing output dropped 37 percent. Consumer spending plunged. Government cutbacks decimated the public works projects. Higher taxes squeezed incomes. It was called the Depression within the Depression, the third worst recession of the century—caused, many said, by the mutual decision of President Roosevelt and the Congress to balance the budget, cut deficit spending, and raise taxes at a time when the economy hadn't fully recovered. Once again it was hard to get jobs and support families. Regardless, people spent their scarce pennies to see a Shirley Temple movie or, even better, head for the ballpark. A 10-cent hotdog at a ball game might be the only meal of the day.

President Roosevelt summarized baseball's effect: "Baseball as a sport has done as much as anything to keep up the spirits of people when they were losing their jobs when they were in the midst of the Depression." Former President Hoover added, "Next to religion, baseball has furnished a greater impact on American life than any other institution."

The game had become more than the national pastime. It lifted people from their troubles and gave them something to look forward to when there wasn't much to celebrate. Baseball took your mind off your troubles. Listening to ball games or, better yet, going down to the ballpark offered a rare chance to cheer, to hope, to see if your team could beat the odds and win. If your team was a winner, you figured maybe you could be too.

The announcers' snappy chatter ended. Josephine's hands tightened on the wheel and her foot pressed against the gas pedal as she rushed to pass a slow-moving black Oldsmobile touring sedan, giving it an admiring if fleeting glance. She had placed her meat orders, and she and Junior were headed back down Carnegie Avenue toward the market. She had much to do. She needed to grind the hamburger meat, clean out the chickens, make her special beef stew, fill the display cases, and advertise the new specials.

Josephine turned north at East 93rd Street and waited at the Euclid Avenue intersection for the streetcar to pass. Euclid Avenue had once been known as "Millionaire's Row," the "Showplace of the Nation"—the place where the John D. Rockefellers and notables like Marcus Hanna, John Hay, Jeptha Wade, and Charles F. Brush lived in extravagant estates overlooking Lake Erie. Mark Twain had described it as "one of the grandest streets in the world" and considered building his own estate there. Now, a half century later, there were few reminders of the grand street it had been. Hardly any elaborate mansions remained. Now tight blocks of merchants, offices, and churches lined the avenue, linked by electric streetcars going to and from suburban communities like Shaker Heights on the east and Lakewood on the west.

Josephine and Junior soon glimpsed the awning that spelled out MORHARD'S QUALITY MEATS and the hand-drawn white letters on the storefront windows advertising the specials: *Ground Beef 21¢, Veal Chops 28¢, Smoked Picnics 21¢, Lamb Stew 12¢.* The exterior looked crisp and clean, just the way Josephine wanted. She'd painted the woodwork white around the windows as a signal that it no longer belonged to her former husband. It had been sterilized.

Josephine stopped the car, got out, and took hold of Junior's hand. As the two of them headed down the aisle they spotted Ed in his usual place at the back of the store, carving a slab of beef. She greeted him with a big smile. "Hi, Ed. The meat is ordered. Anything happen while I was gone?"

"The bank called again. They want you to call back right away."

Josephine knew what that meant. The euphoria of the baseball game was gone.

III: BASEBALL

If you teach a boy what's right, he'll grow up right.
—JOSEPHINE MATHEY MORHARD

CHAPTER ELEVEN

Josephine's Idea

Fall 1937, University Heights, Ohio

Junior's school day was finished. He rushed out of his third-grade classroom and grabbed his yellow bike from the rack near the parking lot. He was happy to get out of the stuffy classroom and taste the brisk air. School was a chore. He could read pretty well now, but arithmetic was a problem, especially when he had to add and subtract large columns of numbers.

The good thing about school was seeing his friends—going outside for morning recess and playing afternoon softball on the school's south field. During recess, Junior and classmates Buddy Myers, Don Green, Joey Phipps, Howard Trau, Don Allen, and Jerry Kurland ran around playing tag and trying to push each other off the dirt pile. In afternoon softball, they played with real bats and balls, even if they weren't hardballs.

Junior hopped on his bike for the ride home—it was seven-tenths of a mile by Josephine's calculation. Leila, the house-keeper, was peering out the window, watching for him as usual. She was nice enough, but he didn't like the way she hovered over him. He wanted to be left alone.

He leaned his bike against the house near the back door, where Leila was waiting.

"Take off your shoes so you won't track dirt into the house," she ordered.

He lowered his head and rolled his eyes. Every day she said the same thing. He hated being told what to do. He pouted and dawdled, but eventually did what he was told. He grudgingly took off his shoes like Leila wanted, went upstairs to his bedroom, changed his clothes, and quickly headed out the door. Joey Phipps was waiting.

Joey lived up at the top of the Traymore Road hill and was in Junior's class at Canterbury Elementary School. They were best friends. Joey was slim with blond hair, and a good head taller than Junior. Some afternoons, they'd climb trees in the woods near their houses. Contractors were building new homes nearby, and scraps of lumber and nails were scattered all around the properties. The boys were using them to build a tree house. Most days, though, baseball was on their minds. The two of them had played catch in the backyard and in the street since they were in first grade.

The Cleveland Indians' season was over after finishing a disappointing fourth in the American League, but that hadn't dampened the boys' enthusiasm for the sport. Junior and Joey scampered over to one of the lots and found a couple of sticks of wood that looked like they'd make pretty good bats. They picked up a bunch of large stones, put them in their pockets, and headed back to their usual spot, the street in front of the Morhard house. Junior grabbed a stone from his pocket and walloped it down the street. Joey bragged he could hit one farther than Junior, and the two of them continued their makeshift version of competitive batting practice for the rest of the afternoon, stopping only when they saw Leila looking out the window, knowing she wouldn't approve of them batting stones.

As the sun began its retreat, the air turned colder and Joey headed home. Junior waited outside on the front steps, watching for his mother's sporty maroon car. Finally, he saw the familiar headlights. She was home.

Josephine had much on her mind. The sharp dip in the economy had dealt a harsh blow to her finances. She'd just started catching up on her bills, and now many of her customers again had to choose between sheltering their families and putting food in their stomachs. Josephine had to choose between keeping the market afloat and making her mortgage payments.

The bank was going to foreclose on her pretty house. Earlier in the year, she finally had the market operating smoothly. The economy was better, customers were coming back, and she finally was making a profit. She was paying off the creditors and starting to bring her mortgage payments up to date.

Now there was no way she could make the back mortgage payments by the bank's deadline. For once, she didn't have a quick solution. She needed a miracle.

She found one in the shape of her younger brother Joseph.

It was late in the afternoon. She was putting the next day's specials on the store windows when she saw him heading her way. Her eyes hinted at a smile. Joseph William Mathey, her childhood fishing partner, had been a willing participant in many of her adventures. He'd come up from his home near Youngstown. She was happy to see him.

Joseph had left the farm after two years of high school to become a machinist at Youngstown Sheet and Tube. Like Josephine, he was smart and worked hard, qualities that eventually propelled him into an executive position. He lived with his wife Teresa and their three children—Ethel, Margery, and William—in a three-story white frame house with a wraparound porch in Struthers, Ohio.

Josephine's sisters Flora, Ethel, and Alice knew she was having a difficult time and told Joseph. He'd come to see if he could help. Josephine would never have asked, but she was glad he offered. She didn't want to lose her home.

Joseph wanted to know what she needed. She told Joseph about the bank and the mortgage and assured him she could make the market profitable again and make the regular payment if she could just get caught up.

Joseph told her he'd see what the family could do. He'd contribute, and he was sure her father, brothers, and sisters would pitch in. He passed the hat around and made arrangements to make the house payments until she could get back on her feet.

Once again the family Josephine left behind came to her rescue. She was grateful and relieved. One burden had been lifted. But the stress lingered.

Junior and Joey were in the street in front of Junior's house, tossing balls to each other. It was sunny and warm, and it seemed like most of the other boys in the neighborhood were riding their bikes up and down the streets.

Mike Albl raced down the Traymore Street hill. He saw the boys, came to a quick stop, booted up his kickstand, and hurried over to join in. Mike lived on Channing Road, which ran parallel to Traymore. He often came over to play ball with the two of them. He was in their class at Canterbury Elementary, and they were all good friends.

Pretty soon, Allen Koenig tore around the corner on his bike. He was older than the others and attended Gesu Catholic School. He had a reputation in the neighborhood for being a bully, for pushing and shoving the smaller kids to show his "seniority," possibly forgetting some of the nuns' lessons. Junior and Joey had been among his targets. He came around whenever he saw them playing in the street. Like the other boys, he loved baseball, and it seemed to channel his aggressiveness. At least he'd stopped taunting them.

Another boy, Jimmy Prior, saw them playing and joined in. Jimmy was a year younger than Junior.

The five of them started to get together regularly after school when the weather, their mothers, and Leila would allow. They tried playing in Junior's backyard, but it was small and they got tired of Leila hounding them that they were going to break a window. None of the boys had bigger yards so they went back to playing in the street.

They found an old baseball bat, broken in two, and nailed it together. It kept cracking near the handle, so they taped it up with black duct tape. They whacked at stones and ferreted away worn tennis balls from their older siblings. One of the boys discovered a baseball that was split at the seams. Electrical tape answered that problem.

Allen Koenig picked up the bat. Mike Albl stood behind him, catching the errant balls. Junior was pitching. Joey and Jimmy waited in back for any balls that came their way.

Junior hurled the ball, Allen missed it, and it rolled down Traymore Road past Mike. As Mike ran to retrieve the ball, a truck carrying construction supplies for the new houses rumbled up the street. Mike let the ball go, and the boys raced to get out of the way. After the truck passed, the boys retrieved the ball, and started to play again. Another truck started up the hill. And another.

It was hard to play in the street with so many trucks and cars passing by. It had been easier before they started building homes up the hill. Now, nearly every time they started to play, they had to stop.

Mike Albl had an idea. There was a vacant lot at the corner of Traymore and Meadowbrook, up the hill near where the new houses were being built. They gathered a few old newspapers to use for home plate and the bases, figuring they could hold them down with stones so they didn't blow away, and trudged up the street to the lot.

The boys took turns pitching and hitting and fielding. They played pepper—with one of the boys hitting grounders to the other boys, who quickly tried to catch the ball and pitch it back to the hitter. The grass was up past their ankles and it was hard to find the ball if somebody didn't catch it. But at least they had a better place to play.

It was Junior's turn. He picked up the rehabilitated bat. Allen Koenig pitched the ball over the makeshift plate. Junior smashed it with all his eight-year-old strength. The boys watched as the ball ascended high into the air, floated past the streetlight at the end of the lot—and crashed through the window of a nearly finished house across the street. An angry construction worker flew out of the house. Junior picked up the bat and started to run. The rest of the boys plotted their escape. None of them got away.

The man demanded to know who broke the window and who was going to pay for it. He took down their names. He told them he was going to call their mothers and they were never, ever to play on the lot again. Junior was in big trouble. The boys were mad at him for losing the lot. He was sure he'd be in bigger trouble when his mother found out.

Josephine arrived home around 6:00 p.m. It had been an exhausting few days. She'd been on her feet all day—grinding meat, cleaning and stuffing chickens, making stew, figuring out specials, filling the meat case, and taking care of customers—but that wasn't what made her so tired. It was the other pressures. If it hadn't been for her family, she would have lost her house. She was still trying to stay one step ahead of the bill collectors. Many of her customers again begged her to let them run up a tab for stew meat or ground beef or chicken to feed their families, which, of course she did. She knew she could handle it; she always did, but she needed a break. The top of her head felt like a vise was clamping down on it.

As tired as she was, she pulled herself together as she came into the driveway. Seeing the children was welcome, especially after the tangle of headaches that clouded her workdays. She greeted them as enthusiastically as she could and asked how their day was. Geraldine expounded on the drama club's latest endeavor. Junior didn't say much, just that he had an "okay" day, leaving out the part about the window.

She'd barely started dinner when there was a knock on the door. Junior bounded up the stairs to his room and shut the door. As he feared, it was the burly construction worker. He put his fingers in his ears but he could still hear his mother's voice, "What?" "How much?" "I'll make sure they don't."

Josephine likely was in no mood to hear the worker's story, but she apologized, said she'd pay for the damage, and assured him the boys wouldn't use the lot again. She called up the stairs, "Albert"—the name she used when he was in trouble—and told him to come right down. She asked why he didn't tell her about the window. She wanted to know what happened. He confessed. She told him she'd pay for the window but he'd need to pay her back by cutting the grass after school. Whether he meant to break the window or not, he needed to take responsibility.

Junior lowered his head and said nothing. Inside, he was fuming. He didn't want to cut the grass. He wanted to play baseball. He didn't mean to break the window, but his mother was punishing him and his friends were blaming him for losing the lot. Everything was going wrong. He was angry, angry at everybody—his mother, the construction worker, his friends—but mostly he was angry because they no longer had a place to play baseball. He stomped his way up to his bedroom and grabbed his BB gun from under the bed. He opened his window and started firing BBs, one after the other, paying no attention to where they were going, each shot taking with it a chunk of his anger. It was dark outside; it looked like he was shooting the BBs into the air.

The next morning Junior was eating breakfast, and Josephine was getting ready for work. They heard a furious banging on the front door. She hurried to open the door. An irate man and his wife stood on the front stoop, glaring at her. She recognized them as the neighbors who lived around the corner. In a loud accusatory voice, the man insisted someone in her house had fired a BB gun at their bedroom window, and he was sure it was her son. Their beautiful leaded glass windows were filled with tiny holes. The only house the shots could have come from was hers. They were furious. They were going to call the police.

Josephine was horrified. She called to her son, who'd heard the conversation and was poised to run out the back door. Dutifully, he obeyed.

"I didn't know I hit anything," he said, fighting off tears. "I was just firing into the air, and it was dark. I didn't mean to hit the house."

Trying to keep her composure, she told the family she was so, so very sorry. She'd pay to have the windows replaced, and asked them, please, not to call the police. She would make certain Junior would never again do anything like that.

Now she had to pay not only for the window he broke with the ball, but also for the expensive leaded glass windows he'd shot with his BB gun. Two more bills to add to her mounting debt. But that wasn't what worried her most.

What was she going to do about Junior?

She had to leave for work. He had to leave for school. But Junior was more important. Exasperated, she went back into the kitchen and talked to Junior about what he'd done, how dangerous it was. There would be no more BB gun. Then an even worse punishment: no playing baseball with his friends for two weeks. She didn't know what else to do.

Josephine was distraught. Using a gun to shoot holes in a neighbor's bedroom window terrified her. What if a BB had hit someone in the eye? What if it had been a real gun and someone had been hurt—or worse? And Junior didn't seem to care that he'd done something so dangerous.

She knew most of the time he was a good boy, obedient and helpful. He was doing okay in school, even if he wasn't as attentive as the teachers would have liked. But now all the fears she had about her young son came tumbling out.

Junior's anger seemed to boil over the same way his father's had. He'd often get frustrated if he couldn't do something right or if things weren't going his way—and the frustration would end up in tantrums. He'd scream or throw things.

Something else bothered Josephine: the way Junior got panicky when she wasn't home. She always tried to be there by dinnertime except on Saturday, but if she didn't get there on time, Leila told Josephine he'd just sit on the front porch or ride his bike back and forth, back and forth, back and forth in front of the house until she got home or it got dark or stormy.

She blamed herself. Once again, she'd married the wrong man. Junior had seen things no young child should see—too much drinking, too much anger, too much violence. Now she was afraid he was beginning to mimic his father. He needed to learn to control his anger. The bad marriage was in the past, but Josephine was afraid its effects lingered with her young son.

She wasn't there enough; she had to tend the market instead of the precious son she loved so much. She worked six days a week. Geraldine had a job and was gone most of the time. She had Leila, but on Saturdays, Josephine worked late, sometimes until midnight, and Junior would ride the streetcar down Cedar Hill to Euclid Avenue, get off at East 93rd, and walk the two blocks to the market. He'd stay with her until closing. She was trying her best to be a good mother, but it didn't seem to be enough.

He was so different from his half sister Geraldine, now in her last year of high school. She was as determined as her mother—determined to close the unhappy chapters of her life and open a new one as the exemplary person her father and stepfather had not been. She'd matured into a pretty seventeen-year-old with bright hazel eyes that dominated her oval face, brown hair cut in a bob to just below her chin, a ready smile like her mother's, and a collection of boyfriends the other girls envied. Her grades were excellent, straight A's, and she was in the Cleveland Heights High School choir and drama club—convinced she would one day be the next Katharine Hepburn or Claudette Colbert. She especially liked acting in the school's Shakespearean plays, no doubt aided in depicting tragic heroines by her tumultuous childhood.

Josephine didn't have to worry about her, thank goodness. All her worry was needed for Junior. She had to find a way to help him. It was one more thing she needed to fix. Everything was on the line.

Sunday, Josephine's day off, finally arrived. It was the only time she had to relax. She sank her hefty frame into the soft, welcoming cushions of her favorite easy chair, her forehead creased and her eyes staring intently ahead, not at anything in particular, she was just thinking, thinking mostly about her son.

She was conflicted. His father had been a terrible role model, but he was his father and he'd disappeared from Junior's life. For Josephine, it was a relief to have him gone. But what about her son? She didn't want Junior to grow up like his father, but she knew he needed the male perspective she couldn't give him.

She'd make some changes. She'd find a way to give him the security and discipline that were indispensable if he was to grow up right—but he needed the influence of men with good character and values, men who were models he could emulate. One thing was sure—she had no intention of marrying again. She was done with that! Her son was the only male she cared about at this stage of her life. Somehow, she would make certain he'd grow up to be an upstanding adult with none of the frailties of her two husbands. She just wasn't sure how.

Josephine lifted her throbbing feet up on the footstool that matched her easy chair and lit one of the filtered Pall Mall cigarettes she kept in her purse. She took a few quick puffs, then pulled back the Priscilla curtains and glanced out the picture window to check on her young son.

There was Junior standing in the driveway, alone, his blue Indians baseball cap sitting precariously atop his curly black hair, clutching the nailed-together taped-up bat and swinging at one of Geraldine's old tennis balls.

Josephine sat up straight and planted her feet firmly on the floor.

Maybe baseball was the answer.

The next day, Josephine was deliberately late for work despite her many chores and the piles of bills. After the kids left for school, she drove up to the University Heights Town Hall, strode through the white double doors, and asked to see Mayor John J. Howard. He was busy, but she'd wait.

Howard had been mayor since 1916 when the only paved streets in the village were the main thoroughfares passing through on their way to Cleveland Heights and Shaker Heights. He'd done wonders for the village. He helped convince John Carroll University to move its campus to the village, which spearheaded residential development. Now charming two- and three-story brick homes, each with its own unique architectural details, were rising as quickly as they could be built. What once had been forest and farmland was transforming into meandering tree-lined streets packed close together with families, many owning their first homes.

The village population had increased tenfold in less than fifteen years, but there were few conveniences for residents. The closest grocery store was Heinen's in nearby Shaker Heights. There were a couple of places to eat and a nine-hole public golf course. Josephine thought maybe Mayor Howard could work his magic to help her find a boys' baseball team—or at least a place where her son and his friends could play.

Josephine introduced herself to the mayor, a silver-haired gentleman with dark bushy eyebrows that would have looked menacing except for the large kind eyes that looked out from behind his round glasses. She told him about the boys, how much they loved baseball, and that they had nowhere to play except in the street.

Mayor Howard didn't know of any baseball teams for boys but said there was some land behind the University Heights Town Hall, nearly two acres. The land sloped down from the Town Hall to a dusty tract of dirt, surrounded by grass and weeds. Luckily, the only nearby structure was the city garage. There were no houses with breakable windows. The boys were welcome to use that.

Josephine happily thanked the mayor. Town Hall was in walking distance for the boys. They'd no longer need to play in the street or be chased off empty lots.

She waited until Junior's punishment was over, then eagerly rushed to tell him and the boys she'd found a place where they could play. They carried their battered bat, the taped-together baseball, and the tennis balls they'd confiscated from their siblings and headed to Town Hall. Large stones sufficed for home plate and the bases. Town Hall was in a visible spot in the village center. More boys saw them and joined in.

Josephine came by to watch whenever she could get away. She started thinking about forming a team, and soon there were more than the nine players needed. They could have real games. But this was still the Depression. The neighborhood kids were playing with the beat-up bat they'd nailed together and baseballs they'd taped where the strings had broken. They needed good bats and balls and gloves and catcher's gear and bases and umpires. They needed teams to play.

The ideas tumbled out. She'd organize things. She'd find them teams to play; she'd get uniforms; most of all, she'd show them how to be good sports—and good boys, especially her own son. How difficult could it be?

When Josephine wanted to do something, she bulldozed through anything that got in her way. Depression or not, she squeezed out money that should have been spent on bills and went over to Cleveland Sporting Goods. There she met Laddie Placek, the head scout for the Major League Cleveland Indians and also a salesman for Wilson's Sporting Goods. She told him she was starting a boys' baseball team and needed equipment but couldn't afford it without a discount. Charmed by the little lady with the persuasive way, big ideas, and charming smile, he gave her a couple of bats, some balls, and gloves at half price.

She asked if he knew of any teams her boys could play. Placek told her there was a Catholic parish in a nearby community with kids who played baseball irregularly. They also were looking for teams to play. She took down the phone number.

She called the mothers of Junior's ball-playing friends and invited the boys and their families down to the Town Hall field. She showed them the new bats and balls and gloves and asked the parents if they were okay with the boys being on her team. They agreed. She told them she'd found a team they could play.

She asked the boys what they wanted to name their team, even though she was sure she knew. "The Cleveland Indians," they cried out. She suggested they call the team the "Little Cleveland Indians" or the "Little Indians," for short.

There was still some good weather left. The two teams played a few Sunday afternoons at the Town Hall while the weather was still warm and made plans to play next spring.

She'd taken the first steps.

As fall turned to winter, Josephine was newly energized. Thinking about the baseball team eased some of the desperation of the past several years. She'd create a real baseball team for Junior and his friends in the spring. But now she needed to get the market going strong again, and she had an idea.

Hackenburg's Grocery had started a delivery service to the wealthier suburbs in the Heights. They only sold groceries, not meat. She'd see if they'd deliver meat from her market too. Hackenburg's owner agreed.

Shaker Heights and Cleveland Heights had some of the most beautiful homes Josephine had ever seen—mansions that seemed to go on forever, set high above the city on acres of perfectly mown grass set off by graceful maple trees and professionally landscaped grounds with clusters of perfectly arranged shrubs, accented by flowers that bloomed in a multitude of colors each spring.

Cleveland Heights, the older of the two suburbs, was populated originally by businessmen who'd moved out of Cleveland as the smokestacks edged closer to their homes. They built huge estates along Fairmount Boulevard. On the other side of the city and extending into East Cleveland, John D. Rockefeller had transformed acres of hilly farmland into a "water cure resort" overlooking Cleveland and Lake Erie. When the resort folded, the property became his summer home, which he called the Homestead.

The Rockefeller home burned down in 1917, and Rockefeller sold the property to his son John D. Rockefeller Jr., who donated some of the land to the two cities and developed a residential community of eighty-one French Norman homes he called Forest Hill.

Later, Cleveland Heights' population swelled with the construction of more modest but attractive Colonial and Tudor Revival homes, bungalows, and apartment buildings. More parks and commercial districts followed. By 1930, the population had reached over fifty thousand.

By this time, Shaker Heights had become one of America's

wealthiest and most renowned communities. Although its founders, the Van Sweringen brothers Mantis and Oris, had lost their money in the Depression and many families had been hurt financially, one Shaker lawyer supposedly told his neighbors "he did not believe there was a Depression, that he had never seen it." While perhaps not Depression-proof, certainly many Shaker Heights residents were in better shape to withstand it.

Shaker had been considered a "utopia" by its early residents, the Shakers, who created a colony there in 1822. They called their settlement the "Valley of God's Pleasure" for the natural beauty of its hills, trees, and lakes. They dammed a brook, using its power for a sawmill, gristmill, and woolen mill. They built a hospital. They found creative ways to solve daily problems by inventing forty products, including the washing machine, clothespin, flat broom, and circular saw. Eventually the settlement died out, not surprisingly since the Shakers practiced celibacy.

The two brothers, Oris and Mantis Van Sweringen, purchased the land and turned it into one of the nation's first planned suburbs with curving tree-lined streets filled with beautiful architect-designed Georgian Revival, Jacobean Tudor, French Provincial, and Colonial homes—each one close to a park, lake, rapid transit, and a school. There were homes for every income level.

The Van Sweringens had strict building standards and rules. Only graduate architects "whose drawings express a thorough technical knowledge of the highest and best in architecture" would be allowed to design Shaker homes. Real estate brokers had to be approved. Even the paint colors of the homes were required to be warm earth colors adapted to the home's architectural style. Superior education was another must, with public and private schools committed to excellence.

Heights residents were the perfect customers for Josephine. She'd turned down an offer a few years earlier from Joe Heinen, a friendly competitor, to buy his Heinen's market on Kinsman and Lee Roads in Shaker Heights. He was planning to open one of the first supermarkets in the state, possibly even the country, across the street. She knew it was a great opportunity, but she didn't have the money.

Because Josephine was so meticulous about the meat she sold, she had to pay more and charge higher prices. That made it hard for business at the store in Hough, where many of her customers had lost jobs or still were only working part time. She'd run up tabs for many of them, not wanting families or their children to go hungry. Those who could pay were buying more ground beef and chickens. Families in the Heights could better afford the meat she sold. They also were more likely to buy the choice cuts of beef that were more profitable. It seemed a perfect solution. The meat delivery would be good for Hackenburg's, her meat market, and the Heights customers.

The mortgage debacle was behind her, but she couldn't forget. She never wanted to go through anything like that again. She wanted some "insurance." Her house had a third floor no one was using. She could make extra money bringing in boarders. There was plenty of room, but the space needed work if she was going to rent it out. She could divide it into separate kitchen/eating and living/sleeping areas. That once again meant spending money she didn't have. Regardless, she took another risk and hired a carpenter and a painter and put in a sink, stove, and refrigerator. She advertised it in the newspaper and soon had it rented to a couple.

It didn't take long for her moves to pay off. She began making enough money to cover her costs with a little extra to spare.

She knew she was fortunate. She also knew many people were still suffering. As she drove down Cedar Hill to the market, desperate-looking men often came up to the windows of cars at stoplights, begging for money. Eviction signs again appeared on homes in the Hough neighborhood. Men again were losing their jobs, depleting their savings. She understood.

She wanted to help, so she organized a soup kitchen, using chicken from her store. Junior often went with her, watching as she dished out meals to the lines of people threading their way toward the long table filled with heaping trays of food.

Many of Josephine's customers became her friends. People liked her outsize personality. She was funny. She was dependable. She'd personally deliver meat long after delivery hours were over. Whatever her customers needed, she'd find a way to get it for them. Rich or poor, it didn't matter.

People said she could charm anyone. Back when she was still married, she'd even made an ally of Police Chief Roy Steinford and the cops she encountered when her former husband had the drunken escapade that landed him in jail. Instead of feeling shamed, as many wives would, she charmed the police who took him in custody. She had the charisma of her former husbands without the damaging side effects.

Before Thanksgiving, she asked her well-off customers in the Heights if they'd donate food baskets for poor families in the Hough neighborhood. She soon had a carful.

On Christmas Eve, Josephine and Junior rode up Meadowbrook Boulevard and Edgerton Road hill in University Heights. They rang the doorbells of homes and left chickens from the market on the doorsteps, quickly running away before anyone knew who had left them. That was the real spirit of Christmas, Josephine told Junior.

They headed back to their own brightly decorated house, greeted by a life-size Santa Claus and tall evergreens sparkling with colored lights. Josephine had wanted to give Junior a Lionel electric train set for Christmas. She'd gone downtown to Higbee's, where the department store had set up a huge platform in one corner of the fifth floor with Lionel and American Flyer trains chugging along on a labyrinth of tracks, their engines smoking as they passed the miniature railroad station, blowing their whistles at intersection lights, and making their way past tiny bridges and houses. Whenever they went to Higbee's, Junior begged to see the trains. She knew how much he loved them, but train sets were really expensive, especially Lionel, which he liked the best. She couldn't afford a whole set, so she bought the tracks and an engine. After Junior went to bed, she laid out the tracks in a circle around the Christmas tree and hid them under the rest of the presents so he wouldn't see them. She wrapped the box with the engine.

The next day, Josephine prepared a Christmas feast, even though there were just three of them—roast turkey from the market, gravy, stuffing, mashed potatoes, cranberry sauce, pumpkin pie, and all the extras.

They gathered around the Christmas tree and opened their gifts, one at a time. Geraldine's eyes brightened and her mouth broadened into a smile as she tore open the colorful wrapping paper and lifted a pretty new blouse and skirt out of the boxes tagged with her name.

Junior picked up his present. It was wrapped in red paper and heavy for its size. As he unwrapped it, he recognized the orange and white box. It was a Lionel engine—the best Christmas present ever. Josephine showed him the tracks, all set up and waiting. Junior spent the rest of the day—and many days afterward—watching the engine race back and forth under the tree, the Christmas lights reflecting their colors on the shiny metal. It was magical.

Every Christmas after that, Josephine took the streetcar to Higbee's and bought another train car until Junior had the full set—a coal car, lumber car, passenger car, oil tanker, and caboose.

CHAPTER TWELVE

Fourteen Little Indians

It was April 19, 1938, opening day for the Cleveland Indians. More than thirty thousand fans piled into their seats inside horseshoe-shaped Cleveland Stadium. The weather was about as good as it gets for an early spring ball game in northeast Ohio. The temperature hovered between 40 and 50 degrees F. Fans could catch a glimpse of the sun's rays shimmering on the blue waters of Lake Erie, which lay beyond the stadium. New Cleveland mayor Harold Burton took the mound to throw out the first ball.

Johnny Allen was the opening day Indians pitcher. He'd gone a spectacular 15-1 the year before, his season spoiled by an unearned run. The sportswriters speculated he might go undefeated this year.

The Indians were playing the St. Louis Browns, whose pitcher was right-hander Bobo Newsom. The Indians didn't have a lot of respect for him, brushing him off as a "cousin," meaning he was "pretty soft picking." The Browns were an improving team though. Like the Indians, they were packed with heavy hitters and good pitching.

The Major League season had begun the day before in Washington, D.C., with the Washington Senators facing the Philadelphia Athletics. President Roosevelt was there with Vice President John Nance Garner. Both of them loved baseball. Roosevelt had been a third baseman in prep school; Garner had played semipro ball. Before the game, Garner stopped by to see the players. Jokingly, he asked Senators' first baseman

Zeke Bonura to hit a home run for him. To his surprise, Bonura did just that, belting one into the centerfield stands in the sixth inning. The home team Senators won 12–8.

As usual, everyone expected the Yankees to lead the American League—and probably the World Series as well. It would be hard to stop them, but other teams were trying. The St. Louis Browns offered the Yankees $150,000 for their young superstar Joe DiMaggio. DiMaggio was holding out. He wanted his salary upped to $40,000 from $15,000. The Yanks offered $25,000. They were at an impasse. The Yankees turned the deal down, knowing DiMaggio was too valuable to their team. DiMaggio sat out the first four games of the season but finally gave in and signed for the amount the Yankees had offered, $25,000.

In the National League, the Chicago Cubs paid the St. Louis Cardinals $185,000 for pitcher Dizzy Dean, an exorbitant sum at the time, convinced Dean's superb pitching would guarantee they'd win the pennant and "kick hell out of the New York Yankees" in the World Series.

The Indians had made some good moves, too, and fans expected big things of their team. The team's new manager, Oscar Vitt, was fresh from leading the Yankees' farm team, the Newark Bears, to the Triple A championship with a commanding record of 109-43.

Cleveland Plain Dealer columnist Gordon Cobbledick predicted the new manager would "hustle more and play smarter ball than either of his predecessors" and said the Indians pitching staff, "headed by Johnny Allen and Bob Feller is considered the best in the game." Headlines blared, INDIANS RATE SECOND TO YANKS ON IMPROVED LEADERSHIP AND HURLING.

Feller was now the Indians' highest paid player, making $22,500 a year. Hal Trosky, Earl Averill, and Jeff Heath were predicted to hit well over .300, and the team had just signed gifted shortstop Lou Boudreau to a first year contract for $1,050.

Not everyone was on the Indians' bandwagon though. Reporters outside of Cleveland agreed that the Indians were loaded with talent but added that some of the players were "problematic," specifically mentioning catcher Rollie Hemsley who'd been suspended for "infractions," a term that usually meant he drank too much, and Frankie Pytlak, the other catcher, who'd walked off the club for a time. Shirley Povich of the *Washington Post* wrote, "If there were an Alcatraz in baseball, the Cleveland club would certainly qualify . . . the Indians are seemingly confirmed violators of the baseball laws. Their faculty for getting into trouble is no less than amazing."

Regardless, it was the Indians' opening day. The possibilities were limitless. It was a day to hope, a good day to be a fan of the perennial second-to-fourth place Indians. They hadn't yet lost a game. This year could be the year.

Josephine scrawled *Go Indians!* on the window of the market next to the prices for her daily specials. Business was slower than normal, and she wanted to leave early to stop and see the boys who were practicing on the Town Hall field. As she headed to her car, she could hear the faint cheers from the crowd at League Park. It was just past three o'clock, near the end of the game. The cheering seemed like a good sign. She turned on the car radio. The game was in the bottom of the eighth inning; the Indians were at bat. Ken Keltner had hit a single, moving Earl Averill to second base. There was one out. The Indians were behind, but it looked like they might have a rally going.

By the time Josephine's car drew close to the field, the game was over and Jack Graney's distinctive voice blared the results of the game. The boys heard the radio and ran to the car. Josephine turned up the volume and opened the door. The boys crowded around.

Graney was wrapping up. It didn't take long for the boys to discover it hadn't been a good day for the Tribe.

Pitching hotshot Allen was erratic. In the fifth, he hit Browns outfielder Mel Mazzera with a pitch, setting up a four-run inning. The supposedly easy "cousin" Bobo Newsome defied the label the Indians had pinned on him and allowed just two runs. The Indians squeaked out a Hal Trosky home run and a fifth-inning Moose Solters single that drove in Johnny Allen, but they lost 6–2. A few of the boys groaned. Junior shrugged.

It was just one game, Josephine reminded them. It was a long season, and Feller was slated to pitch the next game. Hope was reignited.

The boys raced back onto the field. Josephine followed, standing in back of the stone that marked first base. The real games wouldn't start until school was out in June. She had already put together a schedule.

Josephine watched the boys take turns batting, pitching, and chasing balls into the grass and weeds beyond the dirt infield. She could easily see the field wasn't ideal. It was pretty level, but there were stones strewn all over and the grass wasn't maintained. It was high and balls kept getting lost. The outfield was small and sloped down toward the street. Even if the grass were to be cut, the balls would roll into the street. Worse, there were ruts in the ground, and the boys could stumble and get hurt. She was going to try to find the boys a better baseball field.

After they finished playing and started for home, she got back in her maroon Chevrolet coupe, with Junior plopped in the seat next to her. It was almost dinnertime and she headed down Cedar Road, past the rows of neat red brick houses, and stopped at Lenny's Chicken-in-a-Basket at the edge of the village. Going to Lenny's was a special treat for Junior. Even though it was a chicken restaurant, he always ordered his favorite meal, a hamburger, with an ice cream cone for dessert.

They walked toward the restaurant, and Josephine stopped short. Right next to Lenny's was a huge overgrown field she'd seen many times before but never with baseball in mind. Her baseball field stood in front of her. It was thigh-high in weeds and looked more like a jungle than a baseball diamond, but it had potential. She wondered who the owner was.

The next day she contacted the mayor, thanked him for the use of the Town Hall field, but told him she had a real team that was playing games, and they needed a better field. She wanted the boys to have a regulation field like the Indians had, only adapted to the boys' smaller sizes. She told him she'd found the perfect place in a great location and asked who owned the property. The mayor informed her it was Anthony Visconsi, a developer who was building a shopping center on the corner. The property extended way past the location of the shopping center, all the way to the next street. The mayor cautioned her that Visconsi might be planning to develop all the land.

Never one to be deterred, Josephine strutted into Visconsi's office, fixed her hazel eyes squarely on his, and declared that the boys needed the vacant land he wasn't using for a baseball field. She told him all about the boys and how they had a whole team but nowhere adequate to play. After they'd talked awhile, he gave in, letting her use it for a ball field as long as he didn't need it for his shopping center. He wasn't planning to build there right away, but he questioned how the boys could play on a field that looked more like the bush than a ball field.

The field *was* a mess. It wasn't just the high grass and weeds. There were broken whiskey bottles, candy wrappers, crunched-up papers—a lot of trash. But a little trash wasn't going to stop her.

Josephine got the boys together and told them they needed to pull the weeds, clean up the debris, and get the infield in shape as well as they could if they wanted a good place to play baseball. They got rakes and shovels from home, one boy brought a scythe, and they went to work. They cleared space for home plate, the bases, the pitcher's mound. They pulled up the weeds and got the tall grass cut down some, but it was a huge job, too much for the boys and their limited equipment. They could play there, but the field was still very rough. It was hard to run and here, too, the balls were getting lost. The infield was uneven, and it was easy to trip. It was bigger than the Town Hall field, but that was the only benefit.

Josephine was undeterred. She'd find a way to make it work. It was clear it would take more than a bunch of kids to make this into a real baseball field, so she marched back to Mayor Howard. She told him Mr. Visconsi had agreed to let the boys use the lot, but they couldn't play on it like it was. Could the city help her? She had all the boys working on it, but it was too big a job and they didn't have the right equipment. It would be great for University Heights to have a nice ball field for the boys. This was the perfect spot.

Josephine Morhard was a hard lady to say no to. The mayor told her he'd see what he could do.

Before long trucks, bulldozers, and scrapers sporting the name University Heights were on the site—grading the land, smoothing out space for an infield and gradually transforming it. Josephine worked with Cleveland Indians scout and sporting goods representative Latimer "Laddie" Placek to deter-

mine how to adapt regulation Major League field dimensions
for the boys. Laddie was a good sounding board and willing to
help anytime she needed baseball advice. They decided the
pitching mound would be fifty feet from home plate instead of
the big league sixty, and the bases eighty feet apart instead of
ninety. She couldn't afford sandbags so she substituted saw-
dust bags.

Whenever she could, Josephine brought Junior by to check
the progress, pointing out where the bases and the pitcher's
mound would be. Neighborhood curiosity-seekers saw the equipment and watched the progress as the infield was leveled, the outfield brush removed, and fresh green grass put in its place. It was
beautiful; other than the big league ballparks, the nicest field
around, just right for the young players.

Josephine had her field of dreams. But she was far from finished.

On Friday, June 17, 1938, the Cleveland Indians were in first
place, a full game ahead of the feared Yankees. It was Ladies'
Day at League Park and the home team had just whipped Con-
nie Mack's Philadelphia Athletics 8–1. The normally reserved
ladies stood up and cheered for tobacco-chewing right-hander
Johnny Allen, who left his notorious bad temper behind in
homage to the ladies and notched his eighth win in a row. Allen
was back to his old pitching form, firing his curve and fastballs
again at the corners instead of down the middle, where he'd
been giving up homers to sluggers like Jimmy Foxx and Red
Ruffing earlier in the season.

First place! Maybe this, finally, would be the year. The excitement was contagious.

Junior grabbed the sports pages of the newspaper before
heading to school. He pored over the box scores and player
stats. Indians right fielder Bruce Campbell had a twenty-two-
game hitting streak going. Earl Averill led the American League
in hitting. Hal Trosky was back in the lineup after being out
with a lame knee. Newcomer Jeff Heath hit a "skyscraper"
homer. A headline boasted BOB'S BACK, indicating that the
team's other star pitcher, Feller, was back in peak form, winning seven games in a row, fanning seven and walking only
four in his last game.

Josephine was equally immersed in the Indians' winning season. She had the games blaring in the car and at home. Conversations at the market often were more about the team's triumphs than the meat her customers were buying. She loved baseball as much as Junior did, and even though her chaotic life made it hard to get to the ballpark, she made time to take Junior to Indians' games whenever she could get away. On Sundays they'd often listen on the big Philco radio shaped like a mini-cathedral that stood on the maple table in the living room.

The Indians alternated games between League Park and the much bigger Cleveland Municipal Stadium. Weekday games were played at League Park except for opening day and holidays. League Park held thirty-two thousand fans. On weekends, the team moved to the stadium, which could accommodate nearly seventy-five thousand fans for baseball and eighty-one thousand for football. With the Indians winning, it wasn't hard to fill the seats.

The stadium had been completed in 1932, and the Indians originally planned to play all their games there. As the Depression worsened, attendance dropped. Using the stadium was expensive. It cost the team $37,000 for rent and $100,000 more in taxes. At the time it was an easy decision to move the games back to League Park, which the team owned. Taxes there were only $8,000.

In 1937, the All Star game was held in Cleveland Stadium, the Great Lakes Exposition was bringing thousands of people next door, and Bob Feller was becoming a big draw. With all the activity on the lakefront and with attendance climbing, Indians owner Alva Bradley again moved the season opener, holiday, and weekend games back to the stadium. Weekday games remained at League Park.

Eighteen-year-old Geraldine—who wanted to be called Gerry—and her friends were weekend stadium regulars. After the games they'd stick around, hoping to glimpse the players up close. Gerry had graduated from Cleveland Heights High School with honors. She'd tangled with her mother over college—Gerry insisting on going to the University of Iowa to study drama; Josephine refusing to pay for her daughter to study what she considered a useless major like acting. Gerry had excelled at her studies, and her mother thought that she had much better options. Josephine would stretch her finances as much as she could to send Gerry to college, but she declared studying acting was a waste of money.

Gerry was as independent and stubborn as her mother. She was either going to study acting, or she wouldn't go to college. Both of them held firm. Adamantly, Gerry took a job at Parker Appliance Company, leaving her dreams of movie stardom behind.

Josephine sat on the top step of her front porch, all the Little Indians crowded around her. She'd invited them over, telling them she had a surprise.

A balding dark-haired man with glasses perched halfway down his nose got out of his car and started toward the house. He was carrying an armful of boxes. Josephine got up and greeted him.

"Boys, this is Mr. Placek. He has a surprise for you."

Laddie Placek set the boxes down, opened one, and pulled out a long white shirt. Josephine ooohed, "It's perfect; just like the Cleveland Indians." It was a white shirt and had a red "C" with blue trim to the left of the buttons. There were matching pants, striped socks, and navy blue caps emblazoned with a red "C." The uniforms were identical to the ones the major league Cleveland Indians wore, except for the "Little Indians" embroidered inside the "C" on their shirts and the team emblem on the back because the sleeves were too small.

Junior tried his on. He slipped one arm into the shirt, then the other. His shirt boasted the number 19—the same number Bob Feller wore. Josephine reached for a cap and placed it on his head. He already had an Indians cap, but this one was part of a real Indians uniform.

She passed uniforms out to the other boys, who excitedly put them on over their clothes. Now they really were the "Little Indians." They couldn't believe they had real Indians uniforms. No other boys had anything like this.

Josephine had wanted uniforms for the boys as much as she wanted a proper ball field. The boys had been playing in their own shirts and shorts, but Josephine believed that if they were going to be the Little Indians, they needed real Indians uniforms. She wouldn't settle for plain red or blue or white uniforms with block letters spelling out the team's name on the back. Getting real Indians uniforms, though, required permission from the Major League team.

Josephine convinced Placek to help her. She had a way of infecting everyone with her enthusiasm and he became as excited as she was. He loved the idea of the Little Indians team. He got permission from Indians' owner Alva Bradley. Even though the uniforms retailed for $14 apiece, he gave her the wholesale price of $6.70 each. He made sure the uniforms were authentic.

Josephine decided each boy's family should pay for his own uniform. She was already providing the bats, balls, gloves, and catcher's equipment. She believed paying for their uniforms would give the families a stake in the team. They'd be more committed. But if a boy's family couldn't afford it, she made sure he had a uniform.

The boys were more excited than ever. They felt like they were part of the big league team in their Little Indians uniforms. They were inspired. The small boys stood tall.

They were a real team now—fourteen young boys, mostly ages nine to eleven, short and tall, hefty and slim, some with natural talent, others with little more than a love of the game.

All the neighborhood boys who played with Junior in the street, on the empty lot, and at Town Hall were on the team, plus a few more. Freckle-faced Allen Koenig was the shortstop. He was one of the older boys, and though he was small for his age he was naturally athletic and could play any position. Junior's oldest friends, Joey Phipps and Michael Albl, were outfielders. Like Junior, they were among the younger boys on the team, and not yet as well coordinated, but they had promise. Junior was the second baseman and had shown signs of developing a strong throwing arm.

The youngest boy on the team, Buddy Myers, was seven and came to the games mostly to be with his older brother Billy. He wanted to be part of the team, and Mrs. Morhard didn't have the heart to say no. She made him the team mascot.

Billy Myers was in the same class as Junior and one of his best friends. He was a Little Indians' outfielder. Besides baseball, the thing he liked to do most was ride the streetcars. He'd ride them back and forth, back and forth, to Cleveland Heights or Cleveland and back home. He rode them so much, his schoolmates started to call him "Streetcar Billy."

Jackie Heinen was a year older than Junior, and it was easy to see he had natural ability, even at his young age. Tall, blond, and blessed with a strong arm, he was the team's best all-around player. He threw hard, and he could hit the ball. When he pitched, the ball burst out of his right hand like a bullet. There was no question he'd be a pitcher, but Mrs. Morhard wanted to use his hitting and fielding ability too. When he didn't pitch, he played third base. Jackie was focused and serious on the ball field, saving his energy for the games.

Eddie Decker was the opposite—as interested in making the boys laugh as he was in playing baseball. He'd run around the field, clowning, making faces, and flailing his arms to get a re-action. He did. The boys liked him and thought he was funny. Mrs. Morhard liked him, too, but in the outfield, he was easily distracted, often paying more attention to a flashy new auto-mobile driving by than keeping his eyes on the game. He was smaller than most of the boys. That, plus his deficiencies on the field, kept him out of the starting lineup, but Mrs. Morhard gave him a chance to play in every game.

Dave Erickson and King Brown were the tallest boys on the team, unusually tall for their ages. Dave's father had built many of the homes in the area, including the Morhards'. Dave was the team's first baseman. He could catch almost anything, jumping high in the air when his height didn't give him enough of an advantage. He was a good hitter, too, and he'd often pass on tips to the younger boys.

King Brown was almost as tall as Dave, but huskier. He was friendly and eager to play but wasn't terribly well coordinated, and his love for baseball never materialized on the field. Re-gardless, he was one of the team's substitute outfielders.

Ronnie Barth, a good-looking boy with blond hair, was the catcher. Mrs. Morhard wrung more money out of her meat market budget and bought him catcher's equipment. Ronnie had a new facemask and a chest protector that was almost as big as he was. It came up over his shoulders and went all the way down to his knees. When he first put it on, he could barely move, stumbling and nearly falling, looking like someone who'd had too much to drink, but Ronnie was determined to make it work. Soon, he was back crouching behind the plate, confidently catching the balls with everything in place.

Jimmy Prior lived almost directly in back of the Morhards. He was eight years old and subbed for Koenig at shortstop. Likely due to his young age, he'd often cry during games if he thought someone was picking on him, even if they weren't, or if he missed catching a ball or getting a hit. Dick Baumiller was also a substitute, the third baseman when Jackie Heinen was pitching.

Josephine herself was the umpire. She also substituted if a player was absent, standing at home plate, swinging the bat in her dress and high heels. If she got a hit, she'd run as fast as the heels would allow, her hefty forty-seven-year-old body bouncing with each step.

Over the winter, Josephine had located more boys' teams to play. She'd put together a schedule of Sunday afternoon games, given out copies, and called to make sure everyone knew the time and place.

The first game of the season was with a Catholic Youth Organization (CYO) team from St. Joseph's, a Cleveland parish. The CYO team was there on the appointed day with a full squad, ready to play, wearing their bi-color baseball shirts with the parish name imprinted on the front. It was a close game, but the Little Indians won.

The following week the Little Indians waited on their beautiful new field for the next team on the schedule. The game was slated to begin at one o'clock. One o'clock came and went. Two o'clock. No team arrived. Josephine took them off the schedule.

The third team came with only eight players, but Josephine didn't want to disappoint the boys so she let them play. To be fair, she made the Little Indians limit their squad to eight starters too. Both teams used only two outfielders.

The contrast between the teams was stark. Junior's team was decked out in their sharp white Cleveland Indians replica uniforms and caps. Except for St. Joseph's, the boys on the other teams wore whatever they could find in their closets—a couple of them in horizontally striped jerseys and long pants, one in a plaid buttoned shirt that hung over his knickers and most of the others in colored shirts and shorts.

Josephine was getting frustrated with the teams the Little Indians were playing. They'd show up without enough players or sometimes wouldn't show up at all. They'd cancel or want to change game dates at the last minute. It was chaos. She wanted a baseball program that was organized, disciplined, and had a set schedule with regular games the boys could count on. Baseball should be a way the boys could gain confidence, learn teamwork, obtain skills, and be guided by good role models. The way things were, these boys weren't learning anything except disappointment and pandemonium.

She put an ad in the newspaper, stating she was looking for teams to play. She asked around. A few communities had city-sponsored or American Legion teams for teenagers but not for boys as young as the Little Indians. Finally, she heard about a team for younger boys in Cleveland Heights. They called themselves the Hilltoppers and wore dark T-shirts with a huge "T," apparently for "toppers"—and plain baseball caps. It wasn't a real uniform, but it was an indication they were serious about playing baseball.

Then she heard from the mayor that another group of boys was playing ball on the Town Hall field. They called themselves the University Town Hall team. It was a playground group that sprang up there after Junior and the boys moved to their new field. They had just enough players. She added them to the schedule.

Soon afterward, Josephine got a call from a woman who lived in Garfield Heights, about twelve miles to the southwest. She had a group of boys who wanted to play baseball and be on a team.

Mrs. Morhard's league was coming together. She had teams she could count on, a regular schedule, and a beautiful field.

Still, it wasn't enough for her.

CHAPTER THIRTEEN
Growing Pains

Junior was in the batter's box. The count was 0 and 2. He sweated the pitch, his eyes blazing with determination, knowing he'd be out with another strike. He clutched the weighty wooden bat tightly, blood rushing to his fingertips and sweat to the palms of his hands. He was a head smaller than and not yet as coordinated as the older pitchers and hitters, but he wanted to be just as good as they were.

The Little Indians were leading the Hilltoppers 3–1 in the third inning. Mrs. Morhard sat in a folding chair under her outsized blue-and-white-striped umbrella in back of the foul line between home plate and first base, a silver whistle hanging loosely from her neck. She pumped her fist in the air. She wanted Junior to get a hit as much as he did, and Junior wanted one badly. He didn't want to be known as a momma's boy who was only on the team because his mother ran it.

The pitcher wound up and hurled a fastball. It looked like it was coming in high. A ball for sure, Junior thought. He readied his swing, then checked it. The ball whizzed past his shoulder. The umpire yelled, "Strike three!"

Junior threw his bat down, smashing it against home plate. He screamed and cried at the same time, glaring at the umpire. "That was high! You're blind!" He stomped out of the batter's box and walked off the field. His teammates gasped. They'd seen his tantrums before, but this was the worst yet. Sometimes he'd get angry if the lineup card had him batting last, or if he'd been told he was playing second base and he wanted to play shortstop. Even so, they were stunned when he called the umpire blind. Especially this umpire.

Tony Pianowski was a highly respected professional umpire who worked in the Cleveland Indians farm system. The *Plain Dealer* called him "one of the best around—and a disciplinarian." Mrs. Morhard was paying him to umpire Little Indians' games.

She blew the whistle, bolted out of her chair, and rushed toward her son as fast as her heavy frame allowed. She grabbed Junior's arm, marched him to her car, and sat him down in the passenger seat, her finger wagging furiously. She pointed to his bike, and he dutifully headed toward it, angrily kicked up his kickstand, and headed home. She didn't just bench him; he was out of the game.

Josephine came back, motioned to Joey Phipps to take Junior's place at second base, and pulled Pianowski aside. She apologized for her son's bad behavior and told him to treat Junior like all the other boys. There would be no special treatment because he was her son. Junior's tantrums wouldn't be tolerated. Pianowski wasn't planning to give Junior special treatment, but it was good to know Mrs. Morhard was behind him.

They agreed: if Junior started arguing or screaming or walked off the field, he'd be benched or sent home, and another player would take his place in the lineup.

Visibly unnerved by Junior's behavior, Mrs. Morhard blew her whistle to resume play and settled back in her lawn chair to watch the rest of the game. Distracted, she glanced again at umpire Pianowski. He was strict with the boys. It was good to have reinforcement. She hoped Junior would learn the tantrums would need to stop if he wanted to play baseball.

Junior may have been Josephine's biggest problem, but he wasn't her only one.

She blew her whistle again. The Little Indians' Eddie Decker was somersaulting across the outfield. Shortstop Alan Koenig was hurling insults at the pitcher who was behind in the count. Koenig argued with the umpire every time he struck out. Tall, hefty King Brown couldn't quite get his pre-pubescent body coordinated enough to hit the ball. Some of the boys seemed more interested in socializing than playing the game.

The boys had no experience playing real baseball—they'd

only played their own loose brand of ball in the streets, on empty lots, behind Town Hall or on playgrounds in their communities. They were undisciplined and lacked the fundamentals.

Josephine recognized that the boys were young, but she wanted them to learn the game and learn *from* the game—to gain confidence in their abilities, to learn discipline and teamwork, and gain values they could use throughout their lives, whatever they ended up doing. She needed regulations and standards. She needed ground rules that all four teams in the league would comply with.

The games already lasted seven innings, not nine innings like the major leagues. To avoid confusion, she ruled that if teams were tied after seven innings, the game would end in a tie. All the boys on every team would have an opportunity to play at least one inning, even if it meant the team might lose its best players for part of the game. The older boys would mentor and help coach the younger boys. There would be no swearing and no arguing with the umpire. Definitely no fighting. All disagreements had to be settled peacefully. The boys were to show respect for each other and their opponents at all times. When innings changed, the boys should hustle to their new positions. There was to be no dawdling. Above all, she expected the boys to show good sportsmanship.

She set even higher expectations for her own team, the Little Indians. The shirttails of their uniforms had to be tucked in, pants had to be belted, and socks up to their knees. She wanted her boys to learn to be helpful to others as well as play ball. Before a boy was allowed to pick up a bat or ball, he had to tell her about a good deed he'd done for someone the day before. The boys competed with each other to come up with ideas. At Heinen's Grocery Store, boys waited to help carry the bags of elderly customers. They mowed lawns, pulled weeds, and swept out garages. Residents began to wonder what had happened to the village's usually mischievous boys.

Mrs. Morhard was at every game. If anybody got out of line—if they questioned an umpire's call, got in an argument, or started causing trouble—she'd blow her whistle loudly and lay down the law. Everybody knew she meant business.

She demanded discipline and good behavior. She believed if

you taught kids what was right, they'd grow up right. One father complained she'd been too hard on his son. A year later, he thanked her.

She balanced discipline with encouragement. If a boy struck out, she'd tell him to try again. If he didn't get a hit or failed to make a catch, she'd say, "don't be discouraged," "keep trying," "never give up." Before every game, she'd pump the boys up, saying, "I know you'll succeed. You can do it."

Mrs. Morhard had a special way to reinforce that message—her own life. She'd invite the boys to her house, bake a big plate of brownies, and regale them with the stories she loved to tell—the fun ones about the animals on the farm and fishing and rescuing the little piggy—and the tough ones about the backbreaking work, leaving home when she wasn't much older than they were, how she sometimes had nothing to eat except gingersnaps and peanuts and had only a single dress she had to wash and dry each night. She'd say, "Look at what I've been through. Look at what I've done. You can do it too."

She told them the way to be successful at anything was to be honest and truthful, work hard, take no shortcuts, have consideration for other people and, most of all, be determined and persistent.

Beyond the discipline and motivation, she wanted the boys to learn to play the game the right way. She needed someone who really knew the game to give the boys instruction on how to hit, pitch, and throw. And she knew just the right person: Laddie Placek.

Laddie was a professional, the head scout for the Cleveland Indians. She asked if he'd instruct the boys, and a few days later he jogged onto the field wearing a dark blue Indians baseball cap that covered the bald part of his head. He told the boys he was going to show them how to play the game.

He conducted batting practice and held baseball clinics. He taught the boys how to "wield that willow," as Pinky Hunter would say. He picked up a bat, showed them how to hold it and how to position their arms and elbows.

"When you're at the plate, hold your front arm straight, use your elbow, step into the ball, and swing through on an even plane."

He held infield instruction, showing the boys the right way to "pick up that bounder and throw over to first base," telling them, "you need to use your wrist when you throw the ball."

He worked with the young catchers, showing them the snap throw, follow through, and how to crouch behind the plate. He taught the pitchers the overhand throw, complete follow through, and how to confuse the batter.

He knew who had potential and who did not. He helped with the lineups. Mrs. Morhard relied on his advice.

He was the baseball pro. She was the boys' baseball mother.

CHAPTER FOURTEEN

Baseball Idols

Junior heard a car rumbling up the driveway. He peeked out the front window. It was a smart-looking Ford convertible. Gerry was in the passenger seat; the driver was a dark-haired young man wearing a crisp white shirt. Junior figured she had another new boyfriend. This one had a really nice car.

When the two of them walked into the house, Junior thought Gerry's companion looked familiar. He was tall and wore a short-sleeved shirt that showed off his broad shoulders, deeply tanned arms, and bulging biceps. Junior thought he looked like Superman. Then Gerry introduced him. It was Jeff Heath, the Cleveland Indians' rookie left fielder.

Junior stared. He wondered what his sister was doing with a real Cleveland Indian.

Jeff Heath was indeed his sister's new boyfriend. He'd become attracted to the beautiful girl who'd been coming to the games—and she to him.

Jeff was a handsome Canadian native with piercing brown-almost-black eyes, a prominent chin, and a bright baseball future. Cleveland Indians manager Oscar Vitt called him, "the best natural hitter I've seen since Joe Jackson." He was born in Fort William (now part of Thunder Bay) in northern Ontario where the province meets Lake Superior. As a toddler, he moved with his parents to Seattle, Washington, where he eventually became a high school baseball and football star. He was highly recruited by college football coaches, one considering him "the best high school running back in the country." In a surprising move, he chose baseball instead, signing with a semipro team and earning a bid to tour Japan with Les Mann's All-American amateur baseball team. There he posted an astounding .483 batting average. Moving to the Minor Leagues, he continued to wow fans with two brilliant seasons, hitting .383 and .367.

The year 1938 was Heath's first full season in the majors, and he was having one of the best rookie seasons in big league history. He was one of baseball's most exciting young hitters.

Heath and Gerry sat down on the living room couch. Mrs. Morhard was in her usual soft armchair. Junior just stood, listening. After chatting with Gerry and Mrs. Morhard for a while, Heath turned to Junior and asked if he liked baseball. When Junior shook his head yes, Jeff said, "Want to play catch?"

Without another word, Junior hustled to grab the ball and glove from behind the kitchen door. Heath was right behind him. He picked up the bat, and they headed for the backyard. There was green space between the house and the shrubs at the back of the property. Heath headed back as far as he could and zipped the ball into Junior's glove, and Junior used his best overhead throw to fling it back. "Not a bad arm, kid," Heath said, making Junior feel even better than he did when he ate one of his mother's brownies.

They tossed the ball around for a few minutes, and Heath asked Junior if he wanted to know how to swing a bat the right way. Junior had begun to lose his shyness around the baseball star and excitedly said, "Yes."

Heath patiently worked with the young boy, showing him how to position his hands around the bat, how to stand and swing to get the most leverage. Junior was thrilled. Jeff Heath replaced Bob Feller as Junior's baseball hero.

The newspapers reported that Heath could be bad tempered and difficult, especially with Indians manager Vitt, but he loved kids and liked showing them how to play the game. The next time he stopped by to see Gerry, Junior and a few of his neighborhood friends were playing catch in the backyard. Again Heath joined in to the amazement of Junior's friends. Gerry didn't mind. She was pleased he was paying attention to Junior and the boys.

Jeff Heath and Gerry dated throughout the 1938 baseball season, and he'd regularly drop by the Morhard house. Whenever he came over, he always spent time with Junior, playing catch in the backyard or talking to him about the team and the players. He'd give him tickets to the games. Sometimes he'd bring his buddies Bob Feller and Roy Weatherly with him. Feller and Heath roomed together on the road. Heath and Indians center fielder Weatherly had struck up a close friendship. "Stormy" or "Little Thunder" Weatherly was a polished outfielder, fast and a good all-around player. They'd all play catch with Junior and his awestruck friends in the Morhard backyard. To Junior and his friends, Heath, Feller, and Weatherly didn't just look like supermen; they were supermen—their personal superheroes.

It was a sunny day, a good day to see a game. Junior decided to use one of the Indians tickets Jeff Heath had given him. His mother and sister were working, so he rode his bike to the Canterbury Road station and hopped on the Cleveland Heights/Fairmount/Canterbury streetcar that went to League Park. The streetcar line was one of nineteen on the east side of Cleveland and its suburbs. The streetcars looked like freestanding railroad cars that ran on tracks in the middle of the streets, connected to the overhead electric wires that powered them by long curved metal fishing pole–like rods.

The streetcar clanked past Fairmount Boulevard's brick estates and down the steep Cedar Road hill where the tracks swerved to the hillside, then down to the busy intersection at 105th Street and Euclid Avenue, Cleveland's second downtown, packed with stores and movie houses. It continued along Euclid Avenue, ultimately ending up at Public Square in downtown Cleveland.

Junior got off at 66th and Lexington. It was two blocks to the two-story red brick entrance to the park on the corner of Lexington Avenue. The line of ticket booths hid behind bulky concrete columns that held up an overhang that kept fans dry in the rain—or sometimes, an early spring snow. Signs marked "A" and "B" showed the gates to get into the ballpark.

League Park was one of the oldest ballparks in the country, built decades before Boston's Fenway Park and Philadelphia's

Shibe Field. A sign outside the historic ballpark says it "opened on May 1, 1891, with the legendary Cy Young pitching for the Cleveland Spiders in their win over the Cincinnati Redlegs."

Only eight years later, the ballpark faced an uncertain future when its big league tenant, the National League Cleveland Spiders, met a merciful end after owner Frank Robison shipped Cy Young and his other top players to the St. Louis Browns. The Spiders, left with only a few decent players, became known as the "Misfits." The team was so bad, people stopped coming to the ballpark. Only around one hundred fans attended home games during the entire year. Robison changed many of the home games to away games, hoping to attract fans elsewhere. That earned the team other nicknames—the Exiles, the Forsakens, and the Nomads. The Spiders ended the season with only twenty wins, gaining the unique distinction as the worst team ever.

League Park went on despite the Spiders, hosting a succession of other teams in the next few years. The minor league Cleveland Lake Shores played there in 1900. In 1901, the team became the Cleveland Blues and joined the newly formed American League. The Blues became the Broncos in 1902, then the Cleveland Naps from 1903 to 1915, named for Napoleon Lajoie, the teams' popular player-manager.

In October 1907, a semipro team from Vermilion, Ohio, played at League Park while the Naps were out of town. Normally a semipro team wouldn't play in the big-league park, but this team had a special attraction, an eighteen-year-old brown-haired, blue-eyed, and "mighty pretty" pitcher named Miss Alta Weiss. Wearing a dark blue dress with VERMILION across her chest and a skirt that ended just below her knees, the fans cheered her as loudly as they'd ever cheered Cy Young, Lajoie, or anyone else. She struck out five, got a hit, and her team was ahead 7–6 when the game was called because of darkness. The newspapers said her pitching motion was just like that of Naps' pitching star, Addie Joss.

In 1910, the ballpark underwent a major transformation, changing from a single deck wooden structure to a double-decker concrete and steel edifice. On opening day for the new stadium, the Naps' starting pitcher was again the famed Cy Young, now in his forties. He'd returned to Cleveland in 1909 after stints with the St. Louis Browns and Boston Red Sox. Young's Hall of Fame biography claims he "left a legacy as a pitcher that is unlikely to ever be matched"—511 total wins, 30 or more wins five times, 20 or more wins fifteen times, and 3 no-hitters.

Another of League Park's legendary players was Shoeless Joe Jackson. He was with the Naps for six seasons. Jackson has often been called the greatest natural hitter in baseball history. In his first full year with the Naps, he hit .408, still a Cleveland team and Major League rookie record. He got his nickname when he played a Minor League game in his stocking feet because his new baseball shoes were not broken in. He never learned to read or write and signed his contracts with an "X." He married his wife Katie when she was fifteen. She managed his money, read his contracts, and wrote his letters.

Jackson's batting stance was unusual for his era. He kept his feet close together in the batter's box and his hands close together near the knob of the bat, not apart like most players of his time, and took a full swing. Babe Ruth said he copied his swing from Joe Jackson.

Jackson averaged .368 in his years with the Naps. In the off-season 1914–1915, he spent the winter in vaudeville. He liked it so much he refused to report to spring training. He was thinking of giving up baseball for the stage. When his wife filed for divorce because of his decision, he reconsidered, but it was his last year at League Field with the Naps. His batting average declined, the Naps ended up in last place, and the Naps owner was in financial trouble.

Chicago White Sox owner Charles Comiskey offered a blank check for Jackson and he went to the White Sox, where he hit well and helped the team win the 1917 World Series. Unfortunately, two years later he became embroiled in the Black Sox Scandal. He and seven other players were accused of throwing the World Series. Despite being acquitted in a jury trial, all eight players were expelled from baseball for life.

The same year Shoeless Joe left Cleveland for Chicago, the Naps' financially distressed owner sold Napoleon Lajoie to the Philadelphia Athletics. It made no sense for the team to carry the name of the departed Lajoie, so they came up with another name, the Cleveland Indians.

The old Cleveland Spiders had been nicknamed the Indians when the team signed Louis Sockalexis, son of the chief of the Penobscot, Maine, Native American tribe, and the first minority player in the National League. The team believed Sockalexis was destined for stardom. In college, he'd been a triple threat—excelling at baseball, football, and track. After twenty games with the Spiders, he had a batting average of .372. Attendance climbed when he was in the lineup. Unfortunately, his fame was short-lived. His addiction to alcohol ended his career. At one point, he fell out of a window while inebriated. In his last game for the Spiders, he fell down twice in the outfield and was released by the club.

In 1920, the Cleveland Indians won the American League pennant and went on to win the World Series 3–2 over the Brooklyn Dodgers. Four of the seven games were played at League Park. Hall of Famer Tris Speaker was the manager, the starting center fielder, and the team's leading hitter with a batting average of .388. Steve O'Neill, who would later manage the Indians and brought the Detroit Tigers to the World Series in 1945, was the catcher. Pitcher Jim Bagby won thirty-one games, Stan Coveleski won twenty-four, and Ray Caldwell won twenty. Jack Graney, who would become the Indians broadcaster, was an outfielder.

League Park now was the weekday home of the Indians and National Football League Cleveland Rams.

Junior picked up a scorecard and headed for one of the slatted green wooden seats in back of the first baseline. The games were played during the day when most people worked, so League Park was rarely crowded, and he could usually sit wherever he wanted. When he got hungry, he'd run up to the food vendor behind home plate and grab a 10-cent hot dog and a 5-cent Coke.

Junior liked watching weekday games at League Park much better than games at Cleveland Stadium, though he did find the thunderous noise of the many thousands of fans at the stadium exciting. League Park was a better place to watch a game. He sat in the lower deck where he could see every play closely. He could even hear the players talking—and sometimes swearing. They all had wads of tobacco puffing out their cheeks. They chewed it all game long and spit it out wherever they happened to be—in the dugout, at bat, on the mound, or in the field.

Kids in the ballpark's neighborhood climbed the trees behind the left field stands and perched on the branches to watch the games. Others peeked through holes in the wooden fence near center field. Junior felt lucky to have a ticket.

The distance to the right field fence was short, even closer than Fenway Park's Green Monster. Junior was hoping to see Jeff Heath or Hal Trosky hit a ball over the fence. Both were power hitters and did that regularly. He watched Heath at the plate and remembered what he'd told him about holding the bat. Heath swung hard, powered by his muscular arms. He could hit balls far into the upper deck.

His other favorite player was still Bob Feller. He liked to watch the way Feller lifted his left leg when he threw his fastball and wondered if that was his secret. Junior thought he was the Indians' best pitcher, better than Johnny Allen.

Junior wasn't sure what position he wanted to play himself. He had a strong arm and thought he could be a good pitcher, too, but the pitchers on the Little Indians were older, more experienced, and they were really good. Right now he was playing second base, and that was fine.

He checked out the Indians' infielders. Lyn Lary was the shortstop. Junior liked the way he leaped high to grab ground balls and threw in a flash to first base. He also paid close attention to third baseman Ken Keltner, and the way he backhanded ground balls to get the hitter out at first. Watching the players gave him ideas.

The Indians went on to win the game. Heath got two hits but no home run. Maybe next time. Junior got back on the streetcar toward home. He remembered the longest home run he ever saw in the ballpark. The Indians were playing the Boston Red Sox. Jimmy Foxx hit the ball way out of the ballpark and into the trees where the neighborhood kids were sitting. After the game, Junior hustled to his mother's meat market to tell her about it, saying he was glad he was in the ballpark and not in a tree.

On October 2, 1938, Josephine brought Junior to a game at Cleveland Stadium as an early birthday present.

It was a cold Sunday with the temperature in the 40s. The harsh wind howled in from Lake Erie, whirling through the stadium. It was the first game of a doubleheader. The third-place Indians were playing the fourth-place Detroit Tigers. The pennant wasn't at stake, but the stands were full.

The fans gathered to see if baseball history was going to be made. The Tigers' Hank Greenberg was trying to tie Babe Ruth's home run record of sixty home runs. He had fifty-eight. He hadn't hit a homer in his last three games. He needed just two more and he had two games to do it. It wouldn't be easy. He was up against Indians' young ace Bob Feller, who was looking for his eighteenth win.

Mrs. Morhard and Junior had a box seat near the third base-line. Feller was pitching well, getting strikeout after strikeout, but the Indians weren't hitting.

Greenberg struck out his first two times at bat. In the sixth inning, Greenberg walloped a line drive to left center field that hit the wall near the 380-foot mark. In most ballparks, that would be a home run, but in the huge stadium, it bounced back on the field for a ground rule double. The crowd groaned.

In the eighth inning, Greenberg walked. On the Indians side, Feller already had an amazing sixteen strikeouts, close to the Major League record he shared with Dizzy Dean of the St. Louis Cardinals. Detroit's curve-baller Harry Eisenstat was even better than Feller. He was pitching a no-hitter.

Mrs. Morhard, Junior, and the crowd were mesmerized, intent on every pitch. The tension built with each inning. In the eighth inning, Eisenstat's no-hitter ended when he gave up a hit to Indians' catcher Frankie Pytlak.

In the ninth inning, Greenberg came up to bat again. He belted another long ball toward center field. The crowd watched, holding its collective breath. The ball soared. Outfielder Roy Weatherly went way back, reached in, and grabbed it. The great Tigers' slugger hit two long balls but neither made it in for a home run.

Bob Feller was the only one who would go into the record books that day. He notched eighteen strikeouts—a record that stood for twenty-one years. But he lost the game. The winner was Eisenstat of the Tigers, who won 4–0.

In the second half of the doubleheader, the great Tigers'

slugger failed again at his chance for the home run record. It wouldn't be broken until 1961 when New York Yankee Roger Maris hit sixty-one homers.

One afternoon at the end of the season, Jeff Heath stopped by the Morhard house with a special surprise. He asked Junior to come out to his Ford convertible. He opened the car door and pulled out a huge baseball bat—a professional Major League bat like the ones he used in Indians' games. With a big smile, he told Junior it was for him. The young boy was thrilled. The bat was so big he could barely lift it. A real Major League bat!

Despite their promising start, the Cleveland Indians ended the 1938 season with a record of 86-66, in third place behind the New York Yankees and the Boston Red Sox. Both Bob Feller and Mel Harder won seventeen games. Johnny Allen went 14-8. Roy Weatherly ended the season batting .262.

Jeff Heath had one of the best rookie seasons in big league history. He nearly swiped the batting title from Boston Red Sox Hall of Famer Jimmy Foxx, coming in second by only .006. He led the league in triples with eighteen, was third to only Foxx and Hank Greenberg in slugging with an average of .602. Eventually he would make the All Star squad three times.

After the season, Heath and Geraldine parted. Distance was one factor—he went back to Seattle in the off-season. Her mother was another. The ever-vigilant Josephine liked the twenty-two year-old ballplayer but thought he was too old for her still-teenage daughter.

The bat stayed—it became Junior's most treasured possession.

CHAPTER FIFTEEN
They Will Come

They called it Little Indians Field.

It was becoming a magnet for baseball lovers—and that was just about everybody. Families parked their boxy Fords and Packards and Chevys haphazardly along the edges of the field. Kids' Schwinn and American Flyer bicycles squeezed in between them. Moms in flowing dresses, high-heeled shoes, and frilly hats; dads in long-sleeved shirts and ties; and sisters in pigtails watched the young players from foul territory outside the baselines. Neighborhood boys too young to play, clad in short-sleeved shirts tucked into their belted shorts, crowded together on the grass, chomping on Baby Ruth candy bars, pretending to swing bats, and letting out an occasional whoop when a player got a hit or made a great catch.

Watching young boys in sparkling white mini big league uniforms smack their bats against speedy fastballs like pros was irresistible.

The field was on Cedar Road in University Heights, just down from Warrensville Center Road, which was becoming a major intersection. A nine-hole golf course and a small restaurant, Jack-Kraw Steak Sandwiches, were on the northeast corner. Next to the field was the new shopping center Anthony Visconsi was building. It was one of the first in the country set back from the street to allow off-street parking. Visconsi figured the automobile was going to change the way people shopped, that people would soon want to shop in their neighborhoods instead of going downtown.

The field stretched from just beyond the shopping center wall all the way to the next street, Vernon Road. Lenny's Chicken-in-a-Basket was in back of home plate on the corner of Vernon Road.

Going west, Cedar Road led to Cleveland Heights. Toward the south, Warrensville Center Road led past John Carroll University to Shaker Heights. Surrounded by the growing Heights communities, the Little Indians field was in a perfect location.

The interest in boys' teams offered more proof baseball was truly the nation's pastime, no matter how young or proficient the players might be. The field was a magnet for young boys from University Heights and the neighboring communities.

One boy, younger and smaller than the rest, was at Little Indians Field just about every time there was a game. He brought his own bat, ball, and glove and stood as close to the field as he could, mimicking the players' moves. He badly wanted to be on a team. His name was Brad Rogers.

Brad lived just down the road from the Morhard home in a lush wooded area of neighboring Shaker Heights. Unlike the boys on the Little Indians, Brad lived in one of the stately homes on Shelburne Road, a sprawling three-story brick estate set on an acre-plus lot, framed by banks of glossy green-leafed pink and white rhododendrons and surrounded by an expansive lawn as immaculately cared for as the greens of nearby Shaker Country Club.

Brad's mother was a Bradley, a member of the wealthy family who developed much of this area of Shaker Heights and owned twenty Cleveland properties. She was Cleveland Indians' owner Alva Bradley's attractive red-haired sister.

Brad was the youngest of the three Rogers children; he had two older siblings, Anne and Ed. His given first name was Bradley, after his mother's well-established family. The family had a host of servants, including a chauffeur, cook, upstairs maid, and nursemaid, allowing Brad's mother to indulge her passion for decorating homes. She was a distant presence to her children. Their father worked in the tie department of Higbee's department store and was rarely around. Neither spent much time with the children, especially Brad, their last child. Brad's nursemaid, Anna, a Czechoslovakian woman always referred to her youngest charge as "poor Bradley," and cared for him almost exclusively. The family money didn't mean much to the neglected young boy, except that he could go to Indians games any time he wanted.

His parents sent Brad to preschool at the posh Hathaway Brown School, then to another private school, Hawken, for elementary school. He had little interest in academics and often found himself in trouble at school. The one thing Brad loved was baseball. When the wintry Ohio weather finally warmed up enough, he and his classmates would rush outside to play baseball at recess. It was the highlight of his day.

One spring day, Brad was playing in the infield when he suddenly, desperately needed to go to the bathroom. He was bursting inside, but there was no way he would stop playing. Slowly he felt a small trickle seeping down his leg and onto the front of his knickers, ending in a pool on second base. The stern headmaster was appalled. He shamed the young boy in front of his friends and marched him home to his humiliated mother. Brad tried to explain, but his mother wouldn't listen. She gave him the worst punishment she could have given her baseball-crazed son. He wasn't allowed to attend Cleveland Indians' opening day.

Mrs. Rogers was one of Mrs. Morhard's meat delivery customers, and the two of them became friends. They had more in common than their sons and meat deliveries. Mrs. Rogers suspected there was a reason her husband wasn't around much. It certainly wasn't because of his nine-to-five job at Higbee's. She thought he was drinking and running around with other women. She enlisted the sympathetic Mrs. Morhard to help her find out—and the two women would often drive around like Carrie Nation looking for him at local bars.

Baseball-loving Brad was persistent. He'd hang around the Little Indians games and practices, longing to play. He was friendly, always had a big smile when he was around the ball field, but Mrs. Morhard didn't let him play at first. He was too young and small, and she was afraid he'd get hurt. That didn't deter Brad. He kept coming back, day after day, lugging his glove, ball, and bat. Mrs. Morhard finally gave in. He loved baseball so much she couldn't bear to keep him off the team. He became the littlest Little Indian. His older brother Ed joined the team too.

Meanwhile, the boys on other teams in the league wanted spiffy uniforms and big league names like the Little Indians. Before the season began, they also had Major League names and uniforms.

The Hilltoppers became the Little New York Yankees. Mrs. Morhard got them new uniforms, complete with the pinstripes, just like the perennial American League pennant and Major League World Series winners. The boys expected to carry on that tradition with their team. And they had the talent to make that happen.

Their manager was William Lindquist, a former minor league baseball player whose family had owned a semipro baseball team. William had two sons—the older one, Bill, was showing promise as a pitcher. His father spent much of his free time grooming Bill for what he hoped would be a Major League career.

The summer before, to avoid distraction while he was teaching young Bill the rudiments of pitching, his younger son, Ray, went to stay with an aunt in St. Louis. Ray was miserable. He spent much of his time walking up and down the railroad tracks. His aunt said if his family didn't want him, she'd keep him there. That woke his father up. This summer, Ray was home.

Ray Lindquist was one of the best ballplayers in the league. It looked like he might become even better than his brother. His ambition was to someday be a professional baseball player, maybe even in the Yankee organization.

The University Town Hall team became the Little Chicago White Sox. The boys from Garfield Heights were the Little Washington Senators. Quickly, all the teams expanded their rosters with the many new boys who wanted to play. Now all the teams in Mrs. Morhard's league had the names and uniforms of American League ball clubs. The boys were thrilled.

There was nothing like Mrs. Morhard's baseball league anywhere—boys' baseball teams modeled on Major League Baseball, with authentic Major League uniforms, a boy-size regulation field, and professional baseball instruction. Mrs. Morhard had done it all with whirlwind speed.

Mrs. Morhard's phone constantly rang; mothers or fathers whose boys wanted to be on a team kept calling. It wasn't just boys from the neighborhood; families from the other side of Cleveland were calling her. Friends from the meat market wanted their boys to participate. Rosters expanded.

Eight-year-old Jack Anderson and his mother were among the crowds that stopped by Little Indians field to watch the games. Mrs. Anderson was a fine all-around athlete and had become an accomplished tennis player. She was as interested in the teams as her son, maybe even more. She'd come to the United States from Scotland as a child and shared Josephine Morhard's passion for baseball. They became good friends.

Her husband was a physician. He had a good practice in the Carnegie Medical Center at the busy commercial district at East 105th Street and Carnegie Avenue in Cleveland. Even so, with the lingering effects of the Depression, many of his patients were out of work and had to pay him in potatoes and chickens. Nonetheless, he was successful enough to spend his spare time flying his own airplane. Between doctoring, flying, and other pursuits he, like Brad's dad, was rarely around. Mrs. Anderson, too, worried about her husband's "other pursuits." She joined Mrs. Morhard and Mrs. Rogers in their occasional rounds of the local bars.

Mrs. Morhard was impressed with Mrs. Anderson's sports knowledge. She seemed to know more about baseball than most men. Jack wanted to play and his mother was interested in starting a team. There were plenty more kids who wanted to play. Mrs. Morhard organized another team, the Little St. Louis Browns, and made Mrs. Anderson the manager. Now there were five teams in the league. Including Mrs. Morhard who managed the Little Indians, two of the five had female managers.

It was unheard of to have mothers in dresses and high heels running baseball teams, but Mrs. Morhard insisted the two of them could run teams as well as the men. Plus, women had something else to offer the boys: boys as young as these needed a woman's guidance and understanding as much as male influences. She had her own ideas about what boys' baseball should be about. To her, baseball was not just a man's game.

Now that Mrs. Morhard had five teams, she needed another professional umpire.

She spotted a tall, good-looking, dark-haired young man
standing in back of first base. He looked too young to be one of
the fathers, more like a ballplayer himself—he was well over
six feet with the erect carriage and demeanor of an athlete. He
came by himself and seemed genuinely interested in the team.
He chatted with the boys after the game. She wanted to find
out more about him.

His name was Hal Lebovitz, and he was a twenty-two-year-
old schoolteacher. He'd entered Cleveland's Western Reserve
University at age sixteen after skipping two grades in high
school. There he was a star athlete—the basketball team's center, the football team's starting tackle, and sports editor of the
college newspaper. After graduating with a degree in chemistry, he got a job as a high school chemistry teacher, doubling
as the school's football and basketball coach.

He was brilliant and knowledgeable, with an encyclopedic
understanding of the rules of the game. He loved the idea of
the boys' league and enjoyed watching them play. He wanted
to be involved. He'd been umpiring adult sandlot teams for 50
cents a game. Mrs. Morhard asked if he'd do the same for her
games, at the same pay. He agreed.

Mrs. Morhard now had a second paid umpire, but Hal
Lebovitz was more than that. After each game, he returned to
being a coach. He gathered the boys together and gave them
each tips on what they could do to improve their play.

As nice as the field was, Mrs. Morhard wanted to add a regulation backstop so balls wouldn't end up hitting Lenny's Chicken-
in-a-Basket, which was directly in back of home plate. People
were crowding in to watch the games, and there was no place
for them to sit. She thought the field should have bleachers.

She asked the mayor if he'd let her hold an ox roast on the
grounds of the University Heights Village Hall. Ox roasts were
typical Midwestern events, where beef is seasoned then slow-
cooked over a fire, sometimes overnight, until it is delectably
tender.

The mayor may have been jittery at the thought of a huge
fire pit, burning meat, and people tramping all over the village
lawns the workers kept so meticulous, but as he always did
when Mrs. Morhard asked for something, he said yes. He ad-

mired what Josephine Morhard had accomplished in such a short time. She was a miracle worker. She was doing something important for the boys—and for the town. People who'd never heard of University Heights knew about the village now. Best of all, she was bringing the community together and giving the residents something to take pride in.

He agreed to let her use the village property, but he was wary about whether she'd get enough people to come or whether she'd raise any money. He should have known better than to doubt her.

Junior watched the huge slab of beef slowly turning above the long pit of burning wood. It was bigger than he was. *It must be the whole cow*, he thought to himself. The beef had been cooking for hours and now that it was done, its enticing aroma wafted through the crowd of moms and dads, grandparents, neighbors, baseball fans, players, and kids—lots of kids.

There were hundreds of people from University Heights, Cleveland Heights, Shaker Heights, Cleveland, even from communities west of Cleveland. Most lined up near the long tables filled with food—huge trays of potato salad, coleslaw, rolls, lemonade, Mrs. Morhard's special brownies, and the tender slices of beef they'd all come for.

Junior saw a familiar convertible pull up to the grounds. Inside, he saw the faces of Jeff Heath, Bob Feller, and Roy Weatherly. The ox roast's big attractions had arrived, just as Mrs. Morhard promised in the flyers she distributed throughout the village and other nearby communities. Many in the food line forgot their stomachs and joined the mob that crowded around the ballplayers, eager to shake hands and get autographs from baseball stars most of them had only seen at a distance in League Park or the stadium. In return, the players asked them to generously support the Little Indians. They did.

Mrs. Morhard's ox roast made enough money to purchase the backstop and bleachers.

"Just wait until next season," Josephine said as she gathered more names of interested kids, parents, and onlookers.

CHAPTER SIXTEEN

The Junior American League

Little Indians pitcher Dick Kusa kicked his right leg high in the air in his signature motion and fired his fastball like a missile at the hapless batter. Umpire Hal Lebovitz signaled, "Strike three!" The first game of the new season was a win for the Little Indians.

It was May and the crisp, cool air turned the players' cheeks and noses pink despite the sun's lightly warming touch. The outfield smelled of freshly mown grass. The ball field had a smart new look. A backstop stood a commanding twenty-five feet high, ensuring that wild pitches or foul balls wouldn't end up in one of Lenny's chickens in a basket. Onlookers happily celebrated the win in new wooden bleachers that stretched along the first baseline.

A smiling, sharply dressed man in a navy blazer and white open-collared shirt stepped down from the bleachers and walked briskly over to the excited young players. He patted them on the back and spoke to each one, congratulating the winners and lifting the spirits of the losers.

A photographer with a Rolleiflex camera hanging from his neck and a young reporter holding a lined pad quickly joined them. The photographer motioned to the man and two of the Little Indians—little Buddy Myers and shortstop Allen Koenig—to join him at the edge of the field in front of a row of trees. He positioned the boys. Allen Koenig turned around to show the Indians' emblem on the back of his shirt; Buddy

Myers smiled shyly as he faced front to show the big "C" on his uniform. The man knelt down to look more closely. The Rolleiflex clicked, capturing the image of the great Cleveland Indians pitcher, Mel Harder, with the two Little Indians.

Harder was a hero to the boys. He'd been named to four straight All Star teams, was the winning pitcher in 1934, and picked up saves in the 1935 and 1937 All Star games. In the 1937 game, he pitched thirteen scoreless innings against the best hitters in the National League. Harder regularly won at least fifteen games a year and boasted one of the lowest earned run averages in the American League. Born in Nebraska, he joined the starting rotation in 1930 and was chosen to pitch the first game when Cleveland Stadium opened its doors.

Harder lived on Dysart Road in University Heights, near Jackie Heinen's family and about three blocks from the Morhard home. He'd often stop by the ballpark to watch the boys play when he wasn't on the road with the team. The boys idolized him.

After the photo shoot was done, he invited the boys over to his two-story white frame house. They piled into his living room while the great Indians pitcher made them popcorn and served sodas and lots of encouragement and advice on how to play. The boys ate it up—the popcorn and the advice. The most important thing in baseball, he told them, was good sportsmanship. "You should play to win, but have fun while you're doing it. And, most of all, be a good sport."

The next day, the photo popped up in a Cleveland newspaper under the headline No, THE INDIANS HAVEN'T SHRUNK.

Boys' baseball was going big-time.

Mrs. Morhard had worked hard over the winter to make sure everything was well organized for the new season. Laddie Placek helped her order and install the backstop and bleachers. The city installed a flagpole and a large American flag at the far edge of center field. It was the finest ball field around, except for the big league parks.

All the teams in Mrs. Morhard's league had names and uniforms of American League ball clubs. From top to bottom she was modeling her league on Major League Baseball.

It was inevitable that her next move would be to name her league after the big leagues too. It became the Junior American League.

It didn't take long before more press caught on. The Hearst-owned International News Service (INS) syndicated articles on the Junior American League, which appeared in newspapers across the country. The *San Antonio Light* talked about the team's "honest-to-goodness uniforms, umpires, real equipment and even double headers" adding "there will be as much interest in their own pennant race as there will be in the stretch drive for the real American League battle."

The season ran from May through the middle of September. They had a thirty-game schedule. When school was in session, the boys played a doubleheader on Sunday afternoons. After school let out in June, they added two Wednesday afternoon games.

Mrs. Morhard hired another umpire, Paul Kvetko. The league now had three professional umpires. Stern-faced Tony Pianowski was the disciplinarian. He kept the game moving, made sure the players got on and off the field quickly and didn't waste time. Kvetko was the opposite, mild-mannered and laid back. Hal Lebovitz was the umpire-coach. Besides calling balls and strikes, he encouraged the boys and gave them tips—telling them to stand closer to the plate or showing them where to position themselves in the field so they'd be in a better position to catch the ball. If a player made a mistake—like forgetting to swing at a ball when a teammate was trying a clean steal at home—he'd talk to the boy at the end of the inning and ask him what he should have done. The boy usually knew.

Mrs. Morhard made sure each team had a knowledgeable adult manager, scorecards, and lineup cards. The boys got their own lineup cards before every game. To help defray the costs, the players sold $1 booster tickets and charged the adult spectators a small fee. Mrs. Morhard put up a sign on the back edge of the backstop and she'd ask someone, often a player's younger brother, to collect the 25 cents. He'd sit between the backstop and the bleachers holding a box with a slit in the top for the money. He got a small payment for his trouble.

The ties between the Major League Cleveland Indians and the Junior American League teams grew stronger. Owner Alva

Bradley, new manager Roger Peckinpaugh, and the Indians players all loved the idea of the mini-Indians. The big league team provided all the baseballs for the league. Big league scouts and players helped teach the game to their young counterparts. Peckinpaugh's son Johnny and several players' sons joined a team.

Mrs. Morhard was at every game despite her responsibilities at the market, watching from her usual spot—a folding chair under the outsize blue and white umbrella in back of first base. Her face was animated; her keen eyes watched every pitch, every move on the field; her silver whistle hung around her neck. The season had just begun, but she already had ideas for next year. She was going to add a National League.

At the time, Junior wasn't really aware of the scope of what his mother was accomplishing. He just liked playing baseball with his friends and being a Little Indian. He'd undergone a transformation since the early days of the team. There were no more tantrums.

It was clear he had natural ability. He'd always thrown the ball well, but being on the team and learning from the baseball pros were helping him become a better all-around player. He worked hard on hitting and picking up ground balls and was turning into a good second baseman.

He wanted to be the best there was. He was willing to sacrifice whatever he had to, believing the harder he worked, the better he'd become. He remembered what his mother told him: "No matter how many times you get knocked down, you need to keep getting up." It was what she'd done all her life. He was following her lead.

Junior had heard about a speed meter the Cleveland Indians and *Plain Dealer* had developed to measure the speed of a baseball. Two photoelectric circuits at the front and back ends of the machine measured speed as the ball passed between them. Several Major League pitchers had tried the device. Yankees' pitcher Atley Donald had been clocked at 94.7 miles per hour. Bob Feller's first try measured 81 mph (though later tests clocked him over 100 mph).

The Cleveland Indians offered kids a chance to test their pitching speed on the device. Junior wanted to go. Mrs. Morhard drove him down to Cleveland's Public Hall where the event was being held. Junior waited his turn in the lines of boys that stretched halfway down the block.

Each boy got three balls to hurl at a target about fifty feet away. Junior stepped up and tossed his three balls, one after the other, as hard as he could while the machine recorded their speed. One of the men operating the speed meter looked at Junior quizzically after he finished, said "great job," and told him his speed. As Junior walked away, he added, "pretty amazing for a kid." Junior thought it was no big deal. He always threw like that. The next day his feat made the sports pages in a local paper. His pitch speed hit 90 mph. None of the other kids had come close.

The other boys were becoming better baseball players too. On the Little Indians, Jackie Heinen had blossomed into an ace pitcher who doubled as a third baseman on the days he wasn't on the mound. He was a good hitter too. Once he smashed a ball 290 feet into left field—crashing into the wall of the shopping center. The boys were scared the owner, Mr. Visconsi, would be mad and stop them from using the field, but he just shrugged and said, "That's a heckuva long ball for a kid."

Dick Kusa, the other top pitcher, was unhittable much of the time. Dave Erickson, the tallest boy on the team, could "hit a ball a mile." Shortstop Allen Koenig was the fastest, a good fielder and batter. Catcher Ronnie Barth was adept at throwing out players who tried to steal a base. A new catcher Billy Spero had joined the team and become a tough competitor.

The Little Indians were winning most of their games, but the other teams were beginning to catch up.

After the games, Mrs. Morhard would move among the crowd, smiling, chatting, talking about the game. Then she'd congratulate the boys—all of them, not just the winners of the game. She was fond of them all—but she always had that whistle.

In his *Plain Dealer* column, Lebovitz wrote, "When there was a problem, she served as [Commissioner of Organized Baseball] Judge Landis. If any boy got out of line, she'd blow that whistle she always carried, lay down the law and that was it."

Mrs. Morhard wasn't even five feet tall, but everybody paid attention and did exactly what she asked.

* * *

The Little White Sox were turning into the Little Indians' main competition. Their best players were shortstop Wayne Wiggins and first baseman Joe Spicuzza. Wiggins was tall and thin, blond and blue-eyed; Spicuzza was the opposite—dark-haired, dark-eyed, short, stocky, and built like a fireplug.

Wiggins could hit just about anything a pitcher threw at him. He was the league's leading hitter. He and Spicuzza were also Junior's chief tormenters. Both were two years older and had gone through their growth spurt, so they were much bigger.

After school, they hid in the bushes, waiting for Junior to walk by. They jumped out and taunted him, repeating, "Junior Morhard, momma's boy! You wouldn't be playing if your mother wasn't running the league!" If they weren't taunting him, they were beating him up or "pantsing" him—pulling off his pants and hiding them. Junior knew he was good enough to play, so the taunting only bothered him a little. Pulling off his clothes bothered him a lot.

Before one of the games between the Little Indians and the Little White Sox, Junior rode his bike over to the field early to practice. Wayne and Joe were the only other boys there. They dashed over as soon as they saw him. Junior knew he was in trouble. Wayne grabbed him and held his arms while Joe pulled off all his clothes except his underwear. They hoisted them up the flagpole as high as they could. Junior was humiliated. He didn't tell his mother or anyone else; he was going to handle this himself. That afternoon he was so mad, he walloped the ball as hard as he could and had one of his best games. The Little Indians won.

Junior was discovering that having his mother run the baseball league he was in wasn't always a good thing. He knew she'd done this out of love for him, but he sometimes felt he was getting attention he didn't deserve—both bad and good—just because he was her son. He was beginning to want to do something on his own.

Mrs. Morhard, too, was finding success brought new headaches. She'd built the league from nothing and had over a hundred boys participating. She'd brought in Cleveland Indians and former minor league baseball players and scouts to teach the boys baseball skills. Throughout the city, its suburbs, even across the nation, people knew about the Junior American League. The games were covered in the newspapers and widely publicized. Everything was going well. But then a problem emerged in the form of the father of one of the Little Indians. His name was Elmer Kaufman.

Jerry Kaufman was one of the new players on the Little Indians. He was a good pitcher, and his teammates liked him. Elmer always came with him. At first, Elmer tried to be helpful—he offered suggestions on the lineup and gave the boys tips at the plate. Mrs. Morhard listened to what he had to say and was grateful for the help.

Gradually he became more aggressive, even obnoxious. He began telling her what to do and who should be playing. He butted in when she tried to talk to the boys. He attempted to overrule her decisions. He interfered in all aspects of the game. Elmer made it clear: he could run things better than she could. She was a woman. What did a woman know about baseball? A woman couldn't manage a baseball league.

Mrs. Morhard tried to be patient and work with him, but there was a limit.

She'd been through plenty of hard times. She'd fought her way through life since she was a child. She'd dealt with men who attempted to rape her, cheat her, and frame her. She'd married two wayward men who put her through hell. She resurrected a meat market. She survived it all. She'd dealt with much worse than Elmer Kaufman. There was no way she was going to let him or anyone else get the best of her—certainly not take over her team or the league she founded.

They had very different perspectives. She was interested in much more than winning—or trying to mold professional baseball players. Through baseball, boys could learn values and qualities to help them be happy and successful in whatever they chose to do. She wanted them to develop baseball skills and be as good as they could be, but these were young boys. They should enjoy playing and have fun, not be pressured.

Elmer had a different view. He wanted things done his way. Having "fun" playing ball and the other lessons Josephine imparted weren't what boys' baseball should be about. It should be about doing whatever was needed to win games. Josephine wanted every boy to have a chance to play in every game. He thought the best players should be on the field all the time. In his mind there was no question he knew more about baseball than she did. He could run the teams and the league better than any woman.

Finally, Josephine had enough. She confronted him and told him this was her league, and it was going to be run her way. He glared at her and stormed out, yelling to his son Jerry, who was tossing the ball to catcher Ronnie Barth, to come with him. He was going to start his own league. He'd take her players. He'd run it his way, not the way a woman was running it. He told her he was going to form a Junior National League, even though she'd already told him she planned to start a Junior National League.

Josephine Morhard was fuming. She'd done so much to help these boys. Could this man really take it all away?

Then her phone rang. It was Anthony Visconsi, who owned the field where the Junior American League games were played. He needed the land back after the season. The shopping center was doing well, and he planned to add more stores.

It was time for her once again to follow the advice she'd given Junior. *No matter how many times you get knocked down, you need to keep getting up.*

It wasn't in Mrs. Morhard's nature to dwell on her problems or spend a lot of time thinking about them. Her first order of business was preventing Elmer Kaufman from stealing her Junior National League; she'd deal with finding a new field later.

She hightailed it to the office of Stanton Adams, judge of the East Cleveland Municipal Court and a prominent attorney. He had a reputation for being tough. Mrs. Morhard could attest to that; he represented her in her two divorces from Junior's father. Adams was the best person she could think of to head off Elmer Kaufman's attempted takeover.

She leaned on his large walnut desk, her hands moving as furiously as the words that poured out of her mouth. The distinguished-looking Adams listened quietly, focusing his intense eyes on the agitated woman in front of him. He calmly told her he couldn't stop Kaufman from starting his own league. What he could do was incorporate her leagues into the Junior American and National Leagues, Inc. That way Kaufman couldn't use the name. Mrs. Morhard agreed.

Thwarted in using the name he wanted, Kaufman went ahead with his league anyway, naming it instead, the Junior American Association. He planned to set up his league with a president, secretary, executive board, and committees—all men, as was the norm. Kaufman would coach the Toppers. The other teams would be the RedBirds, Mudhens, Brewers, Blues, and Sluggers.

They affiliated with the Cleveland Heights Recreation Department and planned to play at four of the city's schools—Canterbury, Roxboro, and Monticello Junior High Schools and Cleveland Heights High School. Only the high school had a regulation field, which wasn't modified for the younger players. The other schools simply had large fields. They would start their season in June 1941.

The contrast with Mrs. Morhard's approach was stark. He had an organization chart. She had an organization. She was anxious nonetheless, afraid her boys would leave to go with Kaufman. She needn't have worried. Her teams remained intact. This time baseball had given Mrs. Morhard a lesson. From then on, any parents who tried to take control or interfere with her were gently asked to leave.

The season was winding down. Soon, the boys would be going back to school. Mrs. Morhard wanted to end the season with a flourish, to celebrate the Junior American League season and everyone who participated. And she had another reason. The boys' baseball teams were costly and she was carrying much of the burden. The village maintained the field, the Indians provided baseballs, and she collected money at the games, but she'd subsidized much of the league expense with her own meat market funds. She didn't want to ask the boys' families to help. Many of them couldn't afford it.

She could have a celebration and help defray the costs of running the league. People were excited about the league and the young boys in their little big league uniforms. She was sure they'd help.

She enlisted the help of the friends she'd made, including the league mothers, the University Heights Women's Club, and the American Legion, which was sponsoring baseball teams for older teenagers.

They'd have a dinner at the Village Hall. All the boys put on their uniforms and swarmed the village and adjoining community neighborhoods selling tickets, starting on their own streets. Invitations went out to the Cleveland Indians players to be guests of honor. *The Heights Press* promoted the dinner. Other papers followed suit.

The highlights of the evening were the showing of the official American League film, *First Century of Baseball,* and the presence of Indians stars Jeff Heath, Mel Harder, Ray Mack, Roy Weatherly, and the veteran Tribe player-manager who'd brought the Indians to the 1920 World Series, Tris Speaker.

Another season was over. It was on to the next problem. She needed another field. The boys soon wouldn't have a place to play. There was vacant land across the street from the ball field. It was in the village of South Euclid, not University Heights. There was plenty of space there, even enough for two ball fields. Whether that worked or not, she vowed they would have another ball field by the spring.

CHAPTER SEVENTEEN

The Junior National League

Cameras clicked from all over the fields—black boxy cameras, cameras with lenses that unfolded like an accordion, cameras that looked like ten-pound exercise weights with flat tops and bottoms that held the spools of film for moving pictures.

Over 170 smiling boys paraded toward the far end of center field, some looking too small to wield a bat, others on the brink of puberty. They formed a horseshoe on either side of the flagpole, Major League team logos emblazoned across their freshly laundered uniforms—the Little Yankees in their pinstripes, the rest in uniforms like the pro teams they represented. Now there were Junior National League teams too—the Little Brooklyn Dodgers, Little Cincinnati Reds, Little Pittsburgh Pirates, and the Little St. Louis Cardinals.

Parents, league volunteers, team managers, umpires, reporters, and Cleveland Indians' officials crowded around to watch.

It was June 21, 1941, opening day for the Junior American League and the new Junior National League. Two ball fields stood side by side on the South Euclid side of Cedar Road—one for each league. The owner had agreed to let Mrs. Morhard use the land. Boys from all the teams once again picked up stones, pulled weeds, and cleaned up the debris. City trucks, bulldozers, and scrapers again transformed the unkempt property. The backstop and bleachers moved over.

The season opener was later than usual due to delays in constructing the second ball field. The dedication ceremony for the new field was about to begin.

A familiar eleven-year-old in a Little Indians uniform stepped out of the line of boys, clutching a bugle. Junior Morhard had practiced hard for this moment, wanting to salute this occasion like he'd seen soldiers do on special holidays. He begged his mother to let him. He lifted the bugle high, pursed his lips, puffed out his cheeks, and started to blow. Nothing came out. He tried again. This time, a breathy groaning sound. Again. A faint grunt. He lowered his eyes, hid the bugle behind his back as if to hide himself, and slowly squirmed back into place.

Some boys giggled as newly elected mayor Earl Aurelius quickly stepped in front of the retreating boy and motioned the other presenters to join him. Mrs. Morhard signaled an older boy to hoist the flag. The young players crossed their hearts and recited the Pledge of Allegiance when the American flag reached the top of the flagpole.

The mayor cut the ribbon and dedicated the field, extolling everyone from his grounds crew to Mrs. Morhard to the boys who picked up the stones and pulled the weeds. Mrs. Roger Peckinpaugh, wife of the new Cleveland Indians manager, presented a floral wreath.

As the presentations ended, Roger Peckinpaugh came over to Mrs. Morhard and told her the Indians were filming the ceremony. He asked if she'd like them to make a movie of the teams. It would be hers to use as a fund-raiser. He saw potential for other cities to start baseball programs like this; a film could inspire them too. The Indians would do it for her free of charge. She quickly said yes.

Peckinpaugh had a special connection to Cleveland. As a young man, he played baseball, football, and basketball at the city's East Technical High School. After graduation, Napoleon Lajoie, his neighbor and manager of the old Cleveland Naps, signed him to a baseball contract. Three years later he was traded to the New York Yankees, where he became the team captain, then the player-manager—the youngest manager in Major League history.

Eventually he made his way back to Cleveland where he managed the Indians from 1927 to 1933. The Indians went through three more managers after that—including the most recent, the mercurial Oscar Vitt, whose players had revolted against him a year earlier. Vitt was tough and had a bad temper. He often clashed with the players.

In June 1940, things came to a head. Mel Harder was on the mound. Harder had fifteen or more wins in eight consecutive seasons, including two with twenty wins. Vitt raced across the field to relieve him, yelling, "When are you going to earn your salary?" The players' long-simmering anger boiled over. Harder was one of the best liked and best performing players on the team. A dozen of them, including Jeff Heath and Bob Feller, told owner Alva Bradley they could win the pennant if he fired Vitt. He didn't. Vitt kept his job. The Indians finished second.

After the season, Bradley rehired Peckinpaugh, who was known for his calm demeanor. Peckinpaugh quickly warmed to the Little Indians and the Junior Leagues. His son Johnny became a right fielder for the Little Indians. Johnny didn't have his dad's natural talent, but his enthusiasm was infectious. The Peckinpaughs became part of Mrs. Morhard's baseball family.

University Heights' mayor Earle E. Aurelius was another new face. The village had just become a city, after pumping up its population to the required five thousand residents. As mayor, he wanted to leave his own legacy. The baseball leagues were bringing attention to the city. People were coming together to watch the boys. Mayor Aurelius was even more enthusiastic than his predecessor. He quickly gathered his troops to help make the second field a reality and ensure both fields were perfectly maintained. He helped out with pretty much anything the leagues needed. Mrs. Morhard returned the favor, working to get him elected and helping with city projects. On this day he was working the crowd and reveling in the moment.

Following the ceremony, each field hosted a doubleheader. In the Junior American League, it was the Little Browns against the Little White Sox, followed by the Little Indians against the Little Yankees. The Junior National League pitted the Little Dodgers against the Little Pirates. Then it was the Little Reds vs. the Little Cardinals.

The new season was underway.

*   *   *

The most exciting new Junior National League team was the Little Cardinals. Midway through the season, they were undefeated, the only team in either league without a loss. Their shortstop, "Little" Marlo Termini, was one of the main reasons.

Marlo was one of the older boys in the leagues and one of the shortest. He was an orphan and was living in a foster home. His life had been like a series of bloody boxing matches with too many knockdowns.

When he was five years old, a woman found his sister JoAnne shivering, without proper clothing, in the snow outside the family's home. She took her inside and found Marlo and two more siblings unsupervised. She reported the situation to the authorities.

The children's mother was judged mentally ill and sent to Cleveland State Hospital, a barbaric place formerly known as the Northern Ohio Lunatic Asylum. It was a prison-like four-story brick institution with three foreboding towers and two massive wings added to house the growing population no one knew what else to do with. Here patients were warehoused in crowded dormitories lined with hundreds of white iron twin-size beds spaced two to eighteen inches apart. The hospital was known for neglecting and abusing patients and housing them in filthy conditions.

The Termini children's Italian-born father worked long hours at the Northern Ohio Food Terminal, which supplied wholesale fruit, vegetables, meat, and dairy products to groceries, hotels, and restaurants. He spoke little English and was unable to care for the four children.

Catholic Charities took charge. Marlo was separated from his siblings and sent to Parmadale Children's Village, an orphanage for boys in Parma, Ohio, west of Cleveland. Unlike other orphanages of the day, where boys bunked in unhealthy, crowded, unsanitary conditions, Parmadale had a wooded campus and Tudor-style cottages for the boys, believing this would be a more humane setting. The orphanage stressed vigorous outdoor activities like football, baseball, basketball, and track.

Parmadale gave Marlo structure, discipline, and three square meals a day. Its goal was to keep the boys for a short time and either return them to their homes or place them in foster homes. Unfortunately, his mother remained institutionalized, his father was still unable to care for him, and his only U.S. relatives, his cousins, reportedly were into bootlegging. After a year, Catholic Charities placed Marlo and his sister in one foster home and his two brothers elsewhere, still hoping to eventually return them to their own family. That hope soon died.

Marlo's mother was murdered at the state hospital, strangled by a fellow inmate. She was in her forties. Then his father died at the age of forty-two.

Marlo went from foster home to foster home, separated from his sister and brothers. He ended up with a family in a neighborhood of small bungalows and two family homes near 146th Street and Miles Avenue in Cleveland. He attended St. Timothy's, a Catholic school several blocks away in Garfield Heights. St. Timothy's had started a baseball team, and Marlo joined.

He'd often see Indians' center fielder Roy Weatherly around the neighborhood. Weatherly was a polished outfielder, fast and with a batting average close to .300—a good all-around player—but he was also short for a player, only five feet six inches. To Marlo, who barely reached five feet three inches after gaining his full height, Weatherly was an inspiration.

It wasn't long before Marlo started turning heads himself. He could hit. He could field. He could pitch. A St. Timothy parishioner heard about the Junior American and National Leagues and contacted Mrs. Morhard. She told her about their star shortstop, and Mrs. Morhard arranged a tryout.

Like all the boys, he played a full game at different positions. The small dark-haired boy with the big brown eyes looked unimpressive as he strode out to the mound. Then he picked up the ball and began pitching, starting right-handed. In the first inning he struck out the first three batters to face him, then switched to his left hand and struck out the next three to end the second. In the third inning he became the catcher and showed what observers called some of the finest catching they'd ever seen.

There was no question. He'd be on a team. One of the St. Timothy parishioners paid for his uniform. Other St. Timothy's players joined and went on the Little St. Louis Cardinals team.

Marlo became the leagues' leading shortstop. His natural ability set him apart from the many talented players already in the leagues. He could do everything. In the field a ball rarely got past him. He hit nearly every ball that came his way. His batting average was .600. The team had other talented players, but Mrs. Morhard said Marlo *was* the Cardinals.

By August 15, the Little Cardinals were still undefeated, well ahead of the other teams in the Junior National League. The Little Indians were atop the Junior American League standings, followed closely by the Little Senators.

Mrs. Morhard was at every game, encouraging the boys and blowing her whistle. Umpire Hal Lebovitz wondered who minded her meat store. One time she was called to the phone at the adjacent Chicken-in-a-Basket. The sheriff was at the meat market. There was a big problem. "You'll have to wait until the game is over," she told him. "Then I'll be there." He waited.

She had the meat market under control now. Business had fallen shortly after she started the Little Indians. The economy was still sketchy, but there was another factor. She'd been the face of the market—always there, asking the customers about their families, telling them stories about her life, giving them a break when money was tight. Like a beacon, she'd lured customers back after her former husband had nearly destroyed the business. But she'd turned her attention to the baseball teams.

Ed was a good butcher, but he couldn't replace her warm personality. When she wasn't there, the market was just another business. And she hadn't been there much.

But a lot had changed since then. People heard about her and the baseball leagues. They spread the word about the meat market. Frequent articles appeared in the newspapers. The boys' families mostly lived in the suburbs, and Mrs. Morhard's meat delivery business had grown like Jack's beanstalk.

The leagues were well organized now and weren't so all-consuming of her time. The games were only on Wednesdays and Sundays in the summer, and she was back to spending most of her time at her meat market. On Saturdays, she'd go in early and stay well into the evening. Plus, the children were older. Gerry was twenty-one and Junior was eleven, going on twelve. They didn't need her attention quite as much.

The economy was better too. The country began to emerge

from the Depression in the late 1930s. Concern about the war in Europe took its place. Even though the United States was not yet involved in the war, policies like "Lend-Lease," which provided military aid without compensation to help Great Britain, triggered a jolt in manufacturing. A National Bureau of Economic Research study said, "The American economy went to war starting in June 1940." Government spending on defense more than doubled through the fall of 1941.

For Cleveland's economy, this was a boon. The city's metropolitan area was an industrial behemoth, a major producer of steel, iron, tires, heavy machinery, vehicles, and parts—all needed for the war effort. Cleveland had a large, highly skilled manufacturing labor force that was producing tanks, war equipment, and conducting research into improvements for aircraft engines. Industries needed more people, and people needed food.

Hough area residents were back at work. They could afford to buy more than ground hamburger from Morhard's Meats. Many customers paid what they owed on the tabs they'd run up. She didn't need to count only on her delivery business in the Heights although that part of her business still was the most lucrative.

Mrs. Morhard had a special surprise for the boys. She turned down the lights. They waited eagerly as the fifteen-foot reel churned through the projector. Black-and-white images materialized on the white screen—in the background was the Cleveland Indians ballpark; in the foreground, letters spelling out *Mrs. Morhard's Little Indians Present "Bringing Up Baseball." Introducing the Junior Big Leagues*. It was the film the Indians made for her.

The familiar voice of Indians announcer Pinky Hunter began, "Ladies and gentlemen. Mothers and fathers everywhere. Let's watch the birth of the Little Indians or what might better be termed the birth of baseball. Here we find two young fellas in the backyard playfully playing catch. And they look like they might be pretty good little ballplayers at that . . ."

On screen Junior and Joey Phipps were shown playing catch in the Morhard backyard. Mike Albl joined in, then Allen Koenig, Billy Prior, Eddie Decker. The boys played a game of pepper—Junior batted, while the others did the fielding; then they took turns. Before long they began arguing over whose turn it was to bat. Mrs. Morhard appeared on the second-floor balcony and admonished them. They continued to fight. They all tried to grab the bat. Soon she was in the backyard, taking the bat away from them all and settling the dispute.

The film told the story of how Josephine formed and organized the boys' baseball program, how it evolved from two boys to hundreds in two leagues modeled after the majors.

Boys from all the Junior American and National Leagues teams were shown in their Major League uniforms, marching toward the camera one by one as Pinky Hunter introduced the teams. Scenes from the games showed the skilled young players, the ball fields, the bleachers full of onlookers, and the regulation backstop.

Not surprisingly, Junior made the most appearances—playing baseball in the Morhard backyard with Joey Phipps, trying on the new Little Indians uniform, and listening to Indians scout Laddie Placek give instructions on the finer points of baseball.

As the film came to an end, Mrs. Morhard tried to hide the tears welling in her eyes. The boys clapped until their hands hurt.

She told them she was going to have an even bigger surprise for them in a few weeks.

CHAPTER EIGHTEEN

Conflicts Abroad

The big story in every newspaper in America was the war in Europe. The war dominated the front pages; Bob Feller's latest heroics now were relegated to the sports pages. Junior consumed the newspaper at breakfast every morning, reading every word, wanting to know every detail of the war—and of course the Indians too.

By August 1941, France had fallen. Germany occupied Paris in the north and had installed the so-called free Vichy government in the southern portion of the country. Along with the other Axis powers, Germany had devoured nearly all of Continental Europe, Finland, and Norway. On the eastern front, troops were 230 miles from Moscow and moving in on Leningrad—Germans moving in from the south, Finland from the north.

In Western Europe, Great Britain was alone. The country had made a heroic stand against Germany in the Battle of Britain, but London had been bombed mercilessly. The war was taking a devastating toll on the island nation.

Officially the United States was still neutral, but President Roosevelt agonized over the plight of the British and the danger the relentless German aggression posed to the United States. Less attention was paid the Axis ally on the Pacific side, Japan. The president was doing all he could to help Britain, but Congress and the popular America First movement aimed at keeping the country isolationist.

German chancellor Adolph Hitler was sending out feelers

advocating a peaceful resolution while, at the same time, his troops were closing in on a key Russian industrial complex near the Black Sea. Roosevelt had seen this tactic before and wasn't fooled. Attempts at negotiation had only given Hitler time to grab more territory.

On August 15, 1941, Junior read a surprising headline: ROOSEVELT-CHURCHILL PARLEY SPURS FIGHT AGAINST AXIS: TALKS HELD ON WARSHIP.

Roosevelt and British prime minister Winston Churchill had met secretly off the coast of Newfoundland. The two leaders had been communicating regularly, but now the situation was so dire they knew they had to meet. Churchill believed the United States was his only hope of stopping the Axis powers. He needed to convince Roosevelt to enter the war, but Roosevelt's power to do so was limited.

On August 14, they issued a joint statement aboard the British battleship the HMS *Prince of Wales*, which had been involved in the sinking of the Nazi super ship *Bismarck*. The two leaders were no longer willing to talk peace with Hitler. They issued the Atlantic Charter, which firmly established U.S.-British solidarity against the Axis powers and laid out eight visionary principles for the world, assuming a victory over the German Reich and its Axis co-conspirators.

In Cleveland, a vastly different point of view thundered for attention. Aviation hero Charles Lindbergh had been in the city, railing against the "American interventionists" he believed were plotting to "create incidents and situations" that would plunge the U.S. into war under the "guise of defending America." Lindbergh had been a Nazi sympathizer early on and was a leader in the anti-war America First movement.

He was America's golden boy, the first man to fly solo across the Atlantic. When he spoke, people listened. He believed Europeans should be left to determine their own future, whatever that might be. Underlying these views, the blond, blue-eyed Lindbergh made many comments people considered anti-Semitic and racist. He believed in eugenics, a twisted outgrowth of the "survival of the fittest" concept in Darwin's theory of evolution. Eugenics encouraged "selective breeding" and discouraged reproduction by those with so-called undesirable traits. This allied with the Nazi view of creating an Aryan race. His was an extreme position, but it illustrated how divided the country was on the war.

Like Roosevelt, many Americans believed Germany and the other Axis powers endangered America and the entire free world. They were convinced the war would reach American soil if nothing was done.

However, the majority of people believed entering the war endangered America more—they feared American men would be sent off to Europe to be killed just like in World War I. They thought that the oceans on both coasts protected the United States, and the war would never reach our shores.

Junior was proud of being an American, but he worried because he had a German name. And he couldn't help but keep thinking about something he'd seen in the attic crawl space above the third floor. It was dark, and he hadn't turned on the light. He stumbled on a round object lying on the floor—an old beat-up helmet made of metal, kind of an olive-brown color with a long pointed spike on top. It was the Pickelhaube helmet his father had worn in the German army. Next to the helmet, jumbled together in a pile, was a bunch of medals, all different shapes and sizes, hanging from ribbons. He picked them up one by one—staring at the green-and-white and red-and-blue ribbons, studying the German inscriptions even though he had no idea what they meant. He recognized the German Iron Cross. One medal looked like a wreath with a figure inside; others were round or oval and gold or silver. Another was a sharpshooter medal.

Thinking about the helmet and medals clearly disturbed him, making him keenly aware of his father's German heritage, a heritage that now made him uneasy.

The kids at school and on the baseball teams knew his father was German, but they never said anything. It bothered him anyway. He wondered what they really thought, especially Jewish kids like Duke Green.

Duke was one of Junior's best friends. He wasn't on the baseball team, but they'd known each other since kindergarten. He lived a few blocks over on Fenwick Road. Junior and Duke, whose real name was Donald, rode bikes and played tag in summer and pelted each other with snowballs in winter. Both boys were swift runners and loved to race to see who was fastest.

An English boy, Tony Steele, had recently come to live with the Green family and joined Duke and Junior in their escapades. He was one of thousands of children who evacuated from Britain to go to the United States and the British Commonwealth countries. After the fall of France, it seemed certain Germany would invade Britain next. Parents wanted to get their children to a safe haven. Others saw sending children abroad as a way to ensure Britain's survival.

Tony's parents had an even greater reason for sending him to the United States. He was Jewish. Although reports of Nazi persecution had been overshadowed in American newspapers by the war, atrocities against Jews were becoming clear. On November 9, 1938, on the deadly Kristallnacht—the Night of Broken Glass—Jews throughout Nazi Germany were murdered, their synagogues burned, shops destroyed, and thousands arrested. The 1935 Nuremberg Laws had excluded Jews from citizenship in the German Reich; Jewish businesses were taken over by "Aryans" who bought them at bargain prices; Jews were barred from public schools and universities. Now, in 1941, Jews were forced to wear badges with yellow Stars of David on their chests. They were forbidden from leaving the country.

Tony's family worried that the same could happen in Britain. He would be safe in America, but sending him away had been a wrenching decision. Several organizations had been set up to relocate British children. He'd be sent across the ocean to a family he didn't know, with no idea when or if he'd come back or what he'd come back to. Luckily, Tony ended up with the Green family.

Junior thought about his German father, how he'd choked his mother and gone after her with a butcher knife. Germany was attacking other countries like his father had attacked his mother. German Nazis were taking over free countries and slaughtering and persecuting Jews all over Europe. Tony had to leave his English family because of them.

Junior didn't like being part German.

Mrs. Morhard, too, was troubled about the unfolding world events.

The Germans and their Axis accomplices menaced the entire world. The war was affecting the families of people she knew, and possibly members of her own extended family.

University Heights had a large Jewish population, and many of her friends and neighbors were fearful for relatives in Europe. She was horrified by their stories of atrocities toward Jews.

Germany now occupied nearly all of Western Europe, including France, where her father's extended family lived. Her maternal grandparents were from Wales, and Great Britain was under siege. In the German blitzkrieg of London, more than a million homes were destroyed or damaged; forty thousand civilians were killed.

She wanted to find a way to help. Maybe again baseball could offer the answer.

As Cleveland's factories pumped out war supplies, baseball was back on the front pages. It offered an escape from the gruesome news of the war.

It was July 16 and the New York Yankees were in town. They'd dumped the Indians from first place in the American League and now were six games ahead. But that wasn't what had people talking. Yankee superstar Joe DiMaggio was in the midst of his record-setting fifty-five-game hitting streak. The Indians' third baseman, Ken Keltner, had nearly stopped the streak at seventeen back in June. In that game, Joltin' Joe had one hit, and it was off Keltner. Keltner thought he should have made the catch and vowed it wouldn't happen again. Fans wanted to see the matchup.

The two teams played the first game in League Park. DiMaggio got a hit in the first inning, extending his streak to fifty-six games. Keltner wasn't involved.

The next day a record nighttime crowd of 67,468 jammed into Cleveland Stadium for the second game of the series.

In his first at-bat, DiMaggio whacked a line drive deep down the third baseline. Keltner, standing way behind third base and almost into left field, snatched it and tossed to first for the out. Later in the game, DiMaggio smashed another long line drive to practically the same place. Again Keltner was in the right spot, grabbed it, and backhanded it to first. He'd

robbed DiMaggio of two sure doubles. DiMaggio only managed a walk in the game. The record-breaking streak had ended.

Unfortunately, despite Keltner's heroics, the Indians lost
both games.

The team continued its slide into August. On August 15,
Chubby Dean, a distant cousin of superstar pitchers Dizzy and
Daffy Dean, made an inauspicious debut in a game against the
St. Louis Browns. The Indians were ahead 3–2, when a cloud-
burst in the sixth inning delayed the game for an hour and
twenty minutes.

Bob Feller replaced Dean after the delay and gave up a run
that tied the game 3–3. The last four innings were played on a
"field that oozed mud ankle deep and sent water flying head-
high with every step taken by the outfielders." The game mer-
cifully ended in the tenth inning, still tied. The Indians hadn't
gained any traction in the standings.

Back in University Heights, the Little Indians and Little Senators were still battling for the Junior American League lead.
The Little Cardinals remained undefeated in the other league.
The last regular games of the season would be on Sunday, September 14.

In her role as the leagues' "commissioner," Mrs. Morhard
had been making grand plans for the end of the season. Now
that there were the two leagues, there would be playoffs. Following the playoffs, she planned to have a Little World Series!
The 1941 season would end with a smash.

The Little World Series would be a welcome escape from
the bad news overseas. And it could be more than that—it
could help the struggling people in Britain. Americans had just
been through the financial turmoil of the Depression. She
knew hardship well. But neither she nor other Americans had
experienced devastation like Britain and other European countries had undergone at the hands of Germany. Great Britain
now was standing alone.

As a member of the University Heights Women's Club,
she'd worked on many community projects and had contacts
with women from other organizations. One of them seemed
perfect—Young America Wants to Help, the Junior Division of
the British Relief Society. The charity provided clothing to

children affected by the war in England, Wales, Scotland, and Northern Ireland.

She'd been charging a small admissions fee to the regular games to help offset the costs. She could help people suffering from the war instead. Proceeds from the Little World Series would go to Young America Wants to Help. It would be children helping children.

She asked Cleveland Indians owner Alva Bradley for the ultimate favor. The big league club would be on a road trip in late September, about the time she wanted to hold the Little World Series. She wanted to know if she could hold the Little World Series on the Indians own home field, League Park.

Mrs. Morhard was a good salesperson; Bradley said yes. The Little Indians had become like an extension of his own teams. His two Rogers nephews, Brad and Ed, were on a team—so were the sons of manager Peckinpaugh and some of the players. These kids were playing really amazing baseball for their ages. They'd learned from the Indians' own scouts and players. Mrs. Morhard's leagues were a great training ground. Some of the boys might become pro baseball players in the future. A bunch of boys in mini-Indians garb was a public relations boon. It was a win for him in every way.

On Sunday, September 21, 1941, twelve hundred people gathered at the league diamonds for the Junior American and National League playoffs, one of Mrs. Morhard's now-famous ox roasts, and a warm-up to the Little World Series. On the field huge tables were set up outside the first and third baselines so people could watch the games while they were eating. Indians players Bob Feller, Mel Harder, Lou Boudreau, Ray Mack, and Roy Weatherly mingled with the crowd and watched the action on the field.

First, the teams that finished 1-2 in each league played each other. The Little Indians defeated the second place Little White Sox in the Junior American League; the Little Cardinals beat their rivals for the Junior National League lead, the Little Reds.

In the next game, the winners in each league played one another in an exhibition game that was a prelude to the Little World Series, which would be a single game at League Park. University Heights mayor Bill Aurelius threw out the first pitch. In a pitchers duel, the Little Indians defeated the Little Cards 2–1. Little Indians pitcher Jackie Heinen wowed the on-lookers, striking out twelve and only allowing two hits. Little Indian Allen Koenig was the game's leading batter, going 3-for-3. On the losing team, Little Cardinals' Marlo Termini stole three bases and smashed two hits.

But the biggest game was yet to come.

The next Sunday, September 28, would be the actual Little World Series championship game, and the young players would have the thrill of their lives! They would be playing in League Park, where the Major League Cleveland Indians and pro-football Cleveland Rams played! The big league Cleveland and St. Louis baseball teams wouldn't be in the real World Series—the Yankees and Giants would claim the 1941 pennants—but their young counterparts were!

All the players and their families were invited to come, free of charge, whether or not their team was on the field.

Mrs. Morhard and Mrs. Frank Hornickle, chairman of the Cleveland Committee of Young America Wants to Help had teamed up to sell as many tickets as possible. To attend the Little World Series, it would cost 25 cents for children under fourteen, 50 cents for adults, and a dollar for reserved box seats. In addition to selling tickets through their own organizations, they arranged to have them sold at major Cleveland downtown retailers, including the May Company, William Taylor Son & Company Department Store, Bond Clothing, and Rosenblum's.

Mrs. Morhard knew how much it would mean to the boys to play in League Park—what an inspiration it would be. For everyone else, it would be wonderful to see these young boys playing like the pros whose uniforms they wore—and it would even do its tiny bit to help the war effort.

CHAPTER NINETEEN

The Little World Series

Mrs. Morhard's Junior Leagues were in the news all across the country. At the tip of Florida, fifteen hundred miles from Cleveland, people read about Mrs. Morhard's Junior Baseball Leagues in the *Key West Citizen*, right under the Sports section's main headline CARDS KNOCKED OFF TOP; YANKS CLAIM AL FLAG. The International News Service (INS) and Associated Press (AP) syndicated feature stories that popped up in cities across the county from Gallup, New Mexico; to Madison, Wisconsin; to Biddeford, Maine; and everywhere in between. A September 1941 AP feature by Douglas Dies began:

> Cleveland, Sept. 6—Sandlot baseball wears
> major league pants in suburban University
> Heights, home of the Junior American and
> National Baseball Leagues, Inc. On two regu-
> lation diamonds, 170 boys between the ages of
> 10 and 14 wear uniforms copied from nine
> major league teams and play a brand of base-
> ball far beyond your expectations.

The story went on to praise "a batter hitting .714" and "an ambidextrous pitcher who bats .600."

The .714 hitter was Albert's nemesis who'd hoisted his clothes up the flagpole, Wayne Wiggins of the Little Chicago White Sox, a team that boasted seven .400 hitters as well. The ambidextrous pitcher with the high batting average was the

Little Cardinals' Marlo Termini. Also lauded were the Little Indians' Dick Kusa—who'd struck out seventeen of the hard-hitting White Sox in his last outing—Jackie Heinen, the hard-throwing son of Josephine's friend and grocery market competitor, Joe Heinen, and Raymond Lindquist, the Little Yankee shortstop who was the son of William Lindquist, a former pitcher in the St. Louis Cardinals farm system.

Mrs. Morhard's original idea of starting a baseball team to help her son was becoming a national phenomenon.

The day had finally come. It was Sunday, September 28—the day of the Little World Series championship game.

It was a glorious day for a ball game. The temperature was an unseasonably high 84 degrees. The hot sun burned bright in a cloudless Robin's-egg blue sky, shining its luminous spotlight over the ballpark.

Boys from all the teams stepped down from the East 66th Street trolleys or exited cars that pulled up in front of the ballpark, their faces glowing, their uniforms newly cleaned, laughing, and chatting among themselves, accompanied by moms and dads, brothers and sisters, aunts and uncles, grandparents and friends. Some headed for the dugouts; others joined fans and baseball aficionados in the stands. In Mrs. Morhard's brand of baseball, everyone participated in one way or another.

There would be a doubleheader—the first game between the runners-up, the Little Chicago White Sox and the Little Cincinnati Reds. Then the main event, the Little World Series championship game between the Junior National League Little St. Louis Cardinals and the Junior American League Little Cleveland Indians.

The winning team would be hailed as the Little World Series champion and get an impressive $50 Championship trophy. It was about two feet tall and featured a baseball player holding a bat atop a wooden base. Individual members of the winning teams would get medals. The runner-up and winner of the preliminary game would also get prizes.

The ceremony began with great fanfare. The Parmadale orphanage band played "Take Me Out to the Ball Game" as the players marched proudly onto the field in step to the music. The crowd stood up to cheer. The American flag was raised, the band played the national anthem, and everyone recited the Pledge of Allegiance, hands over their hearts. Cleveland mayor Edward Blythin stood near the pitcher's mound to welcome everyone and introduce each player individually. More cheers. Then it was time to play ball.

University Heights mayor Earl Aurelius threw out the first pitch. Cleveland WHK radio announcer Duke Lidyard called the plays.

The Little White Sox won the five-inning preliminary game over the Little Cincinnati Reds by a score of 8–5.

Then it was time for the game everyone had come to see. Junior and the rest of the Little Indians were in the Indians' home team dugout. The Little Cardinals had the visiting team dugout. The teams would play seven innings like they had during the season.

It was the biggest game of Junior's young life. He was playing in the Little World Series championship in League Park— the same place where Babe Ruth belted his five hundredth home run, where Joe DiMaggio cracked records by hitting safely in his fifty-sixth straight game, and Junior's hero Bob Feller was pitching his way to Cooperstown.

He'd been here many times to watch the Indians play, sitting in the green wooden seats. Now, Junior stood at home plate, waiting for the next pitch. It was the first inning. The count was 1 and 2.

To Junior, the ballpark looked much different from the field— bigger, much bigger, and a bit intimidating. The green roof way above him reached more than halfway around the field, its huge metallic arms shielding the occupants of the endless rows of double-decker stands from any rain and gusty winds that might blow in from Cleveland's Great Lake. The faces in the ballpark crowd looked like tiny pebbles in wide hats, white shirts, and colorful blouses.

Junior was a speck in the cavernous space, but he felt bigger as he stood in the same spot where Jeff Heath, Hal Trosky, and Earl Averill usually waited for their next pitch, facing the mound where Bob Feller notched his 260th strikeout. It was pretty awesome.

Straight ahead of him, looking like it was a mile away, stood a massive scoreboard. It was actually 460 feet away in the deepest part of the ballpark. Two sets of bleachers rose to its left. To the right, a 48-foot-high wall of concrete topped with chicken wire stretched along busy Lexington Avenue all the way to the right field foul pole. The wall was the Indians' answer to Fenway Park's Green Monster—and it helped neutralize the short 290-foot distance from home plate, necessitated by the tight checkerboard of streets that surrounded the ballpark. Kids stood outside the wall, hoping to grab any balls that went over.

The base path was perfectly sculpted through a carpet of green grass that was graded from the outer edges of the infield up to the pitcher's mound like the ice cream on the top of a cone. As nice as the University Heights ball fields were, they had dirt infields, nothing like this.

Junior came up after Joey Phipps, who grounded out. There were already two outs in the inning. Junior looked squarely at Jim Fronek, the Little Cardinals' pitcher. He was ready, his knees slightly bent, his left foot about a foot in front of the right, his two hands clutching the bat near the knob, his left arm straight to give him leverage, just the way he'd been taught. He wanted a hit, badly.

The pitching mound rose so high Fronek looked like he was on a pedestal. He started his windup, his second and third fingers on top of the ball, his thumb and other fingers grasping it on the sides. Junior knew Fronek had a wicked fastball, and he was doing his best to be prepared. The spinning ball blazed toward him. Junior was sure it was high and held his bat steady, but the home plate umpire called, "Strike three."

It was Tony Pianowski, the ump whose strike call had angered Junior so much he screamed and walked off the Little Indians field a few years before. Junior's eyes widened and he looked up at the ump quizzically, convinced the ball was outside the strike zone, but he let it go. The inning was over.

Disappointed, he walked slowly back toward the dugout, his forehead crinkled into a frown, his head down.

In the Little Indians home team dugout, Mrs. Morhard was watching, looking like a middle-aged Joan of Arc commanding her troops, only with a silver whistle instead of a sword. She said nothing as Junior passed by on his way to the infield. She'd been pumped for him to get a hit, but she was pleased with the way he'd handled himself. She could tell by the look on his face that he thought the ump should have called a ball, but he accepted it. Baseball had helped him mature.

Junior was eleven, almost twelve now, still younger than almost everyone in the starting lineup. He was playing second base. Dave Erickson was at first base, Jackie Heinen at third, Allen Koenig at shortstop, Ed Rogers in center field, Ray Thompson in left, Joey Phipps in right field. Dick Kusa was pitching and Ronnie Barth was catching.

By the top of the fourth, there were no hits, no runs. It was a pitchers' duel. The Little Cards pitcher, Jim Fronek, was up first. Kusa fired the ball. Fronek walloped it into left center for a single, the first hit of the game. Not to be outdone, the third baseman Novak hit a double to bring Fronek home. The Little Cards went ahead 1–0. Kusa composed himself and got the next three batters out with two strikeouts and a groundout to Junior.

In the bottom of the fourth, the first Little Indian at bat, Jackie Heinen, walked. Then Allen Koenig came to the plate. While Fronek was in the middle of his windup, Heinen stole second. Fronek threw Koenig a curveball. A strike. He fired again, this time hurling a fierce fastball. The ball ripped through the air, wildly. Smack. It hit Koenig instead of the strike zone. Koenig dropped to his knees, holding his forehead; his eyes scrunched tight, his bat crashing down on home plate. Ooohs came from the crowd. Players rushed toward him. Mrs. Morhard headed for the field. Before she got there, Koenig was up, trotting to first base, still holding his head but with a smile on his face.

Ray Thompson was next to bat, then Dave Erickson. It wasn't a good inning defensively for the Little Cards. Their two best players, Termini and Novak, made errors, allowing Heinen and Koenig to score. It was now 2–1 in favor of the Little Indians even though Fronek had yet to give up a hit.

In the fifth the Little Cards went crazy. Novak and Termini hit safely, Englehart walked, and Kerrigan singled. Three runs came in. Suddenly the Little Cards had the lead 4–2.

The Little Indians were out one-two-three in the bottom of the fifth, but the defense did its part to keep the Little Cards from scoring in the top of the sixth. Allen Koenig made a great

play, backhanding the ball and throwing it way across the infield for an out. Ronnie Barth avoided a catastrophe when he
chased a passed ball that went back across the track to the concrete wall. He threw off his facemask and hustled to grab the
ball before the base runner got farther than first base.

Junior was up again in the bottom of the sixth. The Little Indians were still down 4–2. Again Fronek hurled his smoldering
fastball. This time it looked like it might be hittable. Junior
swung at it with every ounce of muscle he had, aiming for the
hole in left field. But there was no crack of ball against bat,
only the smack of the ball hitting the catcher's mitt as the ball
whizzed by. He'd done his part in the field, making an out and
a couple of assists, but he still didn't have a hit. He wasn't
alone; neither did any of his usually hard-hitting teammates.
Jim Fronek was doing his best imitation of Indians' resident
pitching ace Bob Feller. He was pitching a no-hitter. With only
one inning to go, it was looking like the Little Cardinals were
unbeatable.

As the game headed to the last inning, Mrs. Morhard checked
her scorecard. A couple of boys on the Little Indians hadn't
played yet, and the league rule stated that every boy must have
a chance to play. She needed to juggle the Little Indians lineup.
Jackie Heinen would be the new pitcher, replacing Dick Kusa,
who would move to left field. Ray Thompson would move
from left field to third base, replacing Heinen. Billy Spero
would take over for Ronnie Barth at catcher. Eggers would replace Ed Rogers in center field. Ed's younger brother Brad
would come in to replace Phipps in right. She'd bring in La-
Pine as a pinch hitter or runner at some point.

She blew her whistle and headed across the field as quickly
as her high-heeled shoes would allow, heading for the Little
Cardinals dugout. The Cards needed to get all their players in
the game too. She told the manager that any boy who hadn't
played yet needed to go in. The Little Cardinals manager argued, then became angry when she wouldn't budge, yelling,
pointing to his team and crying out. That meant he'd need to
take out his best players. Mrs. Morhard insisted. It was the
league rule. All the boys needed to play, whatever the circum-
stances. Winning wasn't the only thing that mattered.

Grudgingly, the Cards decided to pull center fielder Donaldson and right fielder Holicky, replacing them with Matejka and Elwell. There was no way he'd take out Fronek and deny him a no-hitter—or Termini, who'd stolen a base, had a hit, scored a run, and was indispensable at shortstop—or third baseman Novak, who'd managed a hit nearly every time he was at bat.

Junior was embarrassed that his mother had made such a scene. He hoped she wasn't doing this to help his team win. He put it out of his mind to focus on the final inning. He wanted to win this game the right way. So did his teammates.

Mrs. Morhard had no second thoughts. She hustled back across the field to the home team dugout, undeterred. Both teams had the same rules, and she made sure all the boys on the Little Indians were playing too. She watched her Little Indians head to the field. The seventh inning—the final inning—was about to begin.

Fronek was up for the Little Cards. The new Little Indians pitcher, Jackie Heinen, hurled a fastball for a strike, then flicked his wrist and threw a curveball. It sailed in, but not quite the way Heinen wanted. Fronek walloped it for a double into far center field. It looked like he was trying to cement the victory by himself. Matejka followed and was quickly out on strikes. Third baseman Novak singled and Fronek scored to make it 5–2. The Little Indians looked doomed.

Junior and his teammates made their way to the dugout. It was their last chance. Jackie Heinen was up first. A ball, a strike, a ball, a ball, a ball. Heinen headed to first base.

Ray Thompson headed to the batter's box. Fronek's fastball shot by for a strike. Thompson patiently waited for the next pitch. It came in right where he wanted it. He smashed the ball into shallow left field. Cards second baseman Englehart missed the catch but grabbed it, bobbled it, then tried to get Heinen out at second. Heinen was safe. Englehart was charged with an error. Next up, Erickson grounded out. Spero flied out. But they were beginning to get some wood on the ball.

Dick Kusa, now the left fielder, smacked a double. Heinen and Thompson scored. The Little Indians were only a run be-hind. Things were looking up. The momentum had changed. The Little Cards' pitcher who'd dominated the first six innings appeared to be tiring. Mrs. Morhard put LaPine in to pinch hit for Eggers. He walked. . . . With Kusa on second and LaPine at first base Koenig sauntered to the batters' box. He'd scored once after being beaned and had made some great plays at shortstop. With two outs and two on, it was up to him. The rest of the Little Indians knew what a gutsy player he was and were counting on him. They were all standing, leaning over the dugout fence, cheering him on—Mrs. Morhard in the center, surrounded by the boys.

He set himself for the pitch, giving Fronek a cheeky squinty-eyed stare. Fronek took his time and unloaded his first pitch. A strike on the inside left corner. Fronek wound up again. Another fastball for a strike. The count was 0 and 2. There was silence in both dugouts. Fronek started his windup. The ball flew out of his hand, and thwack, Koenig launched the ball into shallow left center field past Matejka, the Cards' substitute center fielder. Matejka grabbed the ball on a bounce, bobbled it, picked it up again, and threw toward third base, over the head of Cards' regular third baseman Novak, landing on the track. Novak hustled to grab it, but Kusa was already rounding third base on the way home, with LaPine close behind him, Koenig touching the bag at second as Novak hurled the ball toward home. But it was too late. Kusa and LaPine scored, making it 6–5 in favor of the Little Indians. They had won the Little World Series!

The Little Indians rushed out of the dugout, beaming, smiling, hands high in the air, caps falling off their heads. They crowded around the game winners, saving their heartiest cheers for Koenig, the former bully, who'd won the game.

Mrs. Morhard tried to contain her happiness. After all, she ran the whole league not just the Little Indians, but the smile on her face said it all. Her first team, the one Junior was on, had won the Little World Series! She rushed over to congratulate each one, then hustled to the Little Cards dugout to praise them for a great game. Their manager was still miffed about having to replace some of his best players in the last inning, but the boys were happy to see her. She brought them out onto the middle of the field and had the Little Indians join them.

Umpires Hal Lebowitz, Tony Pianaowski, and Paul Kvetko brought out three trophies—one for the Little Indians as Little World Series champs, one for the runner-up Little Cardinals, and one for the winner of the earlier game between runners-up in each league, the Little White Sox. She motioned to the players from all the other teams to come down from the stands and join her on the field to hearty applause from the crowd.

As she looked at the boys and the vast ballpark, she felt an enormous surge of pride. These boys had played in League Park, in League Park! It still seemed surreal. She'd done this, all this! For her boy. For her boys.

It was over for another year. She was busy once again with the market, but she missed the boys and the games. Her boys' baseball leagues weren't forgotten, even in the off-season. She got calls from people all over the United States who'd seen newspaper stories about the leagues and the Little World Series. They wanted to know how to get boys' baseball leagues started in their own communities. Mrs. Morhard gave the callers as much information as she could and sent out copies of the film.

One of the calls to Mrs. Morhard was from a man in Williamsport, Pennsylvania. He wanted to know more about her leagues. His name was Carl Stotz. He had no sons of his own but a couple of young nephews who liked baseball.

When he was a boy himself, Carl had a dream that when he grew up, he'd "have a baseball team for boys, complete with uniforms and equipment." Now an adult, married with a daughter, he'd often stop by his sister's house to play ball with his nephews in their backyard. He wanted to make that long-ago dream come true.

Playing ball with his nephews got him thinking about starting boys' teams that could play one another. He got some of his nephews' neighborhood friends and boys from a local church together and split them into teams.

His boys first played in the summer of 1939 on a "sandlot" with a dilapidated wood and wire mesh backstop. The left field and center field sloped away from the infield and home plate directly faced the setting sun. He made the bases himself. He was working on adapting the field to suit the boys. He named his program "Little League."

Josephine by now had hundreds of boys in her incorporated Junior American and National Leagues, close ties with the

Cleveland Indians, professional baseball instructors and umpires, two beautiful fields with backstops and bleachers, uniforms modeled on the big league teams and bats, balls, gloves,
and catcher's mitts for all the teams. She'd held a Little World
Series championship in a Major League ballpark. Stotz wanted
to know more.

Mrs. Morhard was on the phone for a long time, telling him
everything she could about her Junior American and National
Leagues. When she hung up, she said to Junior, "A man from
Williamsport, Pennsylvania, wants to see our film." She sent it.

She was way ahead of Williamsport, but the fledgling Williamsport teams had one thing she lacked. Mrs. Morhard under-
wrote her leagues with fund-raisers and her own pocketbook.
Each of Stotz's teams had a sponsor, the small local businesses
Lycoming Dairy, Lundy Lumber, and Jumbo Pretzel.

The year 1941 had been great for her baseball leagues. An October 3 headline in the *Heights Press* proclaimed WE CON-
GRATULATE YOU, MRS. MORHARD. It went on to praise her for
her "splendid" job of organizing the leagues, for taking kids'
baseball off the streets, for giving sandlot baseball a more
"classy" touch, and for providing so many happy times for the
kids and the grown-ups.

More than thirty-six thousand people had watched the
games at the Cedar Center fields in 1941. Mrs. Morhard promised that next season would be even better.

Two months later, on December 7, 1941, the Japanese
bombed Pearl Harbor.

IV: THE FINAL INNING

*I went over to the fields the other day and just
sat there looking at them and remembering all they
had meant to the boys and me. I couldn't help it. I
had a good cry.*
—MRS. JOSEPHINE MORHARD,
as quoted in "Mother's Idea Started
Junior Ball Leagues" by Margaret Suhr Reed,
Cleveland Plain Dealer, September 22, 1941

CHAPTER TWENTY

Wartime Brings the End

Overnight, the country changed. War was now a cruel reality. The lingering vise of the Depression had been eclipsed by a more deadly opponent. The suddenness of the attack on Pearl Harbor aroused America, crushing the idea of its impregnability and fostering a patriotic resurgence. The fierce opposition to the military draft melted away. Millions of young Americans enlisted. Cleveland recruiting offices were jammed. The day after the Pearl Harbor attack, Cleveland's army office processed nearly three hundred applications, up from the norm of twenty-five to thirty. The navy recruiting office kept its doors open twenty-four hours a day, seven days a week.

The Cleveland Indians' Bob Feller was one of the first to sign up. He recalled what he did when he heard about the attack on Pearl Harbor in an article he wrote for the U.S. Navy magazine *Proceedings*. He said he was driving to Chicago to talk about his 1942 contract with the Indians when he heard the news, and it made him "angry as hell." He knew he had to enlist right then even though he was one of the best, if not the best, pitcher in the Majors, with a record of 107-54 and a draft exemption.

When he met the Indians' Cy Slapnicka, the talk was not about his contract; Feller told him he'd decided to enlist in the navy. He put in a call to an old friend, former heavyweight boxing champ Gene Tunney, who managed the navy's physical training program, and on December 9, 1941, he was sworn in.

Feller gave up a $100,000 contract to enlist in the navy. His initial assignment was playing baseball to entertain the troops. He wanted to do something more meaningful, so he enrolled in gunnery school and spent twenty-six months as chief petty officer aboard the USS *Alabama*, where he saw combat in the Marshall Islands and elsewhere in the Pacific.

Other Major Leaguers followed his example. Baseball was losing many of its best players, including Hall of Famers. Hank Greenberg was 1940's Most Valuable Player, but he, too, was drafted. He was honorably discharged but re-enlisted and eventually served with a B-29 bomber unit. Ted Williams enlisted in the navy in May 1942, became a second lieutenant and a marine fighter pilot, setting records for aerial gunnery. Warren Spahn fought in the Battle of the Bulge after pitching just one Major League game. Yogi Berra was a Minor Leaguer for the Norfolk Tars with a .396 batting average when he was drafted. He became a gunner's mate and volunteered for the special mission piloting the rocket boats that led the landing craft on D-day.

Team owners scrambled to find replacements for the hundreds of Major and Minor League players they lost. When New York Giants manager Leo Durocher found he had only two regulars left on the team, he put himself in the lineup. A forty-six-year-old named Hod Lisanbee pitched for the Cincinnati Reds. Former prisoner of war Bert Shepard, who had an artificial leg, pitched for the Brooklyn Dodgers. One-armed outfielder Pete Gray was a St. Louis Brown. Former Red Sox slugger Jimmy Foxx came out of retirement to play for the Philadelphia Phillies. Women had an opportunity to play pro ball when Phillip K. Wrigley founded the All-American Girls Professional Baseball League.

Many players not eligible for the draft took part-time jobs in defense industries in addition to playing baseball, including stars like Mel Harder and Enos Slaughter.

In Cleveland, throngs of other young men departed for military training centers from Cleveland's Union Terminal. People bought War Bonds to help pay for the war. Air raid sirens blared and families dutifully turned off lights and appliances so no light would be visible to an approaching enemy.

Well-known businessman Earle L. Johnson shocked Cleveland into realizing an enemy invasion could happen here despite its seemingly secure inland location. A pilot, he loaded up his plane with huge one-hundred-pound sacks of flour, then flew over the city and "bombed" Cleveland's abundance of factories, coating huge swaths of the city whiter than a blizzard, clearly illustrating the destruction that could fall on the city. It created a near panic.

The war became even more personal for Mrs. Morhard and her family. Gerry was happily engaged to a young stockbroker whose darkly handsome looks reminded people of Hollywood matinee idol Tyrone Power. His name was Ralph DeRosa, and he was thoughtful, considerate, and very much in love with Gerry. Mrs. Morhard heartily approved. He was the kind of man Mrs. Morhard hoped her daughter would marry.

Pearl Harbor abruptly changed their plans.

On the advice of a colleague, Ralph had joined the army's 107th Cavalry reserve unit, mainly seeking networking opportunities to attract clients. The unit drilled just once a month at an armory in Shaker Heights.

After Pearl Harbor, the 107th was called to active duty and sent to Fort Ord, California, on December 23, 1941.

Like many couples facing the uncertainty of the war, Gerry and Ralph decided to get married whenever and wherever it was possible. In late March 1942, Gerry and a friend Carmen McNutt, whose husband was also stationed at Fort Ord, set out in Carmen's car for the weeklong drive to California. At 4:00 p.m. on April 4, Gerry and Ralph were married at St. Mary's Episcopal Church in Pacific Grove, near Fort Ord.

The United States was losing the war in the Pacific. The Philippines fell to the Japanese. Corregidor was evacuated. In the Bataan Death March, the Japanese forced sixty-six thousand Filipinos and ten thousand American soldiers to walk sixty-five miles with no food or water in temperatures over 100 degrees, enduring frequent beatings.

Fear of invasion gripped the Pacific Coast. Ralph's unit patrolled the California coast from San Francisco to Carmel, searching for signs of an impending Japanese invasion. The newlyweds began their lives together in Carmel, fearful the scenic coastal town might soon be a target for a relentless Japan.

The war affected all Americans. People knew they needed to sacrifice if the Allies were to be victorious. Japan controlled the Dutch East Indies (now Indonesia), the world's main rubber-producing region, creating a severe shortage of rubber for the Allies. Auto companies stopped making new cars. Tires were rationed, scrap rubber drives held, and people were encouraged to cut out unnecessary driving to save wear and tear, buy retreads when necessary, and drive no faster than 35 miles per hour.

In May 1942, the U.S. Office of Price Administration issued War Ration Card Number One, called the *Sugar Book,* to every American family, limiting the amount of sugar they could buy. Sugar seemed an unlikely item to be rationed, but the military wanted its soldiers to have chocolate bars and chewing gum in their K rations. Sugarcane was also needed to produce gunpowder, dynamite, and other chemical products.

Gasoline was rationed in the eastern states, though not yet in Ohio.

Manufacturing jobs were again plentiful, but small stores selling items like radios and phonographs lost their businesses as production shifted from consumer products to military supplies.

Mrs. Morhard worried about her daughter and new son-in-law, but they were over twenty-five hundred miles away and she could do little. She found out one of her players who'd aged out of the Junior Leagues, Little St. Louis Cardinals star Marlo Termini, had been drafted into the U.S. Army before he'd even finished high school.

At home, her concerns about Junior had faded. He was now twelve. The tantrums were long gone. He'd graduated from Canterbury Elementary School in January 1942 and begun seventh grade at Roxboro Junior High in Cleveland Heights. Every weekday he walked a mile to the streetcar, which took him to school, then back for the long walk home. He had lots of friends, his grades were okay, and he always got his homework done. His teachers told her he could do better with his schoolwork but he was quiet in class, well behaved, paid attention, and showed a great interest in history and civics. His favorite class, still, was gym.

Despite the war, or perhaps partly because of it, the market was busier than ever. Mrs. Morhard could still get the meat she needed; so could her customers. People had jobs and money in their pockets. Relief expenditures were the lowest in ten years.

Cleveland again was an industrial powerhouse. Factories were smoking as they geared up for war. General Motors and the other auto companies had stopped making new cars and shifted manufacturing to producing diesel engines for warships, tanks, military trucks, aircraft parts, and other military equipment. Other companies switched from making consumer products to war materials—a vacuum cleaner company began producing machine gun mounts, a manufacturer of beer coolers now made artillery shells.

The improved economy helped Morhard's Meats' bottom line, but there were other reasons too. Mrs. Morhard had made lots of connections. People on the East side of Cleveland, the Heights communities, and beyond knew about her from the baseball leagues. Thousands had attended her ox roast fund-raisers, which unintentionally advertised the meat she sold. Mayor Aurelius asked her to organize a major community-wide party at City Hall, which attracted over one thousand people. Her Hough Avenue store was thriving; her delivery service was faring even better.

As busy as she was, she missed baseball and the boys. There'd been talk of suspending Major League baseball during the war, and she questioned what she should do the next summer.

On behalf of the Major Leagues, Baseball commissioner Landis wrote President Roosevelt asking his opinion. Roosevelt replied, "I honestly feel that it would be best for the country to keep baseball going. There will be fewer people unemployed and everybody will work longer hours and harder than ever before. And that means they ought to have a chance for recreation and for taking their minds off their work even more than before."

Mrs. Morhard was happy with Judge Landis's decision to move forward despite so many big leaguers signing up to go to war. She went ahead, too, vigorously planning for the 1942 season of the Junior American and National Leagues, Inc. Maybe boys' baseball would bring a small sense of normalcy back.

It was the evening of the Fourth of July, 1942. The warm wind swirled in from Lake Erie across the open end of Cleveland Municipal Stadium into the upper deck where Mrs. Morhard and Junior settled into their wooden seats. They were there to watch the biggest Fourth of July celebration in years, the Festival of Freedom.

More than a hundred thousand people crowded into the stands to see the patriotic spectacular. There was music with film and Broadway star Rosemary Lane, a full orchestra, choruses, and a sing-along. A historical pageant wowed the crowd and, as darkness enveloped the city, the sky exploded with an extravagant fireworks display. Somehow, coming together on the anniversary of the heroic day when the U.S. declared its independence lifted spirits and inspired confidence that the United States would once again be victorious.

It was an unforgettable evening for the two of them. For Josephine Morhard, it provided a few hours when she could relax, celebrate, and give Junior a treat in the middle of a very full, hectic weekend.

She'd closed the market for the holiday and was heavily involved in the Fourth of July festivities in University Heights, which, like most communities, had amped up its celebration this year. The day started with a firebomb display. At 11:00 a.m. Josephine took Junior to watch the parade. The civilian defense corps, police and fire departments, Red Cross, and the Cleveland Heights high school band marched from Visconsi's shopping center to the Fairmount Theater. The theater was showing the war films *Mister Gardenia*, *Lake Carriers*, *Tanks*, *Safeguarding Military Information*, and *Wings of Steel*, and everyone could get in free. Before the films, the district's U.S. congresswoman Frances Bolton addressed the crowd.

The two of them skipped the films to get ready for Mrs. Morhard's contribution to the celebration: four baseball games on the two diamonds at University Square—the new name for the area. Boys were already gathering for the games—two on each field—the Little Browns vs. the Little Senators, Little

Yankees vs. Little White Sox, Little Pirates vs. Little Cardinals, and Little Reds against the Little Dodgers.

At 1:00 p.m., the boys lined up; one of them raised the flag
and everyone recited the Pledge of Allegiance and sang "The
Star Spangled Banner." Then the games began. The Little Indians had a game elsewhere, in Chagrin Falls with a new team
that had formed there. Mrs. Morhard had set it up in the hope
of getting the team to come into her Junior Baseball Leagues.

She had even bigger plans for Sunday, the fifth of July. It
was Dad's Day at the Little Indians ballpark. She'd seen her
own son-in-law called to active duty, ballplayers like Bob Feller
enlist, and young men wrested from their homes to be de-
ployed to places most had never heard of, like Midway Island
and Guadalcanal. Other men—neighbors, her young ballplayers' dads—could be called up. She wanted to give fathers and
their sons a special experience on the holiday weekend.

The leagues now had thirteen teams. For Dad's Day each of
them would play a team made up of their fathers. Josephine's
brother Joseph Mathey, now a key executive at Youngstown
Sheet and Tube and a rabid baseball fan, would take the place
of Junior's long-absent father.

Once again, national as well as local media publicized the
teams. In advance of the events, Associated Press stories and
photos again appeared in U.S. newspapers.

Once again calls came in from people outside Cleveland,
wanting to start leagues like hers in their home areas.

Josephine Morhard was reveling in the success she'd
achieved. She'd started a baseball team to help her son, and it
had mushroomed into two leagues with hundreds of kids. Boys
clamored to join. Some were too young and not ready for the
level of Junior League competition, so she was planning to
start "farm teams" of younger boys.

With all the interest coming from outside Cleveland, she
wanted to set up leagues in other cities, leagues that embodied
her values, taught kids skills, and gave them something con-
structive to do in the summer. She thought about starting traveling teams to play other cities like Pittsburgh, Detroit, and
Cincinnati.

She had big ideas and the determination to make them happen.

The 1942 season for the leagues was running smoothly. The Junior American Association created to compete with Mrs. Morhard's leagues had folded after one season, but there was growing competition. Partly because of her success, Cleveland Heights and other nearby communities created rec leagues for their young residents.

The Cleveland Baseball Federation was reinvigorated and offered teams for boys fifteen and under. She was undaunted. None of them could match her leagues. She decided to have her teams play some of these outside teams during the season. Others became like the farm teams Mrs. Morhard wanted, giving the younger boys early experience before graduating to Mrs. Morhard's celebrated little big leagues, craving the opportunities to learn from and interact with Cleveland Indians personnel and the challenge of competing with the leagues' highly skilled players.

In August, as the season was winding down, Indians owner Alva Bradley invited boys from all the teams to be his guests again—this time at Cleveland Stadium for a Friday evening August 21 game between the Indians and White Sox. For the boys, going to a game in the huge Cleveland Stadium was a thrill. Even better, one of their favorite players, Mel Harder, was pitching. It was just four days after Harder had been hit in the head by a batted ball that had knocked him out of the game. Other favorites, Jeff Heath, Roy Weatherly, and Ray Mack, were also in the lineup. The Indians' shortstop Lou Boudreau was now the player-manager, replacing Roger Peckinpaugh.

The Indians were in third place with a record of 63-56, 15½ games behind the Yankees, and 10½ games behind the Red Sox. It was a close game, but the Indians beat the Sox 3–2. The reliable Harder pitched a complete game, giving up only five hits. Of the two runs, one was unearned. Mack had three hits and one run; Heath and Weatherly scored the other two runs. The boys' special heroes had done their part to win. They liked to think the ballplayers had done it for them.

Two days later, on Sunday, August 23, Mrs. Morhard held her annual benefit. She counted on the benefit to raise funds to cover league expenses during the season. It wouldn't be the usual ox roast this year. The war was on and food supplies needed to be conserved. This year, the benefit would focus on baseball and entertainment.

Five ball games were held in the afternoon and one in the evening. The first game would be an All Star game between the Junior American and National Leagues, followed by games between the Little Browns and Little Senators, Little Yankees and Little White Sox, Little Pirates and Little Cardinals, and the Little Reds and Little Dodgers. Following the games, radio personality Duke Lidyard brought his radio gang and his Junior Show Boat show to the ball fields to entertain. A War Bond was awarded in a raffle. Then the movie, *The Ninth Inning*, was shown. Attendance was good, but had fallen off some from 1941. In late September, there was another Little World Series, but the war began to have an effect.

In December, Mrs. Morhard placed the red sticker with a large white "C" and the words *mileage ration* on her driver's-side windshield. She'd gone down to the U.S. Office of Price Administration and persuaded them she needed more gasoline than was allowed for the "A" category, which was issued to the general public and only allowed three to four gallons per week. The "B" sticker, mostly for businesses, had a limit of eight gallons a week. The "C" was unrestricted, and it was important for her meat delivery business, even if meat delivery wasn't on the official list of qualifying occupations. Mrs. Morhard always seemed to get what she wanted.

Gas had been plentiful in Ohio, even though it was rationed on the East Coast, but in December 1942, gas rationing was imposed nationwide. The problem wasn't a scarcity of gas. It was the severe rubber shortage. If people didn't drive as much, their tires wouldn't wear out. Gas wasn't a problem for Mrs. Morhard, but tires were. Recapping was her only option, and that required a special certificate.

As much as she believed in helping the war effort, she bristled occasionally at the numerous forms, stickers, stamps, and the time it took her away from her business. There were shoe stamps, typewriter rental, stove purchase, bicycle, rubber footwear certificates, and more. It wasn't the rationing that annoyed her; she was fine with that. She'd sacrificed a good portion of her life. Most Americans had to conserve during the Depression. Rationing wasn't much different. It was the paperwork.

At the beginning of the war, the U.S. government had suggested people reduce consumption, but in March 1943 they demanded it. Following Britain's example, the United States began rationing meat, cheese, and fats. That did affect Mrs. Morhard's meat market. Beef, pork, veal, lamb, canned meat, and fish were rationed. Every month, families received sixty-four red stamps, good for two pounds of meat each week. Each cut of meat was given points—the more scarce the cut, the higher number of points. Her customers now had to tear off the required number of stamps in front of her.

She'd established good relationships with Mike and Jack Rose of State Packing where she bought her meat, and had no difficulty getting what she needed for the market, but, as her customers changed their buying habits, she did too. People were buying more chicken, which was not rationed, and hamburger. They weren't buying the choice cuts of beef that were more profitable. Canned Spam, which she didn't sell, became a family go-to meal with dozens of recipes in newspapers on how to make the concoction of pork and ham more tasty.

Despite the restrictions, some of her affluent customers in the Heights found a way to purchase whatever they wanted. They'd order steaks when she was sure they'd used up their stamps for the week. She knew people were trading stamps they didn't need for stamps they wanted. Maybe that's what they were doing. Or they could have been getting them from the growing black market that sold forged ration stamps. She didn't ask.

Rationing was having a dampening effect on her profits, and on her baseball leagues. The war was now all-consuming. People's priorities had changed radically. There was little time for boys' baseball.

As Josephine navigated the streets of University Heights, she checked the sprinkling of blue stars that graced the front windows of many homes, indicating a family member in military service. She thought of Ralph and Gerry and wondered if or when he'd be sent into battle across the ocean. She thought of Marlo. She thought of Junior, and how she'd feel if he had to go to the war, facing enemy fire.

She knew the danger Hitler and the Axis powers posed and the importance of fighting the war, but she ached for the families losing husbands and sons. She silently prayed when she saw a blue star exchanged for the gold one that meant a family member had been lost in the war.

More than 839,000 Ohioans were drafted, enlisted, or on active duty as reservists. It was the fourth highest number of any state. Many of the fathers of boys on her teams were past the age for the draft, then eighteen to thirty-seven, though many brothers and uncles remained eligible.

The loss of men to the war created an acute shortage of labor at the very time industry needed more people to manufacture the military supplies the servicemen needed. Fathers of many of the boys signed up to take second jobs in the evening. Women, exemplified by Rosie the Riveter, took day jobs replacing the men who'd left for the war. They worked on B-29 bombers, making aircraft parts, assembling tanks. Husbands and wives had little time for their families, never mind baseball.

By the summer of 1943, Mrs. Morhard needed to spend more time at the meat market. War rationing was cutting deeply into her business. Her baseball fund-raisers weren't contributing enough money to support the leagues, and she didn't have enough extra money to do so. She asked the families of the boys to help support their own teams.

She reluctantly turned over her role as manager of the Little Indians to Paul Kvetko, who had been one of the umpires. She announced that the Little Indians would begin practice at the end of May and Kvetko would conduct a baseball school every Wednesday throughout the summer on the Little Indians Field. The Junior American and National Leagues would open their 1943 season on June 26. Games would be held every Tuesday and Thursday at 6:30 p.m., with doubleheaders every Sunday at 1:30 p.m.

The games went on, but boys began dropping out. Their fathers were working second jobs; their mothers were working; they couldn't get enough gas, and parents couldn't bring them to the ball field. A few gallons of gas a week wasn't enough for most families to drive to work, do their shopping, errands, and also get their boys to the ballparks for two games a week.

Some of the boys on her original teams were now in high school and had joined older teenage boys on American Legion teams. For all of the war-related reasons, it was harder to recruit new boys. Still, the leagues were hanging on. And so was she.

She had her third Little World Series on Sunday, August 29, but not at League Park. She kept it closer to home on the leagues' two baseball diamonds at University Square. The champions this time were the Little White Sox of the Junior American League and the Little Pirates of the Junior National League.

It was more than the war that was affecting Mrs. Morhard's leagues. Her son, the boy she created the Little Indians for, was growing up. Junior was now a teenager. He didn't want to be called Junior anymore. For one thing, he wasn't really a "Junior" since he and his father had different middle names. Second, Junior sounded too much like a little boy and he wasn't little anymore. His teachers called him Albert, but he didn't want people to call him that either. He made it known he wanted to be called Al.

He'd sprung up to become a muscular five-foot-nine-inch young man who ran around the block every day in the morning before school, did fifty push-ups, and lifted weights. There were no baseball teams at Roxboro Junior High, but there was a football team. He decided to try it. Practices were at the high school in Cleveland Heights. To get there, he needed to take the streetcar, then take a bus. After two practices, he quit. It was too far to go, there were too many kids at practice, it was disorganized, and he wasn't that interested.

A few months later, a nice couple moved into Mrs. Morhard's small third-floor apartment. Their names were Don and Jeannie Greenwood. Don had been a football and baseball star at the University of Missouri. He left to enlist in the Army Air Corps in 1942. Not long afterward, he was in a plane crash, was injured, and received a medical discharge. He then went on to the University of Illinois, where he was a multi-sport star—quarterbacking the Fighting Illini and batting .415 against

Big Ten baseball teams. Don had just signed with the pro football Cleveland Rams and was working in the off-season in the
engineering department of Thompson Products Corporation.

One day, Al and several of his friends were out in the street
playing touch football when Don stopped by to watch. He saw
Al running. After the boys finished, Don called Al over.
"You're really fast, and you can cut. You'd make a great halfback. You should go out for football."

Al explained that he'd been to two practices earlier in the
year and quit. Don pressed on, asking why he quit. Al replied,
"It was too far to go and not much fun." Don convinced him to
give it one more try.

The next year, Al was a sophomore at Cleveland Heights
High School. He did go out for football, but not as a halfback.
A boy named King Matthews had been the starting quarterback
on the ninth grade team, but he was on vacation when practice
began. By the time Matthews came back Al had won the job as
the first string quarterback. When high school baseball rolled
around in March, Al made the varsity team, but it was clear his
interest had shifted.

Mrs. Morhard kept the leagues going as well as she could,
opening the 1944 season on Sunday, June 4. Junior and his
friends were still on the Little Indians, and many of the teams
that were left also had older boys. Others had moved on to the
American Legion teams for teens. She added some of those
teams to her schedule, but the rationing, the loss of men to the
war, and the need for non-drafted men and women to manufacture war supplies had taken its toll. Boys' baseball wasn't a priority for many folks now. It was also getting financially difficult.
She'd had to spend much of her own money on the teams since
the war began.

Then Anthony Visconsi called. He needed the two ball fields
to expand his shopping centers once again. Reluctantly, she decided to end the baseball program after the 1944 season.

Hal Lebovitz later wrote, in an April 3, 1960, *Plain Dealer*
column that, if the leagues had not folded, University Heights–
Cleveland Heights might have been the seat of Little League
baseball today instead of Williamsport.

It had been a magical time. Her "Brigadoon" moment appeared, then vanished overnight. Mrs. Morhard had achieved

what she most wanted. She was the mother of the leagues, nurturing her boys with inspiring stories and, when needed, a shrill whistle.

Baseball had been a tool to help boys grow up the right way. She'd seen her own son transformed from an angry boy into a calm, capable young man. She'd watched a ragtag group of boys—some of them neglected at home, orphans, scrappy neighborhood kids—grow and prosper on the field and off.

The credit for starting the Little League may have gone to Williamsport, but recognition was never what she wanted. Mrs. Morhard's goal had been reached.

Baseball for her boys was a path, not a destination.

CHAPTER TWENTY-ONE

The Reunion

Many years later, the boys let Mrs. Morhard know how much the baseball teams meant to them. In May 1968—right before Mother's Day and thirty years after Josephine started the first boys' baseball league—former Little Indian Brad Rogers, an investment broker, organized a surprise reunion dinner for Mrs. Morhard, then seventy-seven years old.

The "boys" came from all over the country. In the thirty years since she'd watched over them on the baseball fields of University Heights, they had become lawyers, doctors, brokers, coaches, grocery store owners, businessmen, and builders. Two of them had even played in the Minor Leagues. The boys had "grown up right" just as she'd hoped.

Former Cleveland Indians manager Roger Peckinpaugh, Junior American and National League umpires Hal Lebovitz, Tony Pianowski, and Paul Kvetko were there too.

The lessons she imparted through baseball—honesty, hard work, no shortcuts, consideration for other people, determination, don't get discouraged, keep trying—inspired all of them. They also remembered the whistle.

They presented her with a gold pin shaped like a baseball and a real baseball signed by all of them. It was an early Mother's Day present for their baseball "mother." Junior called her "the greatest mom in the world." Mrs. Morhard tried to hold back the tears, but they just kept coming.

When she regained her composure, Mrs. Morhard gave them a sign of her old feistiness. She picked up the whistle she hadn't used since the last game in 1944 and blew it one more time.

The Old Ball Fields

It was 2010. Al Morhard came to this place in University Heights, Ohio, to see where the old ball fields used to be. It had been nearly seventy years since he last played baseball here in his pint-size uniform sporting Bob Feller's number 19 and navy blue cap with a red "C" sitting atop his thick mound of curly black hair.

Though he lived less than an hour away, he hadn't been back to this part of his old town for decades. He stepped out of the car slowly, not that he was feeling his age, but because he needed time to adjust to the now-unfamiliar scene in front of him. His deep-set hazel eyes panned the four corners where Cedar Road met Warrensville Center, trying to change the lens from now to then.

He looked for the spot where home plate used to be, then shifted his gaze past a giant white and red Link Belt digger treading its way over the mounds of rubble that used to be the walls of shops in the Cedar Center strip mall. Somewhere under the dusty wreckage had been one of the fields where he and Joey and Brad and Jackie and the rest of the Little Indians sweated away so many summer afternoons under the watchful eye of his mother Josephine.

On this day, land was being cleared to make way for a trendy retail and office complex. Not long before Corky and Lenny's delicatessen, Cedar Lee Cinema, Marc's discount store, and a checkerboard of retailers served their neighborhood customers. Across Cedar Road, shopping carts rolled in and out of

Whole Foods Market, where the first shopping center used to be. On the southeast corner, a multi-story shopping mall rose from the street like a stark white fortress—masking its forbidding presence with bright, neon letters that spelled out Target, Macy's, Applebee's. The only visible customers waited in an ant-like procession for their cars to enter the limited spaces of a hidden garage.

"Progress," Al murmured as he walked past piles of discarded bricks, slightly shaking his head and kicking away a clump of dirt with a well-worn tennis shoe. He remembered when the stores were built over fifty years ago. Now those stores were being replaced, just like they replaced the old ball fields.

"When I was a kid, this was the country, mostly overgrown fields. The fields were a mess. The weeds were nearly as tall as we were," Al said. "There were broken bottles, candy wrappers, just about anything you can imagine strewn around. My mother was determined to make it into a ball field for us—I guess, mostly for me. She wasn't even five feet tall, but she commanded everyone's attention. If she wanted to do something, she was relentless."

Now in his eighties, Al's face is deeply creased from summers in the sun and one can see traces of both his mother and father—his mother's piercing eyes and slim face, set off by his father's firm chin. He looks a couple of decades younger than his years—his mostly black hair showing only a few silvery strands. His physique is still lean and muscled from the near-daily hour-long weightlifting and turns on the elliptical machine. He still pushes himself to work out nearly as hard as he did when he played.

Al stared again at the site of the former fields, but he was really staring into the past, forgetting the traffic, the noise, the shoppers, the streets full of stores; remembering a time before the Second World War when the city's scrapers were leveling this land for ball fields; when it was full of young boys laughing and pitching and hitting and catching and throwing and striking out; when families from all around Cleveland came to cheer the boys on from the bleachers; when Bob Feller and Mel Harder and Jeff Heath gave tips to the young ballplayers, and when he and the other boys learned lessons that stayed with them their whole lives.

"We were the first, you know, the first boys' baseball leagues, before Williamsport, PA," he said to himself. "It was my mother," he whispered about the remarkably determined woman, who never took "no" for an answer and who began it all for him, her young son whose father was no longer around and who needed the discipline of the game he loved.

"She did it all."

JOSEPHINE MATHEY GERAU MORHARD

Mrs. Morhard never forgot her boys or the baseball leagues. She'd often pick up the phone to call some of them around Christmastime and pretend to be Santa for their kids.

After the baseball leagues ended, Mrs. Morhard continued to run her meat market for a few more years. In 1949, she sold it to her butcher. She was in her late fifties by then, and decided to try something new.

Her cousin Howard Payne had started the Euclid Broom Manufacturing Company and needed help. Howard was blind. He'd lost the vision in one eye playing baseball years earlier, when a ball hit him in the eye. He lost sight in his other one in a freakish accident at Mrs. Morhard's home. He and a friend were putting in an electrical line from her laundry room to the downstairs recreation room. He leaned down to look through the hole where the line was to come through when his friend accidentally pushed the line into his one good eye. Mrs. Morhard was horrified. She felt somewhat responsible since it happened at her house.

She decided to help him grow his broom business. From then on and for years afterward, she was on the phone, calling people whose names she found in her crisscross phone directory and using her persuasive personality to convince them to buy Howard's brooms.

She was devoted to her growing family. She regaled her five grandchildren with the stories of her life—Al's children Sue, Joe, and Kathy, and Gerry's offspring BJ and Tim—and passed on the lessons she'd given Gerry, Al, and the boys. In turn, they were devoted to her. They wanted her to write everything down. She pulled out one of her old steno notepads and began, seemingly with a tinge of regret:

> This is the first day of spring, and it takes me back to my childhood days, full of joy and adventures on the farm.
> How I love to sit for hours and live my life over again.

The hardships of her early life melted away. She wrote twenty or so pages, some in longhand, some typewritten—mainly about her adventures with the farm animals, her adventures with her brother and sisters, and her struggles after leaving the farm. She never finished.

When she was in her late seventies, she developed colon cancer and underwent two successful operations. She lived in the house at 2499 Traymore until she was in her eighties, when she went to live with Al and his family in Gates Mills, Ohio. She still kept the house in University Heights. A third operation, to remove scar tissue that had formed as a result of the cancer, was successful, but her tired body couldn't take the stress.

She died on December 15, 1978, at St. Luke's Hospital in Shaker Heights, Ohio. She was eighty-seven years old.

She still loved baseball.

THE FAMILY

AL (JUNIOR) MORHARD

More than anyone, Al Morhard knows the value of what his mother accomplished. For years, whenever he participated in community events or went to school reunions or even when he walked down the street, former players would come up to him and talk about the teams and his mother. They didn't recall many details of those days but they remembered his mother as a "great lady."

Al went on to play varsity baseball at Cleveland Heights High where his varsity baseball team won the 1947 Ohio State Baseball Championship. He continued to play at Western Reserve University and in the Cleveland Baseball Federation's Class A adult league—a semi-professional league that included former Minor and Major League players—where he played shortstop and third base.

But baseball was no longer his main sports interest. He fell in love with football. He spent hours practicing, throwing a football through a tire in his backyard, running around the block, and lifting weights. He became the quarterback of the Cleveland Heights High School football team, making headlines with his play. In his junior year, he set school records for touchdown passes. In his senior year, he was named one of two All-Ohio quarterbacks. The other, Vic Janowicz, was the 1950 Heisman trophy winner, played pro baseball with the Pittsburgh Pirates, and later, football with the Washington Redskins.

Al's path was different, but equally impressive. Like Janowicz, he was heavily recruited by colleges across the country—including Ohio State, Army, Cincinnati, Miami—but was convinced to stay near home when Western Reserve University decided to launch a major football program, coached by Moe Scarry from the Cleveland Browns. Al accepted a full football scholarship.

The Western Reserve Football program went nowhere—most of the recruits couldn't keep up with the demanding academic requirements. Moe Scarry left after Al had been on the team one year, telling Al he had the talent to become a pro football player. After Scarry left, Al considered going to a better football program but stayed, reaping the school's academic benefits instead. He was a varsity letterman in baseball and football. He was also president of his class, editor of the university newspaper, and selected to be a member of Omicron Delta Kappa, the National Leadership Honor Society. He'd shown his abilities went far beyond sports.

After graduation, Al was accepted at Cornell University Law School, where he graduated with a JD degree. He went on to become a highly successful trial attorney, president of the Cuyahoga County Bar Association, the Cleveland Academy of Trial Attorneys, and a judge. Sports had been simply a path to an enduring career.

His own family is a large one. In addition to his wife, the author of this book, he has three children—Dr. Susan Morhard

Posada, Albert Joseph (Joe) Morhard Jr., and Kathleen Morhard Miller; four stepchildren—Margaret Reid, Gerald (Jerry) Reid, Mary Reid, and Trish Reid—fourteen grandchildren; and one great-grandchild.

GERALDINE (GERRY) GERAU DEROSA

Gerry and Ralph DeRosa spent the World War II years on military bases throughout the United States. They became the proud parents of a daughter Betty Jo (BJ) while Ralph was at the army base in Fort Riley, Kansas. He was about to be shipped overseas when the war ended. They had a son, Tim, a few years later.

Gerry never did fulfill her dream of being on the stage. Instead, while caring for her children, she cultivated other creative skills and became a talented artist. Her artwork was selected for the prestigious May Show at the Cleveland Museum of Art. Later, she became an interior designer, working with firms throughout the Cleveland area.

Ralph remained in the reserves. He was called back into active service in November 1950 for the Korean War and was sent to Korea. Gerry and the children lived with Mrs. Morhard when he was gone and at other times while he was away with army duties. After returning from the war, he taught ROTC at The Ohio State University. Later he worked in sales for a major Cleveland corporation.

ALBERT HERBERT MORHARD

After losing his remaining meat markets in Cleveland, Josephine's former husband headed for Iowa, then New York. He had no contact with Josephine or Al until 1942, when he came back to the Cleveland area and got a job in a Mayfield Heights meat store.

He showed remorse for his past and wanted to be part of his son's life. Mrs. Morhard once again forgave him and invited him to family events and holidays for the rest of his life. He came to all his son's games, sent him spending money when he was in law school, and gave him funds to buy a truck to launch a summer landscaping business.

He developed terrible asthma. One day Mrs. Morhard happened to drive by his apartment and saw him on the porch struggling to breathe. She brought him to the hospital where he died on October 22, 1957.

A FEW OF THE BOYS
(in alphabetical order)

JACK ANDERSON, LITTLE BROWNS

Jack Anderson was always unlikely to end up with a baseball career. His father and grandfather were doctors. That would be his career path as well. He received his Doctor of Medicine degree from the University of Buffalo School of Medicine, did his residency at Boston City Hospital, and conducted research studies at Harvard and Tufts Universities.

He claims he wasn't that good a baseball player, but he enjoyed playing in the boys' leagues. "Mrs. Morhard was a real firebrand. She did a wonderful thing for us. She gave us exact replicas of Major League uniforms. She gave us our own line-up cards. She was organized. She got good people to help. She spent a lot of time with us, and she was always at the games. She was very much in charge."

She even made his mother one of the team managers.

He remembers Hal Lebovitz umpiring and helping teach the kids the game. *The Plain Dealer*'s Gordon Cobbledick helped out too. "The kids listened to him because they knew he worked for the newspaper."

Like Al and most of the boys, baseball was not to be his career, but he played through his early thirties. In the navy he was in the Parris Island Intramural League that traveled throughout the United States and "always won the championship."

When Dr. Jack Anderson opened his medical practice, he had at least two familiar patients from his baseball-playing days, Mrs. Josephine Morhard and Al Morhard. He was Mrs. Morhard's doctor through the rest of her life and Al's until Jack left private practice to become the Cleveland Electric Illuminating Company's medical director. He was on the faculty of the Case Western Reserve School of Medicine for twenty-five years.

His mother, the manager of the Little St. Louis Browns, lived to be over one hundred, still enjoying sports.

JACKIE HEINEN, LITTLE INDIANS

Jackie's father, Joe Heinen, was a butcher like Al's father. He wanted to do more than supply meat, so he opened his own grocery store. He and Mrs. Morhard were friendly competitors.

Jackie was a star pitcher and third baseman on the Little Indians and one of the best players in Mrs. Morhard's leagues. He went on to play high school baseball at University School, and in college at Stanford University, where he played third base as a freshman but impressed his coaches so much as a pitcher, they made that his full-time role.

When his coach decided to test his pitching speed, the results showed he was throwing the ball 100 miles per hour. Thinking the machine was faulty, his coach asked him to come back again the next day. They tested him again—and again the result was 100 mph. Feller was pitching 99 mph.

After college, Jack Heinen played for a Red Sox minor league team briefly, then was drafted. He was stationed at Fort Lee, New Jersey, and assigned to play baseball in the Army League. In his two years in the service, he pitched against many Major Leaguers, including the legendary Willie Mays.

He returned to the Red Sox organization in 1951, playing for the San Jose Red Sox alongside future Major Leaguer Ken Aspromonte. He achieved a 17-7 record and a 2.81 earned run average. On August 20, 1951, he pitched a no-hit game. Newspapers across California praised the "flashy right-hander" who "has a penchant for pitching no-hit and one-hit games." According to his son Jeff, he still holds the record for the most consecutive no-hit innings in the Minor Leagues—seventeen. At the beginning of the 1952 season, he was invited to Red Sox training camp. Every indication was that he would make the team.

By this time Jack had a wife and a child. His father, Joe, told him he had to make a choice—either play the "little boys' game" of baseball (players didn't make much money then) or do the responsible thing—come home, work in the grocery store, and take care of his family. He felt he had no choice. He came home. That was the end of his baseball career.

He eventually took over the grocery store. By the time he passed away in 1994, Heinen's had grown to eleven supermarkets. (There are twenty-three Heinen's Fine Foods stores today in Ohio and Illinois.) His twin sons Jeff and Tom now run the chain. They say they split their father's baseball talent, but they loved to play catch with him. "Catching his curveball was amazing," Jeff said. "Nobody had a curve ball like his."

RAY LINDQUIST, LITTLE YANKEES

Ray Lindquist was another of the boys who went on to play professional baseball. In high school, he was the shortstop on the 1947 Cleveland Heights High School State Championship baseball team. When high school was over for the summer, he played on an American Legion team managed by his father. He went on to Dartmouth University, where he was remembered as "one of the most talented players in Dartmouth history." A college teammate remembers that he was a "skilled shortstop, a productive hitter and a marvelous teammate; the leading talent on our team during his year in Hanover."

Later, he was selected by the St. Louis Browns in the Major League draft and played for the San Antonio Missions in the Texas League and the York White Roses in the Piedmont League. In 1954 he joined the Wichita Indians, a Baltimore affiliate in the Western League and, in 1955 was on the squad of the Binghamton Triplets in the Eastern League, a New York Yankee farm team.

BRAD ROGERS, LITTLE INDIANS

As a young boy, Brad seemed to have everything. He was privileged. His family was wealthy. He was the nephew of Cleveland Indians owner Alva Bradley. But in many ways, he was disadvantaged.

In 1948, his parents divorced, and he was shipped off to private boarding schools—Choate in Connecticut and Kiski in Pennsylvania. In the summer, he was sent off to summer camp. During his teen years, his mother moved to Union, New York, and he lived with her for a short time. She had two homes. She lived in one; he lived in the other. He had six weeks of public school while he was there. He said it was his best school experience until college.

Despite the turmoil of his early life, he had a great personality, a ready smile, and made friends easily. He graduated from Denison College, where he thrived and was president of his fraternity. After college he got a job as a stockbroker.

He soon met and married a smart and lovely blue-eyed girl named Pat. His mother railed against the marriage because Pat was from the west side of Cleveland and a Catholic. But Brad, finally, had his first real home with Pat.

Still loving baseball, he went to work for Hank Greenberg, then the general manager and part owner of the Cleveland Indians. Eventually he joined his brother Ed's Industrial Service Company. Among their products were tarps for Cleveland Stadium.

In 2009, Brad Rogers and Pat were living in South Carolina. It was Al's birthday, and Brad wrote to him:

> There are so many things I remember about you, going back to the late 30's, when we were playing for the Little Indians. All of us referred to you as "Junior." Some even called you "Junie." Those were special times and I remember them vividly, but most of all, I remember your mother. Whenever I think of her, I choke up a bit because she was not only your mother but also the mother to all of "her boys" . . . the whistle—oh boy, did she get the attention of all of us with that thing. How she took care of us!!

MARLO TERMINI, LITTLE CARDINALS

Little Cardinals superstar Marlo was probably the most talented player in either league. He continued his athletic prowess in baseball and basketball at Cleveland's Holy Name High School. While he was still in high school, on April 1, 1944, he was drafted into the army. His basketball team won the division championship that year.

On the military transport train to army camp, he saw a familiar face, the Indians' Roy Weatherly, reminding him of the game he loved but wouldn't be playing for a long while. He was sent overseas to Europe during the war as a member of the U.S. Army Quartermaster Corps, going all the way to the border of Bamberg, Germany.

When he came back from the war, he enrolled at the University of Dayton and made the basketball team as a walk-on, despite the fact that he was only five feet three inches tall. He dropped out to play semipro basketball with the Detroit Clowns for $80 a week, a huge amount of money then. He'd play as many as three games in a day. One of the team's abysmal publicity stunts was to have the five-foot-three Marlo sit on the lap of a seven-foot-two player, both wearing clown makeup. The money wasn't enough to keep him there.

He returned to the University of Dayton, where he graduated in 1952. A year later, he became his alma mater Holy Name's head basketball coach and assistant football coach. His basketball team won the West Senate Division championship in 1956. Later he received a master's degree and became head of the Cleveland State University's Physical Education department and an assistant basketball coach under Ray Derringer. He kept up his interest in the sport of baseball by playing softball. He was a gifted player, elected to the National Softball Hall of Fame after receiving numerous All-Tourney, All-World, All-American, and MVP certificates.

His two sons followed in his path. Mel Termini was a teacher and coach at Benedictine High School for twenty-five years and is now a counselor at a family service agency. Mark Termini heads the noted sports agency Mark Termini Associates and has been named one of the five most influential and high-profile NBA agents. He specializes in contract negotiation and construction and was instrumental in the return of LeBron James to the Cleveland Cavaliers, working with agent Rich Paul of Klutch Sports Group.

THE UMPIRE/COACH

HAL LEBOVITZ

Hal Lebovitz made his mark on baseball and sports, not as a coach or umpire, but as a legend among baseball writers. He's been called one of the greatest columnists in Cleveland sports history. Broadcaster Bob Costas commented, "He was a straight shooter, not a potshot artist. He was the kind of guy who got respect not just for his versatility and knowledge, but for his integrity."

When he was still a high school chemistry teacher, he began contributing to the *Cleveland News,* which hired him as a beat writer for the Cleveland Indians and Cleveland Browns in 1942. He became sports editor of the *Cleveland Plain Dealer* and a columnist in 1964, a position he held until his retirement in 1982. He wrote a column "Ask Hal, the Referee" for the *Sporting News* and was a contributor to *Sports Magazine* and *Colliers.* After his retirement, he wrote regular columns for the *News Herald* newspapers. His books include: *Ask Hal: Answers to Fans' Most Interesting Questions About Baseball Rules from a Hall–of–Fame Sportswriter* and *The Best of Hal Lebovitz: Great Sportswriting from Six Decades in Cleveland.*

In 1999 he was elected into the writer's wing of the National Baseball Hall of Fame "for meritorious contributions to baseball writing."

He died on October 18, 2005, at the age of eighty-nine. He was still writing his baseball column until two weeks before he died.

THE CLEVELAND INDIANS

After years of competing with the Yankees, Red Sox, and Detroit for the top spot, the Cleveland Indians won the American League pennant in 1948 after a one-game playoff with the Red Sox. They went on to win the World Series over another Boston team, the Boston Braves, 4–2. Feller won nineteen games that season. Pitchers Bob Lemon and Gene Bearden won twenty each. Satchel Paige, the legendary pitcher from the Negro National League, who was signed by the Indians late in the season at the age of forty-two, compiled a record of 6-1, pitched three complete games, had a save and a 2.47 earned run average. Mel Harder was the pitching coach.

The Indians reached the World Series in 1954, 1995, 1997, and 2016, but lost the latter two in heartbreaking fashion. As of the writing of this book, they are still waiting for another World Series win. Maybe this year is the year!

BOB FELLER

There's little need to recap the baseball career of Hall of Fame pitcher Bob Feller, named by the *Sporting News* as the "greatest pitcher of his time" and one of the one hundred best players of all time. Another Baseball Hall of Famer, Ted Williams, said he was "the fastest and best pitcher I ever saw during my career." He was inducted into the National Baseball Hall of Fame on the first ballot. Only three players ever had a higher percentage of ballot votes. His statue now stands in front of the Cleveland Indians ballpark.

MEL HARDER

Mel Harder was with the Cleveland Indians for thirty-six seasons, from 1928 to 1963, first as a star pitcher, then as the coach who groomed many of the sport's top hurlers. He even did a quick turn as the Cleveland Indians' interim manager, winning all three games. His was a Hall of Fame career though he never received that honor.

As a player he was a four-time All Star, who consistently notched fifteen wins or more and pitched an Indians' record 582 games. Yankee great Joe DiMaggio said he had more difficulty batting against Harder than any other pitcher. He hit only.180 against him.

As a coach, Harder became known as "Mr. Fixit," helping transform players like Bob Lemon, Mike Garcia, Mudcat Grant, Jim Perry, Tommy John, Gary Bell, Luis Tiant, and Herb Score into some of the most dominant pitchers of their time. Early Wynn, who succeeded Harder as the Indians pitching coach in 1963 said, "Mel Harder made me a pitcher."

For the whole of his career as pitcher and coach, no one deserves more to be in the National Baseball Hall of Fame than Mel Harder. Not long before he passed away in 2002 at age ninety-three, he sent Al a note and a couple of newspaper clippings of him with the Little Indians, reminding Al that he'd often stop by to watch the boys' games.

JEFF HEATH

Jeff Heath became one of the Indians' best players. In 1941, the power-hitting Heath led the league in triples, batted .340, and was third in slugging behind Ted Williams and Joe DiMaggio. He made the All Star team and finished eighth in voting for the Most Valuable Player Award. He became the first American League player to record a "20-20-20" with twenty each of doubles, triples, and home runs. His play would also earn him trips to the All Star game in 1943 and 1945. Despite his great play, he had a bad temper and was considered a troublemaker, which hurt his career.

He was traded to the Washington Senators in 1946 but played only forty-eight games before being traded to the St. Louis Browns. He was traded again to the Boston Braves, even though he'd hit twenty-seven home runs. With the Braves he made it to the World Series in 1948, playing against his old team, the Cleveland Indians. The Indians won, four games to two.

Roy Weatherly

The player they called "Stormy" or "Thunder" Weatherly played for the Cleveland Indians for seven years, 1936–1942, hitting over .300 three times. In 1940, his best year, he came in eleventh for the American League Most Valuable Player award. He was traded to the Yankees after the 1942 season. Like many players, his career was interrupted by World War II. After the war he played for the Yankees and the New York Giants.

THE PRO FOOTBALLER

Don Greenwood

In Don Greenwood's first year with the Cleveland Rams, the team won the National Football League championship. The next year owner Dan Reeves moved the team to California where they became the Los Angeles Rams. Greenwood stayed to join a new team that had formed in Cleveland as part of the All-America Football Conference, the Cleveland Browns. Paul Brown was the coach.

The Browns won the 1946 AAFC championship, Greenwood played halfback on offense and defensive back on defense. He had six touchdowns to tie for the Conference lead. In 1947 he had a terrible collision in a game with the San Francisco 49ers that sent him to the hospital for two weeks. Al Morhard went to see him there. He'd suffered a disabling cheekbone injury and had to sit on the sidelines as the Browns won another championship. His cheekbone healed slowly, ending his career as a player. Later he became an assistant coach at Yale, then head football coach at the University of Toledo.

The Los Angeles Rams became the St. Louis Rams and now they are the Los Angeles Rams once again. The Cleveland Browns moved to Baltimore to become the Baltimore Ravens but kept their name, colors, and logos in Cleveland, where a new Cleveland Browns team was formed in 1999. They, too, are awaiting a championship.

THE LITTLE LEAGUE

The Little League organization we know today began humbly in Williamsport, Pennsylvania, with three teams named after business sponsors who paid $30 each to cover the cost of each team's uniforms. It too suffered during the war, but kept going. It was after World War II ended that the Little League began to grow into the organization we know today. In 1946, the Little League had twelve leagues in its home state of Pennsylvania. The next year, it expanded into New Jersey. Its first Little League World Series took place in 1947 in Williamsport, six years after Mrs. Morhard's Little World Series in Cleveland.

The Little League now has nearly two hundred thousand teams in all fifty states and more than eighty countries.

ABOUT THIS BOOK

Sometimes a gem of a story finds you, like you were meant to write it. That's what happened with this book.

I met Josephine Morhard just a few months before she died. She was a scrappy eighty-seven years old, still driving her Oldsmobile Cutlass, coloring her thinning hair red, and taking a few sips of an occasional Manhattan. She was stocky and short, didn't even come up to my shoulders, but her piercing hazel eyes made me take notice and told me she hadn't lost a step. We began to talk about the grandchildren she was so proud of. Then suddenly she winced and said she had a pain in her side, but "it was nothing."

The "nothing" didn't go away. She'd already had a kidney removed and two bouts with colon cancer. There was scar tissue that needed to be removed. The surgery was successful, but her body couldn't take it. She was gone.

I'd become close to her son Al and was helping the family clean out her house in University Heights when I noticed a large can of 16-mm film that had the words *Bringing Up Baseball* scrawled on the side. I asked about it.

"Oh, that's a film about the Little League. She started it," her son Albert said.

"You mean she started the one in Cleveland," I replied.

"No, she started the Little League. The Cleveland Indians made that film about her and sent it to cities all across the country. The people in Williamsport wanted to see it."

I knew Williamsport was considered the home of Little League baseball, and I was somewhat skeptical. But I was also intrigued. I asked to see the film.

I watched the huge reel of film clank through the rented 16-mm projector. There she was, much younger and heavier—standing on the balcony of the very house we'd just cleaned out, shouting down instructions to the boys playing baseball in her backyard; then standing near the bleachers on ball fields she built in University Heights, watching the Little Indians play the Little White Sox. The film was all about her and the kids' baseball leagues she created and modeled on the Major Leagues.

She did found boys' baseball leagues before Williamsport, but the public no longer remembered. I thought they should. But that was only part of her story. The more I learned about her, the more fascinated I became. Her life was even more compelling than her baseball achievement.

I wanted this book, *Mrs. Morhard and the Boys,* to capture her incredible journey from the young girl who left home at age twelve and faced a hostile world to the confident, feisty woman who created boys' baseball leagues that changed lives. It is a story of adversity, resilience, and determination.

The information in this book has been gleaned from Josephine's own writings; extensive interviews with her son Al, her family, her baseball "boys," their friends and families; the film *Bringing Up Baseball*; media accounts; photographs; and historical archives. I've traveled to the farm country where she grew up, the places she lived, and the sites of the old ball fields to get a "feel" for her world.

Josephine's story is told in the context of the extraordinary times she lived in, from the dawning of the Industrial Revolution to late 1930s and early 1940s when people were reeling from the Great Depression, when World War II was on the horizon, when baseball was truly "America's pastime," and when boys played for the love of the game.

I wish I'd had the chance to know her better when she was alive, but through all of this research, I feel I do. I hope my readers will as well.

ACKNOWLEDGMENTS

My biggest thank-you goes to Al Morhard for his patience and generosity in giving me countless hours of his time as I probed his memories of his mother, the times, the games, and the players—and for his generous support and understanding as I spent many holidays, vacations, weekends, and weekdays tackling the years' long research and writing—at a time when he could have been enjoying retirement.

Another person without whom this book would not be possible is my agent, Laurie Abkemeier, a true miracle worker who has been with me every step of the way, always offering sage advice and knowledge, paring my prose, promptly answering my countless questions, and guiding the book—and me—successfully through the publishing process.

My editor at Kensington's Citadel Press, Denise Silvestro, has been another gem. After a single conversation, I felt she was the right person to handle this book. Now I know she was. She has far exceeded my expectations in every way—with her insight, suggestions, comments, edits, and careful oversight of all aspects of this book. More kudos to Kensington art director Kristine Noble, who captured exactly the right look for the cover; to Ann Pryor, whose marketing and media expertise and vision is getting the book the attention needed to be successful; and Karen Auerbach, who started working on marketing ideas before the contract was even signed.

Thanks to Trish Reid, for the wonderful book trailer.

I'm grateful to Ted Gup, who first suggested I write this book, and to Faith Adiele, Anne Zimmerman, and Otis Haschmeyer who read this book in its early stages and gave me helpful suggestions and gentle critiques. A special shout-out to Rachel Howard, for her guidance and encouragement as I attempted to venture into the publishing world.

Many people gave generously of their time to speak with me. Among the "boys," their families, and others interviewed or contributing information, special thanks go to Jack Anderson, Donna Anderson, Catherine Berlin, Jeff Heinen, Neil Lebovitz, Bill Myers, Brad Rogers, Pat Rogers, Bill Spero, and Marlo Termini. Unfortunately two of the most helpful of Mrs. Morhard's former baseball players, Brad Rogers and Marlo Termini, have passed away since I began this project. Their broad smiles and warm personalities are deeply missed.

I'd also like to thank Mrs. Morhard's grandchildren for sharing their memories: Betty Jo (BJ) Frampton, Timothy DeRosa, Dr. Susan Morhard Posada, Albert Joseph Morhard Jr., and Kathleen Morhard Miller.

For helping with the extensive research necessary to recreate Mrs. Morhard's life and the baseball leagues, I am deeply grateful to the following for their assistance:

For special research projects: Margrit Reid and Trish Reid; for legal guidance: Attorney Raymond Rundelli.

For steering me through the minefields of historical research: Brian Meggitt and the librarians at the Cleveland Public Library; Chuck Collins and the librarians at Heights Libraries; Georgene Fry at Youngstown Probate Court; Kristy Boyles, Youngstown City Health Department; Pamela Speis, Mahoning Valley Historical Society; and various staff at the following organizations: Cuyahoga County Clerk of Courts, Western Reserve Historical Society, Cleveland State University, Michael Schwartz Library, Cleveland Press Collection, Lawrence County (Pennsylvania) Historical Society.

From the moment I began to think about writing this book, our growing family has offered limitless support and encouragement—so here's a high five to Al's and my blended offspring and their families: (in alphabetical order) the Millers: Kathleen, Steve, Daniel, Matthew, Thomas, John, and Andrew; the Morhards: Joe, Kristina, Kristopher, and Lauren; the Posadas: Dr. Susan, Miguel, Alexandria, and Nicholas; the Reids: Gerald, Shannon, and Kelly; Margaret Reid, James Roddy, Dr. Cody, Megan and Josephine Johnson; Mary Reid, Ray Rundelli, Claire and Grace Rundelli; Trish Reid.

NOTES

The most important sources for this book were Josephine Mathey Morhard's written notes and her son Al's recollections of his mother, his childhood, and the baseball leagues.

Josephine Morhard left a steno pad and numerous loose typewritten pages full of stories of her early life, too many to include in this book. Her son Al offered much of the invaluable and detailed information and insight into his mother's life, her marriage to his father, the "boys," and the baseball leagues.

All Mrs. Morhard's quotations are from her notes. I undertook extensive research, beginning in 2012, supplemented her notes, and documented her family history, the people she lived with, her major relationships, marriages, the places she worked and lived, and the times she lived in. Much of this information came from Ohio birth records, U.S. Census Bureau, and other government records, old newspaper and magazine accounts, and historical archives. I traveled to the places where she lived to get a feel for her early world.

The other major sources for this book were first-person interviews, conducted from 2012 to 2017.

Mrs. Morhard's grandchildren contributed their memories. Unfortunately, most of the boys from her baseball leagues are gone. The ones remaining are in their late eighties and early nineties, but I was lucky to find and interview some remarkable men who played in her leagues, including: Dr. Jack Anderson, Bill Myers, Bradley Rogers, Bill Spero, and Marlo Termini; and family members of former players and umpires, including Jeff Heinen, whose father Jack was a Little Indian; Pat Rogers, Brad Rogers's wife; Neil Lebovitz, whose father Hal was an umpire/coach; and Catherine Berlin, whose father Ray Lindquist was a Little Yankee. Some of these people contributed historical documents and photos.

Following are the most important additional sources I've used for historical information.

PROLOGUE: THE BIG DAY

Personal information, anecdotes, and observations of the game are from author interviews and photographs.

Information on Ted Williams's accomplishment can be found here: Bill Nowlin, "The Day Ted Williams Became the Last .400 Hitter in Baseball," *The National Pastime* (July 15, 2013): 76–77.

The Associated Press stories can be found in numerous newspapers, including the following: Douglas Dies, *Associated Press Feature Service*, September 5, 1941; *Cumberland Sunday Times*, Cumberland, MD, September 7, 1941; *Evening Independent*, Massillon, OH, September 5, 1941; *The Key West Citizen*, Key West, FL, September 5, 1941; *The Gallup Independent*, Gallup, NM, September 5, 1941; *Biddeford Daily Journal*, Biddeford, ME, September 5, 1941; *Madison Capital Times*, Madison, WI, September 7, 1941; *Las Cruces Sun News*, Las Cruces, NM, September 9, 1941; and others.

Coverage of the preliminary game of the Little World Series: "Little Indians Top Young Cards, 2-1, in 'World Series,' " *The Cleveland Plain Dealer,* September 22, 1941, 12.

I: EARLY LIFE

CHAPTER ONE: A CRUEL WINTER

Personal information, descriptions, and anecdotes are from Josephine Mathey Morhard's autobiographical notes, photographs, and interviews with her family. Additional information on Joseph Mathey, Messach Butler, and their families from U.S. Federal Census records and New York Passenger Lists, 1820–1957. Birth dates from the Ohio Births and Christenings Index, 1800–1962.

Details about League Park and the Cleveland Spiders 1899 season: Ken Krsolovic and Bryan Fritz, *League Park* (Jefferson, NC: McFarland & Company, 2013), 16–18; Peter Cozzens, "Tangled in Their Own Web: The 1899 Cleveland Spiders, Baseball's Worst Team," *The National Pastime Museum* (July 6, 2016), www.thenationalpastimemuseum.com/article/tangled-their-own-web-1899-cleveland-spiders-baseball-s-worst-team.

The 1899 cold wave is covered in numerous publications, newspapers, reports, online sources, and the National Centers for Environmental Information at the National Oceanic and Atmospheric Administration (NOAA).

The cold wave in Ohio: The record temperature in Milligan, Ohio, can be found in "The Cold, Bitter Truth about Milligan's Bend," *Perry Tribune*, February 7, 2011, www.perrytribune. com/news/article_59df9329-e759-5990-9ed4-f07a44974b6b. html; the Hamilton, Ohio, newspaper quoted is the *Hamilton Daily Republican News*, February 10, 1899; the quote "mother of all cold waves" came from Gregory McNamee, "Relief," *The Akron Beacon Journal,* February 10, 1899, 1.

The cold wave across the U.S.: "The Worst Cold Snap in North American History," Encyclopedia Brittanica Blog, February 11, 2009, blogs.britannica.com/2009/02/february-1899-the-worst-cold-snap-in-north-american-history/; "Relief," *The Akron Beacon Journal,* February 10, 1899, 1; "Climate History: The Great Arctic Outbreak of February 1899," *NOAA*, accessed April 13, 2014, www.ncdc.noaa.gov/news/climate-history-great-arctic-outbreak-february-1899.

The weather system that caused the cold wave: A detailed report of the weather system that caused the cold spell can be found in Paul J. Kocin, Alan D. Weiss, and Joseph J. Wagner, "The Great Arctic Outbreak and East Coast Blizzard," *American Meteorological Society*, December 1988, accessed April 13, 2014, 305–314, doi.org/10.1175/15200434(1988)003<0305 :TGAOAE>2.0.CO;2.

Historical and geological information on the eastern Ohio/ western Pennsylvania region: S. W. and P. A. Durant, *The History of Lawrence County 1770–1877* (Philadelphia: L. H. Everts & Co.); H. S. Williams, *History of the Trumbull and Mahoning Counties Vol. 1* (Mahoning County: H Z Williams & Bro., 1882), 52–82; Wick W. Wood, *History of Lawrence County Pennsylvania* (New Castle, PA: The News Company Limited Steam Printers, 1887), 6–7.

Farm life, farming, and structures in the region: David B. Danbom, *Born in the Country: A History of Rural America* (Baltimore: Johns Hopkins University Press, 1995), 64–65; "Northwestern Woodland, Grassland, and Specialized Farming Region, c. 1830–1960," accessed November 13, 2012, www. phmc.state.pa.us/portal/communities/agriculture/files/ context/northwestern_woodland.pdf.

Welsh immigrants coming to Pennsylvania to work in the mines: Matthew S. Magda, "The Welsh in Pennsylvania, the Peoples of Pennsylvania Pamphlet No. 1," *Commonwealth of Pennsylvania* (1998). Details on South Wales coal mining: "South Wales Coal Mining," *Cuffley Industrial Heritage Society,* accessed November 14, 2012, www.cuffleyindustrialheritage. com/page63.html.

CHAPTER TWO: THE EARLY YEARS

Personal information and anecdotes are from Josephine Mathey Morhard's autobiographical notes and interviews with her family. Descriptions of the areas of Poland, Ohio; Bessemer, Pennsylvania; and New Castle, Pennsylvania; and the schoolhouse from author visits and photographs.

Details about school in the 1890s: "Our Schools," Poland Township Historical Society, accessed November 13, 2012, polandtownship.com/images/historical-society/pdfs/ schools_libraries.pdf; "The Late Nineteenth-Century One-Room School," accessed July 23, 2012, www.heritageall. org/wp-content/uploads/2013/03/Americas-One-Room-Schools-of-the-1890s.pdf; "One Room Schoolhouse in Pennsylvania," ExplorePAhistory.com, accessed November 16, 2012, explorepahistory.com/viewLesson.php?id=1-D-46; H. S. Williams, *History of the Trumbull and Mahoning Counties Vol. 1* (Mahoning County: H Z Williams & Bro., 1882), 52–82.

Children's fashions in the 1890s: accessed July 14, 2012, www.fashion-era.com/Childrens_clothes/1890_ 1900_girls_costume_pictures.htm.

Transformation of America in the late 1800s–early 1900 and the plight of farmers: John Whiteclay Chambers III, *The Tyranny of Change: America in the Progressive Era, 1890– 1920* (New Brunswick, NJ: Rutgers University Press, 2000). Kindle Locations 144–148, 152–163, 171–177, 191–192, 200– 206, 210–217, 217–228, 232–239, 716–726. Kindle Edition: David B. Danbom, *Born in the Country: A History of Rural America* (Baltimore: Johns Hopkins University Press, 1995), 86–90, 149–153, 162.

Bessemer, Pennsylvania, the Bessemer Limestone Company, the ethnicity of workers, and the limestone mining process: Wick W. Wood, *History of Lawrence County Pennsylvania* (New Castle, PA: The News Company Limited Steam Printers, 1887), 133; Joseph Green Butler, *History of Youngstown and the Mahoning Valley, Ohio, Vol. 1* (Mahoning County: American Historical Society, 1921), 727–729.

CHAPTER THREE: MAKING A DECISION

Personal information, descriptions, and anecdotes are from Josephine Mathey Morhard's autobiographical notes, photographs, and interviews with her family. Additional information from U.S. Census Bureau.

Sears, Roebuck Catalog pages: Ancestry.com, *Historic Catalogs of Sears, Roebuck and Co., 1896–1993* [database online]. Provo, UT, USA: Ancestry.com Operations, Inc., 2010. 1903 Original data: *Sears Roebuck Catalogs 1896–1993, Vol. 102–228 K.* Chicago: Sears, Roebuck and Co. 510, 751, 964, 986, 1016,1042.

Change was coming: John Whiteclay Chambers II, *The Tyranny of Change: America in the Progressive Era, 1890–1920.* Kindle Locations 1052–1062. Kindle Edition.

The young resist constraints: John Whiteclay Chambers II, *The Tyranny of Change: America in the Progressive Era, 1890–1920.* Kindle Locations 1517–1525, 1527–1530. Kindle Edition.

Newcastle, Pennsylvania: Wick W. Wood, *History of Lawrence County Pennsylvania* (New Castle, PA: The News Company Limited Steam Printers, 1887), 7–13; History of Lawrence County, Visit Lawrence County, accessed April 13, 2015, visitlawrencecounty.com/about-us/history-of-lawrence-county/"Historic Homes"; *Lawrence County Historical Society,* www.lawrencechs.com/tours/historic-home/; Donald W. Fox, *Bridges to the Past, Lawrence County Historical Society* (State College, PA: Commercial Printing Inc., 1994), 23–25, 39, 50, 68–74, 143–145.

Corn husking: "Harvesting Corn Growing Seasons: An American Farm Family at the Beginning of the Twentieth Century," accessed January 13, 2018, www.growingseasons.com/Growing_Seasons/Harvesting_Corn.html.

II: STRUGGLES

Chapter Four: On Her Own

Personal information and anecdotes are from Josephine Mathey Morhard's autobiographical notes and interviews with her family. Descriptions of Bessemer and Hillsville, Pennsylvania, are from author visits, old photos, and maps. Other information from U.S. Census data and military records.

Bessemer, Pennsylvania, Bessemer Limestone Company, and processes: Wood, *History of Lawrence County Pennsylvania*, 90, 133; Butler, *History of Youngstown and the Mahoning Valley, Ohio, Vol. 1,* 727–729; "Bessemer Limestone & Cement Company—Bessemer PA," Lawrence County Memoirs, accessed November 20, 2014, www.lawrencecountymemoirs. com/lcmpages/395/bessemer-limestone-cement-company-bessemer-pa.

Farmers versus limestone mine workers: Louis S. Warren, *The Hunter's Game: Poachers and Conservationists in Twentieth Century America* (New Haven, CT: Yale University Press, 1999), 2–3.

Medicine Show: Ann Anderson, *Snake Oil Hustlers and Hambones: The American Medicine Show* (Jefferson, NC: McFarland Publishing Company, 2004), 1–2, 31–35, 48–49, 140–143.

Italian hunters, farmers, murder, and the Black Hand: Warren, *The Hunter's Game: Poachers and Conservationists in Twentieth Century America,* 5–8; "The Black Hand, La Mano Nera," Mahoning Township History 1820–1907, Hillsville, accessed March 15, 2012, www.mahoningtownship.net/about. html.

Chapter Five: Bright Lights

Personal information and anecdotes are from Josephine Mathey Morhard's autobiographical notes and interviews with her family. Descriptions of Youngstown, Ohio, are from author visits, old photos, and maps. Other information from U.S. Census data and military records.

Youngstown: Williams, *History of the Trumbull and Mahoning Counties Vol. 1,* 66–69, 92–96, 104, 370–373; Butler, *History of Youngstown and the Mahoning Valley, Ohio, Vol. 1,* 88, 103–104, 117, 180–185, 193–194; Sean T. Posey, *Lost*

Youngstown (Charleston, SC: The History Press, 2016), 12, 19–21, 59–64, 67–70; "In Youngstown We Make Steel (1803–1977)," August 24, 2008, accessed May 28, 2013, www.urbanohio.com/forum/index.php?topic=17134.0.

Youngstown baseball: "Ohio Pennsylvania League, accessed March 12, 2018, www.baseball-reference.com/bullpen/Ohio-Pennsylvania_League; Vince Guerrieri, "Youngstown Baseball Has a History Dating Back to 19th Century," August 14, 2012, didthetribewinlastnight.com/blog/2012/08/14/youngstown-baseball-has-a-history-dating-back-to-19th-century; John Zajc, "Fifty Bucks and a Ball Club," The 1905 Ohio-Pennsylvania League, September 15, 2003, www.sabr.org/sabr.cfm?a=cms,c,412,5,0.

Women's rights, education, work: Eleanor Flexner and Ellen Fitzpatrick, *Century of Struggle, the Women's Rights Movement in the United States* (Cambridge, MA: The Belknap Press of Harvard University Press, 1959, 1975), 7, 22, 25–30, 141–145, 221–225; Jean-Jacques Rousseau, *L'Emile*, ed. W. H. Payne (New York and London, 1906), 263.

Park Theater, Warner Brothers, Burlesque, New Park Theater: Sean T. Posey, *Historic Theaters of Youngstown and the Mahoning Valley* (Charleston, SC: The History Press, 2017), 11–14; "Park Theater," accessed July 4, 2013, cinematreasures.org/theaters/34575; "True Burlesque," trueburlesque.blogspot.com/2012/08/new-park-burlesk-youngstown-ohio-true.html.

Cleveland: David D. Van Tassel and John J. Grabowski, *The Encyclopedia of Cleveland History* (Bloomington and Indianapolis: Indiana University Press, 1987), xxix–xxxvi, 379–380, 547–549, 735; Dan Ruminski, *Cleveland in the Gilded Age: A Stroll Down Millionaires' Row* (Charleston, SC: The History Press, 2012), 11–17.

CHAPTER SIX: THE PROMOTER

Personal information and anecdotes are from autobiographical notes from Josephine Mathey Morhard, Geraldine Gerau DeRosa, and interviews with Al Morhard and family members. Other information from Brooklyn, New York, City Directories, U.S. Census records, Ohio Birth Index, 1908–1964. Carter Hotel and George Gerau descriptions from photographs.

George B. Gerau's physical violence to Josephine Morhard, accounts of her "nervous attacks," and nonpayment of support and disappearance are documented in Cuyahoga Common Pleas Court Case #263928 M663, August 5, and September 25, 1926, "Josephine C. Gerau v. George B. Gerau."

Carter hotel: Cleveland Memory Project, accessed November 1, 2013, images.ulib.csuohio.edu/cdmsingleitem/collection/postcards/id/1962/rec/4.

Chef Boiardi; "Foodimentary," accessed November 1, 2013, foodimentary.com/2012/03/20/a-history-of-chef-boyardee/.

Cleveland Group plan, University Circle: Van Tassel and Grabowski, *The Encyclopedia of Cleveland History*, 654, 998–999; case.edu/ech/timeline/x.

West Virginia Coal Mines: "Big Deal in Coal Mines," *New York Times*, June 18, 1901, 1; "Jonathan Williams, 'East Side Castle,' " *Times West Virginia*, March 6, 2012, accessed February 13, 2016, www.timeswv.com/news/local_news/east-side-castle/article_c68c471e-ffea-5219-b8a5-7c9b4c418663.html.

Patent for a "simple and improved way" to thread sewing machine needles: "Sewing Machine Needle," 1899, accessed December 5, 2013, www.google.com/patents/US623666.

Chief organizer, Protective Labor Union Insurance Company: "Union Labor's Insurance Company Assured Now," *Trenton Evening Times* (Trenton, NJ), January 30, 1910, 14.

1910 in Los Angeles: "Californians at Seaside," *Los Angeles Herald,* May 22, 1910, 38.

July 1910, Lake Arrowhead: "Good Oil Opportunity," *San Bernardino County Sun* (San Bernardino, CA), June 30, 1910; "Patented Oil Lands at $25 Per Acre," *Los Angeles Herald*, July 10, 1910, 27.

Deeds: *San Bernardino County Sun*, June 2, 1910, 9; August 9, 1910, 12; August 20, 1910, 9; January 25, 1911, 9; March 3, 1913, 9.

Estimated cost of drilling: "Coulson Now Oil Magnate," *Petaluma Argus-Courier Petaluma* (Petaluma, CA), August 19, 1911, 5.

New Mexico: "For Sale," *Albuquerque Journal,* March 30, 1912, 3.

None of oil fields produced: "Oil Boom in San Bernardino

Was a Bust," *The Sun* (San Bernardino, CA), July 24, 2017, accessed September 15, 2017, www.sbsun.com/2014/06/09/oil-boom-in-san-bernardino-county-was-a-bust.

Low points: "Undelivered Telegrams," *The Los Angeles Times*, April 3, 1912, 25; "Vain Appeal to Unionites," *The Los Angeles Times*, May 10, 1913, 14; "Arrested for Not Paying Board Bill," *The Sun* (San Bernardino, CA), 8.

Bounced back in a big way: "Gompers Daughter to Wed Local Attorney," *San Francisco Chronicle*, December 5, 1913, 5; "Corporation Attorney Will Wed Miss Gompers on His Birthday," *Salt Lake Telegram*, December 17, 1913, 16; "Rumors of Stage Dispelled: Miss Gompers Is Engaged," *Oakland Tribune*, December 18, 1913, 3; "Miss Sadie Gompers to Marry Attorney of San Francisco," *Washington Herald*, December 19, 1913, 3; "Daughter of Labor's 'Grand Old Man' Is Going to Marry a Lawyer," *Muskogee Times-Democrat,* December 22, 1913, "Samuel Gompers' Daughter Going to Marry Lawyer," *Orlando Sentinel,* December 18, 1913, 2; "'I'm Just a Plain Corporation Lawyer' Says Fiancé of Labor Leader's Daughter," *Wilkes-Barre Times Leader, The Evening News*, January 3, 1914, 9; "Miss Gompers Declares Herself a Suffragette," *The Day Book* (Chicago, IL), February 21, 1914, 23.

Sadie Gompers breaks engagement: "Cupid's Pranks Erratic: Loves Me, Loves Me Not," *Oakland Tribune*, February 4, 1914, 3; "Miss Sadie Gompers, Who Breaks Engagement," *Trenton Evening Times*, February 5, 1914, 11.

Another marriage: www.familysearch.org/ark:/61903/1:1:JDZN-W62, accessed October 4, 2017.

1918 newspaper notice: "Destitute Girl Seeks Location of Father," *San Francisco Chronicle,* May 15, 1918, 10.

Miami Beach, Casa Grande Hotel Company; "Casa Grande Hotel Co. Ready to Sell Stock," *The Miami News*, February 12, 1918, 12.

World War I over: Henry R. Luce, ed., *This Fabulous Century: 1920–1930, Vol. 3* (New York: Time Life Books, 1969), 99, 105–112, 134–135, 175–179.

New clients: "Motor Speedway in Atlantic City," *Trenton Evening Times*, November 5, 1922, 11.

Engine patent: "Internal Combustion Engine," accessed October 9, 2017, www.google.com/pg/patents/US1613990.

Florida land boom: Gregg M. Turner, *The Florida Land Boom of the 1920s* (Jefferson, NC: McFarland & Company, Inc., 2015), 137–142, 156–163; "The Great Florida Land Boom," accessed October 15, 2017, floridahistory.org/landboom.htm; "Ghost Hotel: The Unfinished Ringling Ritz-Carlton in Sarasota," accessed October 15, 2017, accessed October 15, 2017, www.floridamemory.com/blog/2014/04/30/ghost-hotel-the-unifinished-ringling-ritz-carlton-in-sarasota/1-10; "Isman on Florida," *Tampa Tribune,* August 21, 1925, 6.

Optimist Club: "Optimists Club of Tampa Is Chartered," *Tampa Tribune*, February 1, 1924, 3; Ad, *Tampa Tribune*, January 27, 1924, 19.

Ads, articles: "Gulf Frontage at Sarasota on Block," *Tampa Tribune*, March 27, 1924, 11; "Here's a Real Opportunity: Sarasota Gulf Front Property," *Tampa Tribune*, March 30, 1924, 25; "The Rather Deluxe Camp of Attorney and Mrs. George B. Gerau," *The Wilkes-Barre Record*, August 16, 1924.

Mending fluid ads: "New Factory in City: Mending Fluid to be Manufactured on Fifth Street, 50 People Employed," *Hamilton Evening Journal* (Hamilton, OH), January 5, 1926, 12; "VEO Products Is Incorporated," *The Journal News* (Hamilton, OH), February 12, 1926, 11; "Up to Date Methods in Mending," *The Fulton Democrat* (McConnelsburg, PA), May 13, 1926, 6; "Female Help," *The Ogden Standard-Examiner*, June 20, 1926, 23.

Mary Baker Eddy: Gillian Gill, *Mary Baker Eddy* (Cambridge, MA: Perseus Books, 1998), 39–48, 63, 79–80, 82, 105, 133, 167–168; "Mary Baker Eddy 1821–1910: Her Life & Legacy," *The Mary Baker Eddy Library*, accessed October 30, 2017, www.marybakereddylibrary.org/mary-baker-eddy/the-life-of-mary-baker-eddy/; Mary Baker Eddy, "Science and Health with Key to the Scriptures," accessed October 30, 2017, www.mbeinstitute.org/SAH/1910.pdf.

CHAPTER SEVEN: THE BUTCHER

Personal information and anecdotes are from interviews with Mrs. Morhard's son and written documents. Descriptions of the ship, entry into New York, Chicago, and Chicago stockyards are from photos and personal travels. All information on marriages, residences, and so forth is from U.S. Census Bureau and marriage records. Information on Albert H. Morhard's voyage on the SS *Rochambeau*, questions asked, arrival in New York, and destination of Chicago are in the SS *Rochambeau*'s List or Manifest of Alien Passengers for the United States, which sailed from LeHavre, April 19, 1913.

Additional journey information: "The Immigrant Journey," accessed September 16, 2017, www.ohranger.com/ellis-island/immigration-journey; Elizabeth Yew MD, "Medical Inspection of Immigrants at Ellis Island, 1891–1924," National Center for Biotechnology, National Institutes of Health, accessed September 16, 2017, www.ncbi.nlm.nih.gov/pmc/articles/PMC1805119/pdf/bullnyacadmed00114-0060.pdf; Maggie Blanck, "Quarantine," accessed September 16, 2017, www.maggieblanck.com/Quarantine.html.

SS *Rochambeau* and French Line information: "Ship Descriptions," The Ship's List, accessed September 18, 2017, www.theshipslist.com/ships/descriptions/ShipsR.shtml; "A Brief History of the Cruise Ship Industry," Cruise Line History, accessed September 18, 2017, cruiselinehistory.com/a-brief-history-of-the-cruise-ship-industry/; "The Fleets," The Ships List, accessed September 18, 2017, www.theshipslist.com/ships/lines/french.shtml.

New York City, 1913: The Retronaut, "1913–15 New York," YouTube, 3:03, May 26, 2014, www.youtube.com/watch?v=uJoIWicJIaM; Guy Jones, "100 Years ago—January 14, 1913," YouTube, 1:35; Guy Jones, "1911—A Trip Through New York City," YouTube, 7:45, April 7, 2018; Devin Gannon, "From oysters to falafel: The complete history of street vending in NYC," www.6sqft.com, accessed November 23, 2017,

www.6sqft.com/from-oysters-to-falafel-the-complete-history-of-street-vending-in-nyc/; Brian Hoffman, "A Brief History of Street Vending in New York City," midtownlunch.com, accessed September 17, 2017, midtownlunch.com/2011/11/30/a-slice-of-street-vendor-history/; Upton Sinclair and Eugene Brieux, "Damaged Goods," gutenberg.org, accessed September 17, 2017, www.gutenberg.org/files/1157/1157-h/1157-h.htm#link2H_4_0002; Ezra Bowen, *This Fabulous*

Century: 1910–1920 (Alexandria, VA: Time-Life Books, 1969), 42–46; G. Fenske, "Woolworth Building Was the Highest Building in New York in 1913," Woolworth Tours, accessed September 17, 2017, woolworthtours.com/about-woolworth-building.

Baseball in New York City, 1913: "Ballpark Chronology," The Official Site of the New York Yankees, newyorkyankees. mlb.com, accessed July 13, 2017, newyork.yankees.mlb.com/ nyy/history/ballparks.jsp; "Ebbets Field," Ballparks of Baseball, accessed July 14, 2017, www.ballparksofbaseball. com/ballparks/ebbets-field/; Lily Rothman, "See How the Female New York Giants Made Baseball History," *Time*, accessed October 13, 2017, time.com/4539351/new-york-female-giants-baseball.

New York's Darker Side: Susanna Broyles, "Power, Corruption, and Tammany Hall: Sketches of Lesser Known New York City Mayors, 1869–1913," Museum of the City of New York, accessed October 13, 2017, blog.mcny.org/2013/11/05/ power-corruption-and-tammany-hall-sketches-of-lesser-known-new-york-city-mayors-1869-1913/; Thomas Hunt, "DeMarco, Joseph (c1876–1916)," The American Mafia, accessed October 14, 2017, mob-who.blogspot.com/search/ label/DeMarco; Thomas Hunt, "Genovese, Vito (1897–1969)," The American Mafia, accessed September 16, 2017, mob-who.blogspot.com/2011/04/genovese-vito-1897-1969.html.

Grand Central Station: Sam Roberts, "100 Years of Grandeur: The Birth of Grand Central Terminal," *New York Times*, accessed September 16, 2017, www.nytimes.com/ 2013/01/20/nyregion/the-birth-of-grand-central-terminal-100-years-later.html.

Alsace and Mulhouse history: Encyclopedia Brittanica ed., "Alsace" Encyclopedia Brittanica, accessed September 18, 2017, www.britannica.com/place/Alsace; Encyclopedia Brittanica, "Mulhouse," accessed September 18, 2017, https:// www.britannica.com/place/Mulhouse.

Turner Club: Claire E. Nolte, "The German Turnverein," Ohio University, accessed September 17, 2017, www.ohio. edu/chastain/rz/turnvere.htm.

Chicago, 1913: "La Salle Street Station," Chicagology, accessed September 20, 2017, chicagology.com/goldenage/gold-enage108/; Whett Moser, "Smoke Monsters: Chicago 1913, Beijing 2013," *Chicago Magazine,* accessed September 17, 2017, www.chicagomag.com/Chicago-Magazine/The-312/January-2013/Smoke-Monsters-Chicago-1913-Beijing-2013; Ronald Dale Karr, "Rapid Transit System," Encyclopedia of Chicago, accessed September 20, 2017, www.encyclopedia.chicagohistory.org/pages/1042.html.

Chicago stockyard: Rick Halpern, "Race, Ethnicity, and Union in the Chicago Stockyards, 1917–1922," *International Review of Social History,* Vol. 37, no. 1 (1992): 25–58; Louise Carroll Wade, "Meatpacking," Encyclopedia of Chicago, accessed September 20, 2017, www.encyclopedia.chicagohistory.org/pages/804.html; Upton Sinclair, *The Jungle* (New York: Doubleday & Co., 1906); Theodore Roosevelt, "Special Message June 4, 1906," The American Presidency Project, University of California, Santa Barbara, accessed September 20, 2017, www.presidency.ucsb.edu/ws/index.php?pid=69670&st=&st1=; Mark L. Wilson, "Union Stock Yard & Transit Co.," Encyclopedia of Chicago, www.encyclopedia.chicagohistory.org/pages/2883.html; Allen Cornwell, "Chicago 1900: Pickled Hands and Much Worse," Our Great American Heritage, accessed September 20, 2017, www.ourgreatamericanheritage.com/2015/09/disease-death-and-child-labor-the-birth-of-the-meatpacking-industry-in-chicago; Ron Grossman, "Hog Butcher for the World," *Chicago Tribune,* February 19, 2012, www.chicagotribune.com/ct-per-flash-stockyards-0219-2-20120219-story.html.

CHAPTER EIGHT: ANOTHER TRY, AND ANOTHER

Personal information, descriptions, and anecdotes are primarily from interviews with Mrs. Morhard's son, family, photographs, and written documents. All information on marriages, divorces, residences, and so forth is from U.S. Census Bureau, marriage and divorce records.

Chicken in every pot: "Chicken in Every Pot," Dictionary of American History, Encyclopedia.com, accessed April 21, 2018, www.encyclopedia.com/history/dictionaries-thesauruses-pictures-and-press-releases/chicken-every-pot.

Health department complaint: "Butcher Draws Fine: Convicted of Using Meat Preservative," *Cleveland Plain Dealer*, October 15, 1928, 2.

CHAPTER NINE: HARD TIMES
Personal information, descriptions, and anecdotes are primarily from interviews with Mrs. Morhard's son, family, photographs, and written documents.

Hough Neighborhood history: "Region II," *Cleveland Planning Commission,* 92–93, accessed October 3, 2017, planning.city.cleveland.oh.us/cwp/2000/assets/Civic_Vision_2000_RegionII.pd; Krsolovic and Fritz, *League Park,* 8–12, 68–70.

Cleveland in the Depression: Marian Morton, "It Was the Worst of Times, It Was the Worst of Times: Cleveland and the Great Depression," Teaching Cleveland Digital, accessed October 3, 2017, teachingcleveland.org/it-was-the-worst-of-times-it-was-the-worst-of-times-cleveland-and-the-great-depression-by-marian-morton; "Great Lakes Exposition," *Encyclopedia of Cleveland History*, accessed October 4, 2017, case.edu/ech/articles/g/great-lakes-exposition; Laura J. Gorretta, "Homeless, Vagrants and Tramps," Case Western University, accessed October 7, 2017, case.edu/ech/articles/h/homeless-vagrants-and-tramps/.

CHAPTER TEN: THE GAME
Personal information, descriptions, and anecdotes are from interviews with Mrs. Morhard's son, photographs, and written documents. Recreations of the September 28, 1937, baseball game are from box scores and newspaper accounts. Jack Graney, Pinky Hunter dialogue is authentic from recordings of their broadcasts of Indians games though. Descriptions throughout come from old photographs. Team records and player statistics are from baseball reference materials.

Radio broadcasting history: Tony Silvia, *Baseball Over the Air: The National Pastime Over the Air and in the Imagination* (Jefferson, NC: McFarland & Company, 2007), 35–42, 45–48, 50, 53–55; Charles A. Alexander, *Breaking the Slump: Baseball in the Depression Era* (New York: Columbia University Press, 2002), 75, 97, 110, 167; Dave Zirin, *A People's History of Sports in the United States* (New York: The New Press,

2008), 69; James R. Walker and Pat Hughes, *Crack of the Bat: A History of Baseball on the Radio* (Lincoln: University of Nebraska Press, 2015), 142–170; Fortune Editors, "Big League Baseball," *Fortune, 1937*, June 2, 2013, accessed April 20, 2016, fortune.com/2013/06/02/big-league-baseball-fortune-1937; Pat Doyle, "Baseball Broadcasting from Another Day," *Baseball Almanac*, accessed April 20, 2016, www.baseball-almanac.com/minor-league/minor2004a.shtml.

Warner and Swasey Company: Van Tassel and Grabowski, *The Encyclopedia of Cleveland History*, 1027–1028.

Cleveland's Terminal Tower: Van Tassel and Grabowski, *The Encyclopedia of Cleveland History*, 279.

Indians announcers Jack Graney and Pinky Hunter and their typical banter can be found in: "Ex-Tribe Voice Graney, 91, Dies," *The Cleveland Plain Dealer*, April 21, 1978, 61, 67; Ted Patterson, "Jack Graney, the First Player-Broadcaster," *Society for American Baseball Research*, accessed June 20, 2016, research.sabr.org/journals/jack-graney; "Jack Graney," National Baseball Hall of Fame, accessed June 20, 2016, baseballhall.org/discover/awards/ford-c-frick/2016-candidates/graney-jack, retrieved June 2016; "Was Jack Graney the Best Indians Announcer Ever?" Cleveland.com, August 4, 2011, www.cleveland.com/remembers/index.ssf/2011/08/was_jack_graney_the_best_india.html; Wayne Mack, "Radio," Van Tassel and Grabowski, *Encyclopedia of Cleveland History*, 813.

Election Day: "200,000 Expected to Cast Ballots Today," *The Plain Dealer*, September 28, 1937, 1–2.

Bob Feller's baseball career: C. Paul Rogers III, "Bob Feller," *Society for American Baseball Research*, accessed June 22, 2016, sabr.org/bioproj/person/de74b9f8; "Bob Feller," National Baseball Hall of Fame, accessed June 22, 2016, baseballhall.org/hall-of-famers/feller-bob; Alexander, *Breaking the Slump: Baseball in the Depression Era*, 124.

1937 baseball season, New York Yankees, Major League baseball teams, and players other than the Cleveland Indians: Alexander, *Breaking the Slump: Baseball in the Depression Era*, 2, 122–123, 125–127, 137–145; "1937 Just Push Press for Repeat," *This Great Game: The Online Book of Baseball*, accessed June 21, 2016, www.thisgreatgame.com/1937-baseball-history.html; Lawrence Baldassaro, "Joe DiMaggio," *Society for American Baseball Research*, accessed June 21, 2016, sabr.org/bioproj/person/a48f1830.

937 Indians players: Charles Alexander, *Breaking the Slump: Baseball in the Depression Era*, 117, 142; "Earl Averill," *National Baseball Hall of Fame*, accessed October 5, 2016, baseballhall.org/hall-of-famers/averill-earl; Dennis Yuhasz, "Earl Averill Biography," *Baseball Almanac*, accessed October 5, 2016, www.baseball-almanac.com/players/earl_averill_biography.shtml; Bill Johnson, "Hal Trosky," *Society for American Baseball Research*, accessed October 5, 2016, sabr.org/bioproj/ person/9a6065ce; John Weeks, "Johnny Allen," *Society for American Baseball Research*, accessed October 5, 2016, sabr.org/bioproj/person/4bb1afb9.

Dizzy Dean quote "two greatest crooks in baseball": Alexander, *Breaking the Slump: Baseball in the Depression Era*, 137.

Recession in 1937–1938: David M. Kennedy, *Freedom from Fear: The American People in Depression and War, 1929–1945* (New York: Oxford University Press, 1999), 163–168, 350–352; T. A. Watkins, *The Great Depression: America in the 1930s* (New York, Boston, London: Back Bay Books, 1993), 306–312; Robert Higgs, "America's Depression within a Depression 1937–39," *Foundation for Economic Freedom*, accessed October 10, 2016, fee.org/articles/americas-depression-within-a-depression-193739/.

President Franklin D. Roosevelt, baseball: Nancy Beck Young, William D. Pedersen, and Byron W. Daynes, *Franklin D. Roosevelt and the Shaping of American Political Culture, Vol. 1* (New York: Routledge, 2001), 119.

President Franklin D. Roosevelt quote: "Baseball as a sport has done as much . . .": Franklin D. Roosevelt, 1932.

President Herbert Hoover quote: "Next to religion, baseball has furnished a greater impact on American Life than any other institution": "Hoover on Baseball," The National Archives Hoover Heads, The Blog of the Herbert Hoover Library and Museum, accessed June 12, 2016, hoover.blogs.archives.gov/2015/10/28/hoover-on-baseball/President Herbert Hoover.

Euclid Avenue Millionaires' Row: Dan Ruminski and Alan

Dutka, *Cleveland in the Gilded Age: A Stroll Down Millionaire's Row* (Charleston, SC: The History Press, 2012), 13–51.

III: BASEBALL

CHAPTER ELEVEN: JOSEPHINE'S IDEA

Personal information, descriptions, and anecdotes are from interviews with Mrs. Morhard's son, family, photographs, and personal documents. Details on population and residences come from U.S. Census documents.

Mayors, history of University Heights: "The History of University Heights," City of University Heights, accessed June 23, 2016, www.universityheights.com/history.

Rockefeller summer home: Michael Rotman, "Forest Hill," Cleveland Historical, accessed April 11, 2018, clevelandhistorical.org/items/show/83.

Shaker Heights history: David G. Molyneaux and Sue Sackman, *75 Years: An Informal History of Shaker Heights* (Shaker Heights, OH: Shaker Heights Public Library, 1987), 15–34.

CHAPTER TWELVE: FOURTEEN LITTLE INDIANS

Personal information and anecdotes are from interviews with Mrs. Morhard's son, family, former players, written documents, photographs, and the film *Bringing Up Baseball* about Mrs. Morhard's Junior American and National Leagues. Descriptions throughout come from old photographs. Team records and player statistics are from baseball reference books.

Cleveland Indians April 19, 1938, opening day: "Burton and Indians Open Fire Today," *The Cleveland Plain Dealer,* April 19, 1938, 14.

Browns offer for Joe DiMaggio, Cubs acquiring Dizzy Dean: "Rejects $10,000 Bid for DiMaggio" and "Dizzy Cost Cubs $185,000 in Cash," *The Cleveland Plain Dealer,* April 19, 1938, 14; "Joe Dimaggio Confronted Same Issues Players Face Today," *New York Daily News*, November 5, 2007, www.nydailynews.com/sports/baseball/yankees/joe-dimaggio-confronted-issues-players-face-today-article-1.255170.

U.S. President and Vice President at Washington Senators

opening day: "Senators Prime Pump for 12 Runs," *The Cleveland Plain Dealer,* April 19, 1938, 14.

Gordon Cobbledick quotes on new manager and pitching staff are in: *The Cleveland Plain Dealer*, Friday, April 15, 1938, 16.

Perceptions of reporters outside Cleveland on Cleveland Indians in 1938: Bill Nowlin, "Ossie Vitt," *Society for American Baseball Research,* accessed February 20, 2018, sabr.org/bioproj/person/128a662b.

Opening day 1938 game results: "Indians Outhit Browns in Opener, 6–2," *The Cleveland Plain Dealer,* April 20, 1938, 1, 12, 14.

Indians in first place: "Feller Clicks as Hemsley Catches," *The Cleveland Plain Dealer,* June 17, 1938, 1, 14.

Indians alternating games between Cleveland Municipal Stadium and League Park: Krsolovic and Fritz, *League Park*, 98–104, 108–112.

CHAPTER THIRTEEN: GROWING PAINS

Personal information and anecdotes are from interviews with Mrs. Morhard's son, family, former players, written documents, photos, and the film about Mrs. Morhard's Junior American and National Leagues. Descriptions come from old photographs. Other information is from baseball reference books.

Tony Pianowski, called by the *Cleveland Plain Dealer* "one of the best around": "Hal Asks Do Kids Forget," *The Cleveland Plain Dealer*, May 12, 1968.

Boys carrying the bags of elderly customers: "Mother's Idea Started Junior Ball Leagues," *The Cleveland Plain Dealer,* September 22, 1941, 10.

CHAPTER FOURTEEN: BASEBALL IDOLS

Personal information and anecdotes are from interviews with Mrs. Morhard's son and former players. Descriptions are from photographs. Cleveland Indians' and player statistics are from baseball reference books.

Biographical information on Jeff Heath: Russell Schneider, *The Cleveland Indians Encyclopedia, third ed.* (Champaign,

IL: Sports Publishing, 2004), 185; C. Paul Rogers III, "Jeff Heath," *Society for American Baseball Research*, accessed March 27, 2018, sabr.org/bioproj/person/50c16cd1.

Oscar Vitt quote "best natural hitter since Joe Jackson": Schneider, *The Cleveland Indians Encyclopedia, third ed.*, 185.

Cleveland area streetcars: James R. Spangler and James A. Toman, *Cleveland and Its Streetcars* (Charleston, SC: Arcadia Publishing, 2006), 85, 100.

The history of League Park can be found in: Krsolovic and Fritz, *League Park*, 8–25, 38, 32–36, 41–43.

Biographical information on Shoeless Joe Jackson: Krsolovic and Fritz, *League Park*, 43–46; David Fletz, "Shoeless Joe Jackson," *Society for American Baseball Research*, accessed March 28, 2018, sabr.org/bioproj/person/7afaa6b2.

Biographical information on Louis Sockalexis: Krsolovic and Fritz, *League Park*, 15, 49; Fletz, "Louis Sockalexis," *Society for American Baseball Research*, accessed March 28, 2018, sabr.org/bioproj/person/2b1aea0a.

1920 World Series win: Krsolovic and Fritz, *League Park*, 68–70.

October 2, 1938, game at Cleveland Municipal Stadium: "Feller Strikes Out 18," *The Cleveland Plain Dealer*, October 3, 1938, 1, 14.

CHAPTER FIFTEEN: THEY WILL COME

Personal information, anecdotes, and descriptions are from interviews with Mrs. Morhard's son Al Morhard, Pat Rogers, Catherine Berlin, Jack Anderson, Neil Lebovitz, written documents, photos, maps, and the film about Mrs. Morhard's Junior American and National Leagues.

"Just wait until next season" quote: "Mother's Idea Started Junior Ball Leagues," *The Cleveland Plain Dealer,* September 22, 1941, 10.

CHAPTER SIXTEEN: THE JUNIOR AMERICAN LEAGUE

Personal information, anecdotes, quotes, and descriptions are from interviews with Mrs. Morhard's son Al Morhard, former players, written documents, photos, and the film about Mrs. Morhard's Junior American and National Leagues. Mel

Harder at the game is from a letter from Mel Harder to Al
Morhard in 1993 and a photograph he enclosed that appeared
in an unknown Cleveland newspaper. The quote is from former
players' memories of what he said to them.

Mel Harder career: Mark Stewart, "Mel Harder," *Society for
American Baseball Research*, accessed December 14, 2017,
sabr.org/bioproj/person/e1c50572.

Information on speedmeters: "The Historic Quest for Speed
in Baseball," *Scoutee*, accessed January 23, 2018, scoutee.co/
the-historic-quest-for-speed-in-baseball/; "Meter to Record
Feller's Speed," *Richmond Times Dispatch* (AP), June 6, 1939.

Quote "When there was a problem, she served as Judge
Landis": "Hal Asks Do Kids Forget," *The Cleveland Plain
Dealer*, May 12, 1968.

Elmer Kaufman's new Junior American Association organization announcement: *Heights Press*, June 13, 1940.

Village Hall dinner: "Little Indians on the Warpath," *Heights
Press*, August 13, 1939.

CHAPTER SEVENTEEN: THE JUNIOR NATIONAL LEAGUE

Personal information, anecdotes, quotes, and descriptions
are from interviews with Mrs. Morhard's son Al Morhard,
Marlo Termini, other former players, written documents, photos, and the film about Mrs. Morhard's Junior American and
National Leagues.

Opening day, Junior American and National Leagues: "Two
Junior Baseball Leagues to Start Play in University Sunday,"
Heights Press, June 19, 1941.

Biographical information on Roger Peckinpaugh: Peter M.
Gordon, "Roger Peckinpaugh," *Society for American Baseball
Research*, accessed January 19, 2018, sabr.org/bioproj/per-
son/829dbefb, reprinted from David Jones, ed., *Deadball Stars
of the American League* (Washington, DC: Potomac Books,
2006).

Players' revolt against Cleveland Indians Manager Oscar
Vitt: Alexander, *Breaking the Slump: Baseball in the Depression Era*, 249–251; Brad Sullivan, ed., *Batting Four Thousand: Baseball in the Western Reserve* (Cleveland, OH: Society
for American Baseball Research, 2008), 37–42.

Mayor Aurelius: "The History of University Heights," *City*

of University Heights, accessed November 23, 2017, www.universityheights.com/history/.

Cleveland State Hospital: Van Tassel and Grabowski, *The Encyclopedia of Cleveland History*, 273–274.

Parmadale Orphanage: Marian J. Morton, "The Transformation of Catholic Orphanages, 1851–1996," *The Catholic Historical Review*, January 2002.

Marlo Termini: Douglas Dies, "Sandlotters Play World Series, Too," Associated Press articles in numerous newspapers, September 5, 1941; Terry Pluto, "Hall Of Famer, Hailed As Athlete, Teacher, Coach, Loved People," *The Plain Dealer*, March 22, 2018.

Quote, "You'll have to wait until the game is over": "Hal Asks Do Kids Forget," *The Cleveland Plain Dealer*, May 12, 1968.

Pinky Hunter quote: "Bringing Up Baseball" film about Mrs. Morhard's Junior American and National Leagues, Inc., 1941.

CHAPTER EIGHTEEN: CONFLICTS ABROAD

Personal information, anecdotes, quotes, and descriptions are from interviews with Mrs. Morhard's son Al Morhard, Marlo Termini, other former players, written documents, photos, and the film about Mrs. Morhard's Junior American and National Leagues.

The war in Europe and U.S. neutrality: David G. McCullough, ed., *World War II, Volume I* (Washington, DC: American Heritage Publishing Co.), 88–93, 97–101, 112–117, 131–135.

Roosevelt-Churchill talks on warship: "Sea Parley Spurs Fight Against Axis: Roosevelt-Churchill Talks Held on Warships," *The Cleveland Plain Dealer*, August 15, 1941, 1, 5.

Lindbergh: "Crowd at Airport Greets Lindbergh," *The Cleveland Plain Dealer*, August 9, 1941, 1.3; A. Scott Berg, *Lindbergh* (New York: Berkley Publishing Group, 1998); Susan Dunn, *FDR, Willkie, Lindbergh, Hitler, the Election amid the Storm* (New Haven, CT: Yale University Press, 2013), 43–56.

Evacuation of British children during World War II: Julie Summers, *When the Children Came Home* (Simon & Schuster

Ltd., 2011); "Children's Overseas Reception Board," The National Archives, United Kingdom, accessed January 24, 2018, webarchive.nationalarchives.gov.uk/20090218044210/; yourarchives.nationalarchives.gov.uk/index.php?title=Children%27s_Overseas_Reception_Board.

Joe DiMaggio's fifty-six-game hitting streak: Ray Robinson, "Baseball '91; 1941 An Unmatchable Summer," *The New York Times*, accessed March 15, 2018, www.nytimes.com /1991/04/07/sports/baseball-91-1941-an-unmatchable-summer.html?pagewanted=all; Krslovic and Fritz, *League Park*, 117–118.

The Little Indians and Little Cardinals standings: "Indians Leading University Loop," *Heights Press,* August 15, 1941.

Little World Series benefit: "Young American Wants to Help: It's a Junior Affair," *The Cleveland Plain Dealer*, September 17, 1941, 14.

Coverage of the Junior American and National League playoffs and ox roast: "Little Indians Top Young Cards, 2–1, in 'World' Series," *The Cleveland Plain Dealer,* September 22, 1941.

Tickets for the World Series sold at stores: "Series' Tickets Ready," *The Cleveland Plain Dealer*, September 24, 1941, 24.

CHAPTER NINETEEN: THE LITTLE WORLD SERIES

Personal information, anecdotes, and descriptions are from interviews with Mrs. Morhard's son Al Morhard, other former players, printed schedules, written documents, newspaper articles, and photos. The game was recreated from newspaper accounts and box scores.

Various International News Service and Associated Press articles on the Little World Series, including: Douglas Dies, *Associated Press Feature Service*, September 5, 1941; *Cumberland Sunday Times*, Cumberland, MD, September 7, 1941; *Evening Independent*, Massillon, OH, September 5, 1941; *The Key West Citizen*, Key West, FL, September 5, 1941; *The Gallup Independent*, Gallup, NM, September 5, 1941; *Biddeford Daily Journal*, Biddeford, ME, September 5, 1941; *Madison Capital Times*, Madison, WI, September 7, 1941; *Las Cruces Sun News*, Las Cruces, NM, September 9, 1941; and others.

Little World Series program, results, and box scores: "Little Indians Rip No-Hit Bid to Win." *The Cleveland Plain Dealer*, September 29, 1941, 14, 20.

League Park and Babe Ruth's five hundredth home run: Krsolovic and Fritz, *League Park*, 32–36, 85–86.

Little League in Williamsport, Pennsylvania: Carl E. Stotz and Kenneth D. Loss, *A Promise Kept: The Story of the Founding of Little League Baseball* (Jersey Shore, PA: Zebrowski Historical Services Publishing Company, 1992), 1–47.

Congratulatory article: "We Congratulate You, Mrs. Morhard," *Heights Press*, October 3, 1941.

IV: THE FINAL INNING

CHAPTER TWENTY: WARTIME BRINGS THE END

Personal information, anecdotes, and descriptions are from interviews with Mrs. Morhard's son Al Morhard, other former players, printed schedules, written documents, and photos.

Recruiting offices jammed: "No Hurrahs as City Grimly Accepts War," *The Cleveland Plain Dealer,* December 9, 1941, 1, 4.

Bob Feller enlists: "Feller to Decide Service Tonight," *The Cleveland Plain Dealer*, December 9, 1941, 1; "Feller Proud to Serve in Time of War," *The New York Times*, December 16, 2010; Bob Feller, "Answering the Call," U.S. Naval Institute's Proceedings, accessed February 15, 2018, www.military.com/veterans-day/bob-feller.html.

Greenberg, Williams Berra war duty: David Nye, "13 Professional Baseball Players Who Became War Heroes," *Business Insider*, accessed February 17, 2018, www.businessinsider.com/13-professional-baseball-players-who-became-war-heroes-2015-7.

Replacement baseball players in World War II: Marc Z. Aaron, and Bill Nowlin, *Who's on First Replacement Players in World War I* (Phoenix, AZ: Society for American Baseball Research, 2015).

Earle Johnson flour "bombing": Brian Albrecht and James Banks, *Cleveland in World War II* (Charleston, SC: History Press, 2015), 15.

Gerry Gerau, Ralph DeRosa marriage: "Mrs. Ralph A. DeRosa Jr.," *The Cleveland Plain Dealer,* April 12, 1942, 46.

107th Cavalry patrolling California Coast: "History of the 107th Mechanized Cavalry, 107th Mechanized Cavalry Reconnaissance Squadron 1940–1945," accessed February 7, 2018, www.107thmechcavsqd.com/history-of-the-107th-mechanized-cavalry/.

Rubber shortage in World War II, war rationing: Paul Wendt, "The Control of Rubber in World War II," *Southern Economic Journal* Vol. 13, no. 3 (January 1947): 203–227; Steven W. Sears, "Sorry No Gas: How Americans Met the First Great Gasoline Shortage—Nearly 40 Years Ago," *American Heritage*, October–November 1979; Jeff Nilsson, "Could You Stomach Americans Wartime Sugar Rations—75 Years Ago," *The Saturday Evening Post*, accessed January 18, 2018, www.saturdayeveningpost.com/2017/05/05/history/post-perspective/stomach-americas-wartime-sugar-ration-75-years-ago.html; McCullough, *World War II, Volume I*, 473–473.

Cleveland industrial powerhouse: Albrecht and Banks, *Cleveland in World War II,* 54–57.

Suspending baseball during the war: Gerald Bazer and Steven Culbertson, "When FDR Said 'Play Ball,' " *Prologue Magazine*, National Archives, Spring 2002, accessed January 18, 2018, www.archives.gov/publications/prologue/2002/spring/greenlight.html.

July 4 Festival of Freedom, University Heights festivities: "Festival of Freedom to Honor Brave," *The Cleveland Plain Dealer*, July 4, 1942, 1, 3; "Fourth of July in University Heights," *Heights Press*, July 2, 1942; "14 Baseball Games Will Be Feature on Dad's Day," *Heights Press,* July 2, 1942.

Example of nationwide coverage: "Little Majors" and "Giving Help," *Evening Star* (Washington, DC), July 2, 1942, 20.

Bradley invitation, ox roast, five ball games: "Little Indians Nine to Stage Baseball Festival for 4th Annual Benefit," *Heights Press*, August 21, 1942.

World War II rationing: "Rationing in World War II," U.S. Office of Price Administration, November 1946, accessed January 18, 2018, cdm16007.contentdm.oclc.org/cdm/singleitem/collection/p16007coll21/id/68/rec/45.

Blue stars, gold stars: Albrecht and Banks, *Cleveland in World War II*, 71.

Ohioans in WWII: "World War II," Ohio History Central, accessed February 22, 2018, www.ohiohistorycentral.org/w/World_War_II.

Don Greenwood bio: "Don Greenwood (American Football)," American Football Database, accessed March 2, 2018, americanfootballdatabase.wikia.com/wiki/Don_Greenwood (American_football).

League finally folded—might have been the seat of LL baseball instead of Williamsport: Hal Lebovitz, "Little Leagues, Like Suburbs, Need Room to Expand," *The Cleveland Plain Dealer,* April 3, 1960.

CHAPTER TWENTY-ONE: THE REUNION

This chapter is from the Hal Lebovitz article in *The Cleveland Plain Dealer*, "Hal Asks, Do Kids Forget," *The Cleveland Plain Dealer*, May 12, 1968, and interviews with Al Morhard and other former players.

EPILOGUE: THE OLD BALL FIELDS

The information here has been gleaned from a visit to the old ballparks with Al Morhard, interviews with Morhard family members, former junior league players, umpires, and their family members, and baseball and football biographies.

ABOUT THE AUTHOR

Ruth Hanford Morhard was memorizing the batting and earned run averages of Major League baseball players when other girls were playing with dolls. She still loves baseball.

She spends her days as a marketing and communications consultant to national, regional and local human services and arts institutions. Her previous book, *Wired to Move: Facts and Strategies for Nurturing Boys in Early Childhood Settings*, was published in 2013. She has also written several institutional histories. She has a Certificate in Creative Nonfiction from Stanford University and a Bachelor of Arts degree from Skidmore College.

She is married to Al Morhard, the son of Mrs. Josephine Morhard. Their blended family includes seven children, fourteen grandchildren, and one great-grandchild.